# LEO STRAUSS AND THE AMERICAN RIGHT

SHADIA B. DRURY

ALSO BY SHADIA DRURY

*The Political Ideas of Leo Strauss* (1988)
*Alexandre Kojève: The Roots of Postmodern Politics* (1994)

# LEO STRAUSS AND THE AMERICAN RIGHT

SHADIA B. DRURY

ST. MARTIN'S PRESS
NEW YORK

JC
251
.D78
1997

ISBN 0-312-12689-1

**Library of Congress Cataloging-in-Publication Data**

Drury, Shadia B., 1950-
    Leo Strauss and the American right / by Shadia B. Drury.
      p.   cm.
    Includes bibliographical references and index.
    ISBN 0-312-12689-1
    1. Conservatism—United States.   2. Strauss, Leo—Contributions in
political science.   I. Title.

    JC251.D78  1997
    320.53'0973—dc21                                     97-11580
                                                         CIP

Design by Acme Art Inc.

First edition: November, 1997
10  9  8  7  6  5  4  3  2  1

*For*
*John W. Yolton*

# Contents

## Acknowledgments

I am indebted to the work of Jack Gunnell who has done more than anyone else to explain the impact of the German émigrés on American political science. I have also appreciated his friendship and his encouragement. My discussions with Ken Reshaur of the University of Manitoba have been a pleasure. I am grateful for the time he took to read the manuscript and the hours he spent discussing it with me. I owe a special thanks to my colleague, Carol Prager, for reading the manuscript and for giving me her valuable advice. I would also like to thank Fred Wall for his incisive commentary and suggestions. Thanks also to Laura, Gail, and Greg Esselmont of Falcon Lake for correcting the final proofs. I was fortunate to have had the opportunity to attend the course on American Government given by Michael Martinez when he was in Calgary on a Fullbright Scholarship; his delightful lectures had the uncanny ability of conveying the spirit of American government and not just its factual mundanities. I am also grateful for the encouragement and advice of Michael Flamini of St. Martin's Press. I have benefited from conversations with Harry Jaffa, Harry Neumann, Margie Lloyd, Gordon Lloyd, Bill Allen, Morton Frisch, Terence Ball, Peter Euben, Gordon Schochet, Joyce Appleby, David Braybrooke, Ross Lence, Morton Schoolman, Michael Gibbons, Jane Bennett, and William Connolly. I have also profited from my affiliation with Stephen Randall and the discussions of the American Studies Group that he established on this campus. I am indebted to the University of Calgary's Killam Fellowship Award for providing me with teaching release for one term in order to complete this work. As usual, John Yolton was a most valuable source of inspiration and support. And, as always, he sets the scholarly standard to which I continue to aspire. Most of all, thanks to my daughter Kelly and my husband Dennis for their love and support.

# PREFACE

It is something of a puzzle that a seemingly reclusive German Jewish émigré and scholar has been declared the godfather of the Republican party's 1994 Contract with America in the pages of the *New York Times*. And in its exhaustive account of the most influential men in American politics, *Time* magazine concluded that, "perhaps one of the most influential men in American politics is the late Leo Strauss, the German émigré political philosopher who taught at the University of Chicago in the 1950s and '60s."[1] The power and influence of Strauss's students in Washington is a well-documented fact. This is not a book about them, or their exploits in Washington. It is a book about ideas. My goal is to explain the role that Strauss's political thinking has played in the political triumph of neoconservatism in America.

The irony of this situation is that the political ideas of this very influential man are shrouded in mystery, partly because he was preoccupied with secrecy and esotericism, and partly because his students treat his work as sacred texts rather than objects of critical analysis and debate. Their writing about him amounts to an impenetrable and totally unenlightening hagiology that is often more obscure than his original work. And to confound matters even further, he was not a man who was eager to be understood. It is therefore not surprising that there is no agreement among his students about the meaning of his work. In this book, I will examine the ways in which Strauss's followers have applied his ideas to American history and politics. I will show how Strauss's ideas have provided a generation of American scholars and writers with their conceptions of themselves and of their country. And more importantly, I will show how Strauss's political ideas are intimately linked with the political rise of American neoconservatism. I will argue that Strauss has provided American neoconservatism with its distinctive qualities: its sense of crisis, its aversion to liberalism, its rejection of pluralism, its dread of nihilism, its insistence on nationalism, its populism, its dualism, its religiosity, and more.

The first chapter is a brief account of Strauss's political thought in general and its relevance to American liberalism and conservatism. Haunted by his experience of Nazi Germany, Strauss rejects American liberalism as a dangerous, if not disastrous state of affairs in which the likes of Hitler could emerge victorious. This experience is related to the major themes of his political thought—the preoccupation with nihilism, the emphasis on religion, and the role of intellectuals in politics. In this brief sketch of Strauss's political thought I rely on my previous work, *The Political Ideas of Leo Strauss.*

Chapter 2 is devoted to an analysis of Strauss's experience of living in America as a Jew, his conviction that assimilation is both impossible and undesirable, his celebration of Jewish nationalism, his rejection of Enlightenment wisdom, and his endorsement of religion as a political tool.

Chapter 3 examines Strauss's debt to two German contemporaries—Martin Heidegger and Carl Schmitt. This discussion explores what Strauss learned from the Nazi holocaust. I argue that he did not learn much, and that his political thought is dangerously close to Heidegger's and much more radical than Schmitt's.

Chapter 4 focuses on the application of Strauss's political ideas to American history and politics. It examines three different ways in which Americans responded, assimilated, and applied Strauss's political vision. And even though these three reactions are distinct, they are not mutually exclusive. The first reaction of Strauss's American followers is denial—denial that America is awash in liberal modernity. The second reaction is characterized by a deep melancholy that has its source in the conviction that the great tradition of Western civilization has been lost and cannot possibly be recovered. America is seen as the personification of the decline of the West, and as the world's only superpower, she is quickly leading the world astray like a Pied Piper. The third application of Strauss's political thought to American history and politics is a distinctively American approach to bad tidings because it resolves to avert disaster by taking action. This approach opens the way to neoconservatism, which has become the leading ideology of the Republican party.

Chapter 5 is an analysis and critique of American neoconservatism as represented by the work of its leading spokesman, Irving Kristol. I will show how the major themes and preoccupations of neoconservatism echo the political ideas of Leo Strauss. I will argue that there is nothing conservative about America's Strauss-inspired neoconservatism. On the contrary, it is radical and reactionary; its political aspirations are nothing short of the radical reversal of the American liberal tradition. Instead of rescuing liberalism from its suicidal tendencies, instead of providing an atmosphere of stability and sobriety, neoconservatism destabilizes American politics. Gone is the cautious, modest, and moderate spirit that accounts for the attraction of conservatism. I began by writing a book on Leo Strauss's influence on American conservatism, but I concluded that there was little or no conservatism in America. And if there was, then it was not the legacy of Leo Strauss. Instead, Strauss has contributed to the development of the American right.

Historically, the right was conservative and the left was radical. In the French National Assembly of 1789, those who sat on the right were eager to conserve the status quo and were therefore opposed to change, while those who sat on the left were eager for radical change. As a result, right and left came to refer to divergent political attitudes toward political change. But history has made these labels obsolete, because the success of the liberal revolution in France, as well as the rest of Europe, means that the right has lost, and in the bitterness of its defeat, has become radical. It no longer has an aversion to change, but is eager for radical change that would reverse the liberal revolution. Neoconservatism is the classic and most powerful expression of the American right. Far from being moderate or conservative, it bristles with a sense of urgency and crisis that is the hallmark of radicalism.

# LEO STRAUSS AND THE AMERICAN RIGHT

SHADIA B. DRURY

## CHAPTER ONE

# STRAUSSIANS
# IN WASHINGTON

LEO STRAUSS (1899-1973) WAS A GERMAN-JEWISH PHILOSOPHER who fled Germany when the Nazis came to power. He eventually settled in the United States where he taught political science at the University of Chicago. He specialized in the history of political philosophy; he wrote on Plato, Aristophanes, Aristotle, Alfarabi, Maimonides, Averroës, Machiavelli, Hobbes, Locke, and others. His prose was often turgid and his ideas rather mysterious and elusive.

His claim to fame is an eccentric thesis according to which philosophers can never afford to say just what they mean, and that the wisest of them never did. In Strauss's view, a real philosopher must communicate quietly, subtly, and secretly to the few who are fit to receive his message. But why all this secrecy? One part of Strauss's answer is that the philosopher has to be secretive in order to avoid persecution. But this is not the most interesting part of his thesis. The interesting thing is that even Strauss, living as he did in one of the freest societies known to history, claimed that he had to be secretive—that he himself wrote esoterically or in code.[1]

What could possibly be the reason for this secrecy? Strauss may have been afraid of persecution in the milder sense of ridicule and ostracism; for in spite of his fame, that was something that he had to endure in America. But there is an even deeper and more interesting reason for Strauss's secrecy—his belief that the truth is not salutary, but dangerous, and even destructive to society—any society.

There is no doubt that his eccentric ideas, coupled with the inestimable appeal of secrecy, explain his popularity in the academy. But his fame and his popularity notwithstanding, Strauss and his disciples were and continue to be ridiculed and dismissed. Part of the reason is that their views are so far removed from the liberal ideas that prevail in the academy that they seem laughable. Living in a liberal democracy, Strauss had no use for liberalism and little use for democracy. His political ideas are radically elitist. Yet he knew that there was not much tolerance for elitist ideas in America, and he was quite right. Nevertheless, much of the ridicule his ideas have endured was largely brought on by his own disregard of the academic ethos itself. It was not just the fact that Strauss attracted a large following but that his following tended to have the attributes of a cult—its secrecy and faith in the authority of Strauss and of the ancient philosophers he supposedly followed. The ridicule of the Straussians in the academy is connected to their unquestioning devotion to a set of ideas that they cannot or will not defend except to those who are already convinced. It is therefore not the case that they are simply being persecuted for thinking differently, it is for disseminating their views in a manner that is destructive of intellectual life itself. For they do not want their ideas discussed openly or even known to anyone outside the charmed circle of initiates.

Strauss's impact on academic life in North America has been something of a phenomenon; historian Gordon S. Wood described it as the largest academic movement in the twentieth century.[2] Nor is this influence confined to political philosophy. It extends into religious studies, literary criticism, intellectual history, classics, American history, and American constitutional law. In 1987, the year of the two hundredth anniversary of the US Constitution, Wood observed that the Straussians, as they are known in the academy, dominated the conferences; they were well-organized and well-funded. And even though most of them were political scientists by training, they outnumbered historians when it came to giving papers and organizing conferences on the American founding, which is a topic of great *political* and not just historical significance for the Straussians.

Strauss's students have not confined themselves to antiquarian topics. In fact, their interest in the past is integral to their attempts to understand problems of the present. This is not an unusual practice, especially for conservatives. Even someone who is not conservative, and who has no desire to revere or emulate the past, must admit that the past is instructive. Strauss's students have focused on America's past in order to understand her present and to shape her future. Indeed, they have become the leading spokesmen of the conservative intellectual movement in America. They include writers such as Harry V. Jaffa, Joseph Cropsey, Allan Bloom, Harvey Mansfield, Willmoore Kendall, and Irving Kristol. All of them were either students of Strauss, or admirers, associates, and collaborators who acknowledge his profound influence on their thought.

What seems more surprising than his influence inside the academy is the influence that Strauss has exerted on American politics. Strauss's students and their students have occupied important positions in the Reagan and Bush administrations and continue to play a significant role within the Republican party. Prominent figures on the American political scene include Reagan's ambassador to Indonesia, Paul Wolfowitz; Caspar Weinberger's former speechwriter, Seth Cropsey; National Endowment for the Humanities Deputy Chairman, John T. Agresto; National Security Council advisor Carnes Lord; Assistant Secretary of State for International Organization Affairs, Alan Keyes; legal scholar and judge Robert Bork (whose nomination to the Supreme Court by former president George Bush was defeated by the Democratic majority in the Senate); Justice Clarence Thomas of the Supreme Court; former Secretary of Education William Bennett; former Education Department Chief of Staff, William Kristol (later former vice-president Dan Quayle's chief of staff and then the chief pundit and policy maker of the Republican party).[3] Journalists have been fully cognizant of this influx of Straussians into Washington and of the power they have within the Republican party.[4] So much so that the *New York Times* has dubbed Leo Strauss the godfather of the Republican party's 1994 Contract with America.[5]

Journalists are bewildered by what all this could possibly mean. How could an obscure German-Jewish biblical scholar, historian of ideas, admirer of Plato, Alfarabi, and Maimonides become the leading intellectual inspiration of America's Republican party?[6] What are the political implications of Strauss's philosophy? Why does he have such an antipathy to American liberal democracy? Will his followers succeed in replacing the reigning liberal elite with a conservative one? How does Straussian conservatism differ from other varieties of conservatism? What is the connection between Strauss and the neoconservatives? What are the implications of Straussian conservatism on public policy? These are some of the questions that I will address in this work.

In what follows, I will give an account of Strauss's political assumptions—his rejection of liberal democracy, his fear of nihilism, as well as the heady mixture of elitism and populism implied by his philosophy. I will conclude by providing a sweeping account of liberalism and conservatism in America. This is intended to set the stage for the final argument of the book—namely that American neoconservatism, the ideology that dominates the Republican party, echoes the themes of Strauss's political thought.

## THE GHOSTS OF WEIMAR

Strauss abhorred liberal democracy because he associated it with the Weimar Republic whose constitution was drafted at the end of World War I.[7] Germany had no liberal or democratic traditions to fall back on, and the Weimar Republic was crippled from the start by critics on every side who had no use for parliamentary government. Conservatives preferred the monarchical and bureaucratic system of the *Kaiserreich*; nationalists such as Hitler and his party were opposed to the Weimar constitution because they were opposed to parliamentary government in general, supposedly on the grounds that it was divisive, that it led to the fragmentation of the body politic, and that a dictatorship alone can accomplish the necessary social change and promote the national interest; Communists saw parliamentary politics as a bourgeois institution that should be superseded by the dictatorship of the proletariat. Weimar was therefore threatened on all sides from its very inception. Both the Communists and the National Socialists made great electoral gains, but by 1932 Hitler's party had the largest number of seats in the Reichstag. By 1933, Hitler had become the chancellor as well as the leader of the majority party. Within a year he had abolished the power of the state governments and brought all of German life under Nazi control. Strauss's experience in Germany confirmed the political teaching of his beloved Plato. A great enemy of democracy, Plato described it as the second worse form of government, and was convinced that it inevitably leads to tyranny. For Strauss as for Plato, democracy is a licentious state of affairs in which a multiplicity of conflicting and irreconcilable appetites compete for dominance.[8] Plato described a society torn apart by insatiable and conflicting appetites, and he surmised that in this state of disorder, one master passion was bound to become supreme and rule despotically over all others. The scenario described by Plato, whereby democracy gives way to tyranny, mirrors the scenario where Weimar sets the licentious stage for Hitler to emerge victorious.

Strauss understood both Weimar and America in terms of Plato's analysis of how democracy gives way to tyranny. The licentious quality of the American love of freedom and its resemblance to the freedom of Weimar was therefore a reason for disquiet.

Strauss saw liberal society as devoid of any authoritative truth. He saw it as a world in which all opinions, all preferences, and all religions were of equal worth. He felt that this state of affairs creates a vacuum at the heart of liberal society. As the vacuum grows, the struggle to fill it intensifies, and the desire to have it filled becomes irresistible. Under such circumstances, the most single-minded, ruthless, and daring are bound to emerge victorious.[9] In other words, there is a great danger that America might repeat the errors and terrors of Europe.

The comparison of American liberalism to Weimar is not original to Strauss. It is expressed again and again by German refugees such as Theodor Adorno who believed that America is a duplication of Nazi Germany—the only thing missing is the brutality of the police. Instead of leading him to question the legitimacy of the comparison, the absence of coercion only succeeds in making Adorno marvel at the extent, sagacity, subtlety, and near invisibility of the American style of domination. This phenomenon was immortalized in a film with Rod Steiger called *The Pawnbroker* (for which he won an Academy Award). In the film, Steiger portrays a refugee from a Nazi concentration camp who lost his children and watched his wife forcibly used as a prostitute by Hitler's men before she was finally gassed. Everything in America seems to him like a spontaneous version of the camps. New York is portrayed as if it were Nazi Germany without the Gestapo. However, the skill of the filmmaker makes it clear that the protagonist is so haunted by his past that he cannot be trusted to have a sound grasp of the world around him. This may be equally true of writers such as Theodore Adorno and Leo Strauss. Writers such as Allan Bloom and Hiram Caton acquire these ghosts secondhand.

In a disturbing essay, Hiram Caton praises Strauss for having understood the fact that American liberalism is a re-creation of the spineless liberalism of Weimar. In America as in Weimar, he argues, liberalism has created a moral vacuum in which a nightmarish regime of eugenics is gaining the upper hand. A conspiracy of "humanists" and "feminists" have turned women against reproduction. The result is to remove reproduction from the "chance play of matrimony" and place it in the hands of experts who will decide what sorts of people there will be. At the same time, the movements in favor of abortion and euthanasia undermine the commitment to the sanctity of life and open the way to the destruction of unwanted people. In this way, a regime dedicated to the defense of human rights may well be transformed into a regime that liquidates millions. In Caton's view, the similarity between American liberalism and the liberalism of Weimar is that they both suffer from the "passivity of civilized men" when faced with criminal politics. The result is to undermine the sanctity of life, and to legitimize the destruction of undesirable people.[10]

The identification of America with Weimar is also a central theme in Allan Bloom's *The Closing of the American Mind*. In this best-selling book, Strauss's most famous student popularized the ideas of his teacher. Bloom uncovers subtle reflections of Weimar in American popular culture. For example, Louis Armstrong's "Mack the Knife" is a translation of "Mackie Messer" from *The Threepenny Opera*, "a monument of Weimar Republic popular culture."[11] And the all-American expression "stay loose" is really a translation of Heidegger's *Gelassenheit*.[12] And more than anything else, America's nihilism is a German import. Max Weber brought it to America in the innocuous form of value-free social science, and Woody Allen Americanized it by giving us nihilism without European angst. Bloom's book is full of dark premonitions about America that reveal the extent to which he has inherited the ghosts of Weimar that haunted Strauss.

At the heart of Strauss's antipathy to liberal democracy is the belief that it exposes us to the dangers of fascism. Strauss is convinced that Hitler came to power by "democratic" means and that it was a liberal democracy that paved the way for the regime that had no other purpose than the destruction of the Jews.[13] But it could equally well be argued that Hitler came to power by a colossal contempt for Weimar's constitutional principles—by deceit, fraud, abuse of political power, and disregard for democratic fair play.

Nevertheless, Strauss is right in thinking that the terrors of Weimar are ever present. I am inclined to think that a democratic society is always vulnerable to the appearance of a demagogue who preys on the fears, prejudices, and insecurities of the people. By the same token, the comparison of American liberal democracy with Weimar is not fair. Weimar had no traditions of either democracy or liberalism. The political institutions established at Weimar after World War I were foreign to German culture, so the odds were stacked against them. There were no traditions sanctifying the inviolability of individual rights and freedoms. These are liberal in origin, and for the most part, they are important in limiting the excesses of democracy understood simply as majority rule. But as I will show, Strauss had an even greater antipathy to liberalism than to democracy.

## HOW LIBERALISM DESTROYS
## RELIGION AND INVITES NIHILISM

Strauss's critique of American liberal democracy was not simply based on his association of liberal democracy with Weimar. It was based on the belief that liberalism has the effect of eroding religious faith and that the latter is an essential ingredient in a viable political order.

Strauss was grateful to America for giving him shelter, and was not eager to criticize her too openly. As a result, his criticism was indirect and took the form of a critique of "modernity." But there was one rare occasion when Strauss expressed his view of America most candidly. In a commentary on a Jewish-Protestant Colloquium sponsored by the Divinity School of the University of Chicago, Strauss gave one of the clearest statements of his objections to liberalism in general and American liberalism in particular.[14]

Whether Protestant or Jewish, all of the participants at this conference felt that America needed a revival of religious faith to stem the tide of anomie, alienation, and meaninglessness engendered by secular society. But being full-blooded Americans, the participants naturally dismissed the idea of a national religion out of hand. They had no intention of imposing their own religion on others. A state religion would simply be un-American. It would contradict the establishment clause of the American Constitution, according to which "Congress shall make no law respecting an establishment of religion, or prohibiting the free exercise thereof." Consequently, they arrived at a solution that is distinctively American. It consisted of the desire to revive a diversity of religious faiths in the belief that they could exist not only with mutual tolerance but with mutual respect.

Strauss shared the sentiments of the participants about liberal society. Like them he believed that liberalism breeds rootlessness and alienation and that America is badly in need of a revival of religious faith. Yet in his reflections on the conference, Strauss expressed serious reservations about this American naivete that goes by the name of liberalism. The whole idea of a plurality of religions coexisting with one another seemed illogical. For Strauss, the question was, which faith?

Strauss's argument against religious pluralism is as follows. Every religion is based on a particular revelation of truth. And every revelation of truth is bound to clash with every other revelation of truth. In light of this state of affairs, how could one faith respect another without doing violence to its own respect for truth? As a Jew, Strauss tells us that he cannot possibly respect Christianity—especially in view of the role it has played in the massacre of Jews, not only in the distant past, but in this century. This is why society cannot contain a multiplicity of coexisting religions.[15] The result is the demise of all religion and the entrenchment of secularism with its attendant sense of loss and alienation. At the root of this sense of loss and alienation is nihilism or the belief in nothing. For Strauss, this is the worst affliction that could befall any polity, as I will explain.

## LIBERALISM, NIHILISM, AND THE NAZIS

Strauss was certain that the Nazi barbarism we have witnessed had everything to do with the demise of biblical religion and the ascendancy of nihilism. He was convinced that liberalism cultivates nihilism, and makes it the foundation of its polity. In Strauss's view, this is the achievement of modernity. In other words, Strauss thought that the holocaust was not so much a departure from the traditions of Western civilization, but the logical outcome of the ascendancy of modernity. In their naivete, the moderns have unleashed reason, thinking it was harmless. But religious faith could not withstand the scrutiny of reason. The result is that reason has destroyed faith. In Strauss's view, the "crisis of modernity" that is the "crisis of our time" has its source in the fact that reason has destroyed biblical morality; and in so doing, it has dissolved the veil of illusion that protected Western civilization from collapsing into barbarism. The Nazis broke through the protective atmosphere and discovered the sordid truth—namely, that there is no God and no moral order. The world is a vacuum and those who have the courage or the audacity will create it in their own image, and shape it according to their will.[16]

Strauss and his followers never tire of claiming that liberalism has its foundation in nihilism and skepticism. In other words, liberalism is based on the belief that there is no such thing as truth; and in light of this state of affairs, we should regard all opinion as being equally worthy of respect. In theory, this is simply false. Classic liberals such as John Locke or John Stuart Mill were not moral skeptics or nihilists. On the contrary, Locke argued that there was a natural right to liberty independent of governmental decree. And Mill upheld the primacy of liberty not because there was no truth, but for the sake of truth. Mill argued that only freedom can create conditions in which the truth can emerge. Imposing a single public orthodoxy that cannot be criticized or questioned is tantamount to forfeiting the search for truth along with human progress and happiness.[17]

So why do Strauss and his followers continue to paint liberalism as nihilistic and skeptical? The answer lies in the fact that liberalism has a skeptical temper where politics is concerned. For the sake of truth, liberals reject the imposition by those in power of a single and indisputable reality. This liberal stance conflicts with the Straussian conviction that society requires unwavering faith and unflinching devotion. And even though the result is zealotry and fanaticism, Strauss does not flinch from it; for zealotry and fanaticism are preferable to nihilism and skepticism, because the latter weaken society, while the former strengthen it.

One would have expected that the horrors of the Hitler regime would have had a profound effect on a German Jew. One would have expected such a man to embrace liberalism with open arms. After all, liberalism has its roots in the European experience of religious persecution. In England, the ascendancy of a Catholic monarch such as Queen Mary I (or "bloody Mary" as she is more commonly known) to the throne in 1553, meant that Protestants had to declare their allegiance to Rome, and those who did not were burned at the stake. And when Queen

Elizabeth I came to the throne and reestablished her father's Church of England, Catholics could not declare their allegiance to Rome and were forced to conform to the Church of England. The state was not impartial where religion was concerned. And even though England became a Protestant country, many Protestants found the Church of England, with its Episcopal hierarchy, almost indistinguishable from the Catholic Church they had repudiated. Queen Elizabeth managed to avoid religious strife, and this meant that the Elizabethan age was prosperous. But less than 40 years after Elizabeth's death, England was in civil war. Liberal ideas emerged as a response to this condition of civil strife. And while Thomas Hobbes (1588-1679) suggested some remedies, it was generally agreed that his cure was worse than the disease. It was John Locke (1632-1704) who provided the definitive solution that inspired liberal politicians everywhere, especially in America.

Simply stated, Locke's solution consisted in the separation of church and state. Locke suggested a secular politics that allows citizens to pursue their mutual well-being in conditions of freedom, peace, order, and security. Liberated from the oppression of a state religion, citizens would be free to worship in accordance with their faith and their conscience. After all, can a religion be worthy of the name if it is not freely embraced?

It would be easy to assume that Strauss was something of a cynic. In other words, it would be plausible to think that he was too sagacious and discerning to believe that liberalism could provide a solution to the perennial human problem of mutual hatred and antagonism. But this is not the case. His antipathy to liberalism does not have its source in the belief that the liberal ethos is impossible to attain, or that it is too high an ideal to be humanly possible. Strauss repudiated liberalism not because he thought that it could not work, but because he was afraid that it might! It was the ideals of liberalism itself—secular politics, human rights, equal dignity, and individual freedom—that he did not relish. In his view, secular politics led to nihilism and meaninglessness; equal dignity is a recipe for mediocrity; and setting a premium on individual freedom invites licentiousness, disorder, and the dissolution of society. Instead, Strauss advocated a social order steeped in religiosity, a hierarchically ordered society intended to reflect the inequalities of nature, and emphasized civic virtue, fanatical devotion, and unqualified commitment.

## STRAUSSIAN POLITICAL ASSUMPTIONS

What is presupposed by Strauss's critique of American liberalism and his recipe for reform can be described as follows. Every society needs a single public orthodoxy or a set of ideas that defines what is true and false, right and wrong, noble and base. Religion is the traditional and most powerful instrument for the inculcation of such values. If a political society is to hold together and function as a unit, it must have a set of shared truths that are inculcated by one religion or another. Although he has some reservations about the political utility of Christianity, Strauss believes that almost any religion would succeed in accomplishing the political task at hand. He is therefore not too particular about which religion it should be. But one religion or another is necessary to give society the needed concord and cohesiveness. Moreover, religion links the political order to ultimate truth or reality, and this provides that order with an exalted status that inspires citizens to fight and die in its defense. This is why every society needs gods that would bestow sanctity on its laws.

At first blush, Strauss's criticism of liberal society sounds familiar. Like many other conservative and Communitarian critics of liberalism, Strauss believes that a healthy society is one that is bound together by a single authoritative truth that provides the citizens with shared values and a common way of life. Moreover, the state must preserve this social fabric and nourish it like a rare flower. What is usually left unstated is that the state must use its coercive force to uphold the truth of society and to suppress contending visions. All this is classic conservative fare. But Strauss adds quite a number of original touches that distinguish his position from the standard conservative view.

In the standard conservative view, the social fabric is a very mysterious and delicate affair that takes hundreds of years to develop. But sadly, it can be torn asunder in a moment of thoughtless revolutionary fervor. What makes the social fabric so precious and so worthy of preserving is that it is a product of the cumulative wisdom of the ages. And without this accumulation of civilized habits that we call tradition, mankind would be indistinguishable from the beasts.

But Strauss represents a new breed of conservative for whom tradition is not the repository of the wisdom of the ages. On the contrary, tradition is the conscious creation of philosophers-lawgivers-prophets—or what Nietzsche called Supermen. These are men of great sagacity who know just what sort of remedy their times need and they are ready and able to provide it in the form of some glorious myth, noble lie, or pious fraud. So, whatever classic conservatives may say about the mysterious origin of tradition, the new breed of conservatives knows that every tradition begins somewhere, even if it is useful to perpetuate the mystery of the origin.

In Strauss's view, the trouble with liberal society is that it dispenses with noble lies and pious frauds. It tries to found society on secular rational foundations. It teaches that society is an invention that exists for our mutual benefit, and that it is in our mutual self-interest to abide by the rules that will promote order and liberty. But Strauss is not impressed by this sort of thinking. He believes that there is an irresolvable conflict between the interests of the individual and the interests of society. He thinks that the conflict can only be camou flaged by lies and deceptions, and that the greatest among these is religion. The reason is that human beings are selfish and self-centered and will not be willing to sacrifice themselves for others in the absence of belief in a god who punishes the wicked and rewards the just. Further, Strauss believes that the existence of such a god cannot be established by reason or philosophy. The gods of "shuddering awe" are necessary to civilize humanity and to turn natural savages into husbands, fathers, and citizens.[18] What is needed is something grand enough to capture the human imagination, something magnificent and majestic, something splendid and sublime, such as Judaism, Christianity, or Islam.

Karl Marx maintained that religion is the "opium of the people" because it makes them placid and accepting of social inequalities and injustice. He thought that those who were willing to bear life as a burden and wait for their salvation in the beyond are not likely to be inspired to bring about a revolution intended to safeguard justice in *this* world. Strauss values religion as a source of order and stability in society. He believes that religion provides the majority of people with the comfort they need to bear their harsh existence. He does not disagree with Marx that religion is the opium of the people, he just thinks that the people need their opium.

In the American context, the pressing question is, Which religion is supposed to act as the opium and the glue that keeps the polity united and placid? In Strauss's view there can only be one religion, but since America is made up of a plurality of religious groups, it seems that the whole American experiment is doomed. Even if the different Christian sects can be united under a single umbrella, what would be the fate of the Jews? As we shall see in the next chapter, Strauss thinks that the Jews are a living symbol of the human problem for which there is no solution. Persecution is the Jewish lot, and there is a sense in which it defines them.

In my view, Strauss overestimates the utility of religion in politics. First, he is quite mistaken in thinking that religion is always or necessarily a unifying force. Even a people who share the same religion may come to disagree about its meaning, and if the meaning is linked to the political order, then the political order will be ripped asunder in the struggle to determine which interpretation is to be authoritative—which interpretation will form the basis of the official religion that is defended by all the powers at the disposal of the state. Second, Strauss is equally mistaken in thinking that religion is the opium of the people. Far from making people placid and easy to manipulate, religion can inspire civil disobedience and even armed resistance. The Branch Davidians in Waco, Texas, and numerous other militia groups across the country are far from placid. They are not in the least interested in leaving their salvation in the hands of God. They are eager to take up arms themselves.

Strauss is also mistaken in thinking that the interests of the individual are in conflict with the good of the community. On the contrary, social life makes possible the cultivation of human excellence and the fulfillment of human potentialities. Society is the route to individual happiness and completion, at least under normal circumstances. Of course, unusual and unhappy events could befall us, and we may be compelled to sacrifice our life for the society that nourished us. But this is a chance we must take. Social life is like love, it comes with its joys and its risks. Love may be disappointing and cruel, but this is not a reason to forfeit all chances of happiness altogether; nor is it healthy to be deceived by romantics and liars into thinking that love transfigures the world and rescues us from every conceivable disappointment.

## ELITISM OR POPULISM?

Strauss was not as reclusive an intellectual as some believe. He was convinced that ideas make the world. He also believed that it was the ascendancy of a certain set of ill-conceived ideas in the history of the West that has led to the "barbarism we have witnessed." He associated these ideas with modernity, liberalism, and the rationalism of the Enlightenment. He believed that these ideas have triumphed at the expense of ancient wisdom, and that their success had everything to do with the holocaust. In other words, the holocaust was a logical outcome of the ascendancy of Enlightenment rationalism, nihilism, liberalism, and secularism. The task at hand was to turn the tide, or reverse the trend. For that, the right kind of intellectuals were necessary, and Strauss was particularly adept at training them. Indeed, he is reputed to have graduated more than one hundred doctoral students in political philosophy, mostly at the University of Chicago. But intellectuals cannot be effective unless those in power are willing to lend them an ear. In other words, luck is necessary for philosophy to be effective in shaping the world. This luck came in the form of the presidency of Ronald Reagan. And Strauss's students were quick to recognize the opportunity.

Strauss's critique of liberalism is usually expressed as a critique of modernity. And there is no doubt that for Strauss, as for almost everyone else, America is the embodiment of modernity. As Strauss's collaborator and literary executor Joseph Cropsey wrote: "The United States is the microcosm of modernity." She is an "arena in which modernity is working itself out."[19] But it is important to point out that in Strauss's scheme of things, the most or the least that could be said of America is that she represents modernity in its youthful exuberance. In the United States, the drama of modernity has not yet concluded in catastrophe. Here, there is still hope. So while this is cause for optimism, it is also a reason for dismay. For America poses the greatest obstacles to her own salvation: she is enchanted with modernity. She clings to modernity with all her heart. Deprive her of it, and you might cut out her soul, and destroy her very being. Nevertheless, Strauss knows that America's love affair with modernity is bound to end in disaster. However, it is difficult for him to convince her of that because modernity has not yet had the opportunity of disappointing her. Only someone like Strauss who comes from the old world can be disillusioned with modernity. How can he tell

America that her beloved will betray her? Strauss does not tell her (he leaves that to his American disciples). Instead, he flatters her; he tells her that of the two superpowers in the world, she is the greater.[20] Strauss is sincere; for him, the Soviet Union has represented modernity in its more advanced and hence more decadent stages.[21] In its early phase, modernity still contains small remnants of ancient wisdom.

The role of Strauss's American disciples is to arrest America's development in the direction of more advanced modernity, and to enhance the small remnants of ancient wisdom that America's early stage of modernity still contains. America is to be divested of her modernity—gently, almost imperceptibly, without trauma and without violence. And since this is a supremely un-American activity, it is a very dangerous proposition and must therefore be undertaken with utmost care, not to mention secrecy. It requires great tact and a multiplicity of resourceful strategies, for it is nothing short of a counterrevolution. The Straussian revolution must be a quiet one. This is one reason that the popularization of Strauss's ideas in the best-selling book by Allan Bloom, *The Closing of the American Mind* is reason for consternation. It is certainly a betrayal of the pledge to secrecy and discretion—and would have been more so had its thesis been clear and unambiguous.

Some of Strauss's disciples are unwilling to accept the un-American nature of their political program, while others only refuse to admit it publicly. The accusation of being un-American is not restricted to Straussian conservatives; conservatism has always been suspect in America.[22] Since America has its origins in a revolution against the aristocratic and authoritarian model of European society, it is legitimate to ask: Can there be an American conservatism that does not betray the American heritage? With a few exceptions, Strauss's disciples are sensitive to this sort of criticism. They tend to address this criticism by reinterpreting the nature of the American regime and the intentions of its Founding Fathers. The object of this reinterpretation is to prove that America is not modern or liberal at all, but ancient and conservative to the core. This is the reason that the study of historical documents such as the Declaration of Independence, the Constitution, and *The Federalist Papers* are the focus of the attentions of Straussian conservatives. If they can convince America that she is not the modern liberal she believes herself to be, then their efforts to divest her of her liberalism will be easier to accomplish.

Straussians are not in total agreement on the nature of the American founding. They argue about whether America is fundamentally liberal and modern or conservative and ancient. But they all agree that her liberalism needs to be severely curtailed, if not totally eradicated.

For love of America, Strauss hopes to save her from the harmful effects of her own liberal modernity. The question is how can America's salvation be secured? How can the task of divesting her of her liberalism be accomplished? Strauss's political solution is to create an aristocracy in the midst of American liberal democracy. Hopefully, this elite might divest America of her liberalism—quietly, without discord or difficulty. Strauss's project is premised on the assumption that the mass never rules, but no one can rule without its consent. Every democracy has its ruling elite—an elite that shapes the opinions of the mass. This is what Straussians call the "ennobling" of democracy.[23] The idea is based on creating a wedge between *liberalism* and *democracy*.

Strauss is quite right to distinguish between liberalism and democracy. Liberalism is concerned with securing the greatest possible freedom for individuals. And this may very well be accomplished by a constitutional monarchy. Liberalism is therefore not logically wedded to democracy. Democracy is the rule of the people, or rule according to the will of the people or the majority. Of course, there are democrats such as Jean Jacques Rousseau who are eager to distinguish between the will of the people and the will of the majority, but for the most part, this is a difficult distinction to sustain in practice. Democracy always contains the threat of the tyranny of the majority over minorities and individuals and this is the reason that liberals such as John Stuart Mill have been generally suspicious of democracy. Liberalism and democracy are therefore an odd couple. Nevertheless, they manage to coexist in American society. In my view, it is the liberal ethos that ennobles democracy; liberalism creates a political environment that protects the rights and freedoms of individuals against the potential tyranny of the majority. But Strauss's conservatives would like to undermine liberalism and use democracy to further their quiet revolution.

Populism is the cure for America's liberal malaise. The idea is to use democratic means to undermine America's attachment to liberalism. This explains why the Straussians are willing to make their peace with democracy, but not with liberalism. It also explains how the Straussian brand of conservatism combines elitism with populism.

I am not suggesting that the populist cure is a sinister plot devised by the new elite. On the contrary, populism is a means undertaken in good faith or out of love for America. The trouble is that the cure could prove to be worse than the disease. There are at least two dangers associated with this cure: one has its source in the people, the other in the elite. First, once the populace is aroused, there is no telling what the political consequences might be. Second, there are serious doubts that Strauss's brand of elitism is salutary for American society, or for any society.

The radically elitist nature of Strauss's thought is quite well known and incontestable. But in my view, there is nothing particularly pernicious or sinister about elitism itself. It has always been part of traditional conservatism as well as liberalism. Indeed, it may be argued that there has never been a society that did not have some kind of elite or other. Even liberal democratic societies, such as the United States, have their elites—they elect representatives to govern, and they approve of differentials in wealth based on luck, effort, and skill.

What sets liberals apart from conservatives is not that they are not elitists, but that they believe that opportunities should be open to talents, and as a result, they are committed to equality of opportunity. In contrast, conservatives believe that equality of opportunity is unattainable, and that we should make our peace with the fact of inequality. By the same token, traditional conservatives believe that those who have been blessed with opportunities for education and self-cultivation through the accident of birth and wealth, owe a debt to the society that has provided them with these privileges. This is the idea of noblesse oblige. What is disturbing about the new conservatism, or neoconservatism, is not so much that it is elitist, but that it cultivates an elite that is self-righteous, an elite that deludes itself into thinking that it is a natural aristocracy, that all its privileges are deserved, and that it has no obligation to the have-nots in society. Strauss has contributed a great deal to the development of an elite that is intoxicated with its own self-admiration.

Strauss's elitism is a melange of the ideas of Plato and Nietzsche. Strauss believes that every culture and its morality are human fabrications designed by philosophers and other creative geniuses for the preservation of the herd. Because the truth is dark and sordid, Strauss maintains that the philosophic love of truth must remain the hidden preserve of the very few. But in their public posture, philosophers must pay lip service to the myths and illusions they have fabricated for the many. They must champion the immutability of truth, the universality of justice, and the selfless nature of goodness, while secretly teaching their acolytes that all truth is fabrication, that justice is doing good to friends and evil to enemies, and that the only good is one's own pleasure. The truth may be deliciously savored by the few, but it is surely dangerous for the consumption of the many. This is why Strauss insists that philosophy must be kept hidden, and that all great philosophers were esoteric writers whose books contain a dual message—an esoteric or clandestine message for the few and an exoteric or salutary message for the many.[24]

Allan Bloom castigates the American universities for failing to educate either the few or the many. What he finds particularly dangerous is the tendency of liberal education to subject the norms of society to the scrutiny of reason. For Bloom as for Strauss, liberal education succeeds only in cultivating a dangerous open-mindedness that erodes the wholehearted attachment to "one's own" traditions and prejudices. A true education must inculcate the values of society as absolute and inviolable, while teaching the truth to a small elite intended to govern the society indirectly through the influence it exerts on the powerful. Since Bloom shares Strauss's view that the great books of the Western tradition contain a dual teaching, he defends an education based on these books as the best vehicle for educating both the few and the many.

In the final analysis, Strauss and Bloom see culture as a house of cards that is easily blown over by philosophical hot air. This explains why they are eager to cultivate an elite that makes a virtue of lying and dissembling. It is not surprising that they are sympathetic to Richard Nixon for whom dissembling and chicanery were the most vital political tools. In truth, the education Strauss and Bloom espouse is little more than a blind and thoughtless adherence to a doctrine whose secrecy shields it from scrutiny and criticism. When ideas are inculcated by whispering to boys in corners, the result is not just corruption, but stupidity. I contend that the pernicious influence of Leo Strauss has its source in the *kind* of elite he cultivates—an elite that is not fit for power because it is neither wise nor good. It is not wise because it cannot defend its beliefs before the tribunal of reason; it preaches only to the converted. It is not good because it is a manipulative elite that eschews the truth in favor of lies and deceptions, and because it exempts itself from the moral standards it imposes on others—and this is the road to tyranny.

## ALLIANCE WITH THE CHRISTIAN RIGHT

Strauss has given his students a totally extravagant faith in the capacity of the right thinking elite to determine the will of the people. The key is to use the most artful and most reliable techniques that history has made available. And in Strauss's view, nothing has ever proved to be more effective than the influence of religion.

In view of Strauss's emphasis on the importance of religion for the harmony and well-being of political life, it is natural to find that Strauss inspired neoconservatives such as Irving Kristol are supportive of the religious right. As I will show, Kristol shares Strauss's view that a healthy dose of religious enthusiasm is indispensable for transcending the nihilism that is at the root of America's troubles. He is so convinced of the political utility of religion that he is blind to the immoderate nature of groups such as the Moral Majority of Jerry Falwell or the Christian Coalition of Pat Robertson and Ralph Reed. Kristol has encouraged the Republican party to embrace the religious right; and the party has been listening.

There is no doubt that religion often exerts a wholesome influence on human conduct. And it may even serve as a small protection against tyranny and the abuse of power because persons committed to the moral life may prefer to risk their lives than to collaborate with wicked schemes. But it is also the case that religious fervor often turns political and even militant. Religious groups are not always satisfied with the religious freedom that liberal society affords them. They are not content to gather together, worship, sing, play, and educate their children as they see fit. They are interested in imposing their vision of private morality on the rest of society. What they want is not freedom of religion, but conformity to their religious views. This has been a perennial problem in the history of America as well as in the history of Christianity itself. Christians have wavered between extremes: on one hand, withdrawing from the world, focusing on their own inner purity, thinking that they are in the world but not of the world, insisting that this world is beyond redemption, enduring the evils of existence, and waiting for salvation in the beyond. On the other hand, they have been eager to conquer the world for Christ. Their current mood is overtly political if not altogether militant. The Christian Coalition, founded by Pat Robertson and then led by his protégé Ralph Reed, is a case in point. Its "leadership school" does not waste much time on prayer, but on the political process and how best to manipulate it. Grassroots leaders in hundreds of counties in every state are instructed in the modern art of quick communication— phone, fax, and modem. These leaders are trained to mobilize their troops into rapid-response networks intended to "blitz" or bombard congressmen with the values of the coalition.[25]

There is no doubt that the Christian Coalition has had a great deal of power within the Republican party; it may well have provided the margin for as many as half of the Republicans' 52-seat gain in the House of Representatives in the 1994 election. With its 1.6 million active supporters and a $25 million annual budget it had a virtual veto power on the Republican nominee for president in 1996. William Lacy, the chief strategist for Robert Dole's presidential bid of 1996, admitted to the press that a Republican candidate needs the support of the Christian right to win either the nomination or the general election.[26] Presidential candidates in 1996 were reputed to be seeking the advice of Ralph Reed. Coalition lobbyists were among a group who met regularly in Republican House Speaker Newt Gingrich's suite to discuss the strategy to pass the party's Contract with America of 1994.[27] And despite his choirboy image, Ralph Reed has been doing just as much to push the Republican party further to the right as his predecessors, Pat Robertson and Jerry Falwell, did. School prayer, recriminalizing abortion, stripping known homosexuals of their civil rights, teaching creationism in the schools, and censoring libraries and the press are just the beginning of the "contract with the American family" as Reed calls his political agenda. This would indeed constitute the dismantling of liberalism in America.

The power of the Christian right may explain why politicians are eager to court its leaders, but it does not explain why Jewish intellectuals such as Irving Kristol, William Kristol, and Midge Decter are eager to defend the likes of Pat Robertson. The latter's zealous anti-Semitism is a matter of public record. In his book, *The New World Order*, Robertson gives an account of world history (from the Reign of Terror to the Nazi holocaust and the two World Wars) as a conspiracy of Jews, Freemasons, and "international bankers."[28] It seems to me that people in the grip of such theories are dangerous in positions of power. One hopes that it was the prevalence of good sense, and not just good luck, that led to Robertson's failure to win the Republican party's presidential nomination in 1988.

The willingness of Jewish conservatives to defend Pat Robertson does not simply have its source in the fact that they share the same enemy—namely liberalism—but that these conservative intellectuals who were nourished on the ideas of Leo Strauss, are convinced that religion is a necessary cement for society. And even if this is true, it must be admitted that religion is not an unmixed blessing, and that it contains attendant dangers. There is no doubt that Strauss's fears about America repeating the errors of Europe are not totally far-fetched—not for the reasons that he provides—but simply because demagoguery is an unavoidable risk of democratic politics.

American conservatives such as William Buckley and William Bennett fool themselves in thinking that the Christian right is simply interested in safe streets, good schools, strong families, nonintrusive government, and a chummy Communitarian atmosphere. But that is not the case. They are very much interested in governmental interference to uphold and enforce their own values and preferences, not only in matters pertaining to public morality, but in private morality as well. But their political tactics call their ethics into question. For example, Ralph Reed has defended the "stealth campaigns" of Christian Coalition candidates who have disguised their political agenda by campaigning on issues such as crime or taxes, but have revealed once in office that their real interests are in gay rights, abortion, and creationism.

Reed justifies such deception as a type of "guerrilla warfare."[29] He flatters himself into thinking that his stealth campaigns are a matter of using the tactics of a guerrilla war against Satan. Those who paint their political opponents as the forces of evil and regard themselves as the defenders of good, are inclined to justify any means as necessary to defeat their opponents. The urgency of vanquishing the satanic forces, and the sheer immensity of the task, blinds them to the fact that such mendacious and duplicitous conduct is a blatant disregard of Christian virtue.

The conception of politics as a struggle between cosmic forces of good and evil is not confined to religious groups. Republican Speaker of the House Newt Gingrich is in the habit of speaking of his political opponents as the enemies of Western civilization. By the same token, he paints himself as the self-appointed knight in shining armor whose duty it is to rescue Western civilization from decline and degeneration and restore it to its former glory. In *The Contract with America,* he echoes Strauss's sense of crisis when he declares that "what is ultimately at stake . . . is literally the future of American civilization as it has existed for the last several hundred years."[30] The issue is "whether or not our civilization will survive."[31] This sense of crisis leads to fudging the distinction between war and politics, and this in turn leads to the refusal to play by the rules—supposedly all is fair in love and war.

Oliver North is a good example. When he ran unsuccessfully for the Senate in the elections of 1994, he told supporters of his "redemption campaign" that if he wins, then the war begins. In war there are few rules, and no one to enforce them, so all that is left is power and cunning. But politics is supposed to be a triumph over war. It is supposed to replace the violence and chaos of war by a rule-regulated contest for power. Political order begins to give way to chaos and war when these rules are blatantly discarded. It seems that Oliver North has learned nothing from his conviction in the Iran-Contra scandal of the 1980s.

The American Right feels as if it is being held hostage by liberal society. This beleaguered mentality goes hand in hand with a world-view that is as demonic as it is dualistic. It is demonic in the sense that it sees the world as overrun by the forces of evil (now called liberalism) and dualistic because it regards its political opponents as the incarnation of cosmic evil. The beleaguered pose as the saviors and defenders of the world against the looming threat of the demonic forces. The right-wing militia groups that have gained prominence in the United States in the 1990s are classic cases in point: the South Michigan Regional Militia, the Texas Constitutional Militia, the Florida State Militia, the Constitutional Defense Militia in New Hampshire, the Guardians of American Liberties in Boulder, Colorado, Police Against the New World Order in Arizona, and others are united in their opposition to gun control, the federal government, and the United Nations.[32] One of the largest and most militant of these is the Militia of Montana, headquartered in the Cabinet Mountains, which they believe to be the place where the war against the government of the United States will begin. John Trochmann, one of the founders of the group, accuses the government of secretly building concentration camps, and advises his readers to stock up on the three *Bs*—boots, beans, and bullets. The militia's newsletter, *Taking Aim,* also contains racial overtones; it claims that sometime in the next century "America's white population will perish."[33] Supposedly, the government is in league with the nonwhite races and the whites have to arm themselves for purposes of self-defense.

The literature of these militias has apocalyptic overtones and abounds with conspiracy theories. The militias accuse the federal government of treason for collaborating with the Soviets to create a world Socialist government. The collapse of the Soviet Union makes the literature laughable, and some militia groups have substituted the United Nations for the Soviet Union in their account. The trick is to create an atmosphere of impending catastrophe, even where there is no perceptible danger. The media is perceived as collaborating with the enemy; the most powerful propaganda machine in all of history has sold its soul to the devil, and uses its power and ingenuity to portray the advance of the global tyranny in the most innocuous light.

The trouble with these groups is that they use politics to give life cosmic purpose and intensity. But since they don't find politics either exciting or intense, they resolve to replace it by war. And if the enemy is formidable enough, struggle is bound to be as heroic as it is endless.

There is a connection between Leo Strauss and the beleaguered sense of crisis that characterizes the American right. The dominant theme of his work is the "crisis" of the West, which has its source in liberal modernity. In a commentary on Carl Schmitt's *The Concept of the Political,* Strauss agrees with Schmitt that liberalism has turned life into entertainment, and has deprived it of its seriousness, intensity, and struggle. As I will show, Strauss shares the controversial Nazi jurist and political philosopher's view that the fundamental distinction in politics is that of *friend* and *foe.* Schmitt admires the Nazis because they understood the importance of this distinction and they proceeded to exterminate their enemies, including "internal" enemies. Like Schmitt, Strauss believes that politics is first and foremost about the distinction between WE and THEY.[34] Strauss thinks that a political order can be stable only if it is united by an external threat; and following Machiavelli, he maintains that if no external threat exists, then one has to be manufactured. Had he lived to see the collapse of the Soviet Union, he would have been deeply troubled because the collapse of the evil empire poses a threat to America's inner stability. There is certainly some truth in this; nevertheless, it is dangerous to think of politics, as Strauss does, in terms of groups that are culturally, religiously, and linguistically cohesive. To the extent that such cohesiveness does not exist in the world, politics becomes a perennial struggle to destroy the internal foe, the other, the different. This is the reason that nationalistic politics is so radical and why it is a classic manifestation of the beleaguered mentality. As I will show, Strauss's understanding of politics is nationalist and profoundly at odds with liberal pluralism.

It is important to point out that pluralism is not the invention of liberals, even though they are the first to champion it as an asset. I doubt that too much diversity is the asset that liberals think it is, but plurality is a fact of human existence, and the attempt to eradicate it is positively dangerous because it turns politics into an endless struggle.

It is a mistake to expect politics to provide life with significance, seriousness, and intensity. It is not the business of politics to give life meaning, mystery, and magic. Art, love, or religion can accomplish that, but not politics. Relying on politics to invest life with meaning, has the effect of turning life into a living hell.


## LIBERALISM AND CONSERVATISM IN AMERICA

American conservatism is a post–World War II phenomenon that is largely a reaction to developments in the history of liberalism in general, and American liberalism in particular. Liberalism began as a successful revolution against absolute monarchy, against the power of the Church and its religious intolerance, against feudalism, and against the mercantilist system. As was usually the case in European politics, England led the way. First, it severed itself from the power of the Catholic Church, thanks to Henry VIII and Elizabeth I. Then the Puritans led a revolt against absolute monarchy in the English Civil War of the 1640s that ended in the beheading of Charles I. But English civil liberties were not secured until the Glorious Revolution of 1688, and whose spokesman was John Locke. In the atmosphere of European life in the seventeenth and eighteenth centuries, liberal ideas swept Europe like a fresh breeze, blowing away the moldy institutions and oppressive traditions associated with medieval life. Politically speaking, liberalism curbed the absolute and arbitrary power of the state by insisting on the protection of the natural rights to life, liberty, and estate. Civil liberties meant equal protection of all citizens under the law. Religiously speaking, it undermined the authority of the church. By introducing a wedge between church and state, it prevented the state from using religion to buttress its power; but it also prevented the church from relying on the violence of the state to punish heretics and protect orthodoxy. Liberalism was not an attack on religious life itself; it was meant to guarantee religious liberty and provide a solution to religious strife and persecution.

Economically speaking, liberalism swept away the mercantilist system that was deeply rooted in power, birth, and privilege. This meant more competition, industriousness, and a degree of social mobility that undermined the occupational determinism that was the iron law of the old order. In short, liberalism delivered the death blow to the crumbling and corrupt medieval order. In its three-hundred-year life it has been one of the headiest and most successful revolutions in history; and in some circles, it shows no signs of abating.[35] But nowhere did it take root or succeed as quickly as it did in America.

The second phase of the liberal revolution was epitomized by the writings of John Stuart Mill (1806-73) in the nineteenth century. Mill was not satisfied with civil liberties alone. He thought that a liberal society should provide its citizens with *personal liberty*. The latter presupposes a distinction between the public and the private domains. Mill divided human actions into those that were self-regarding and those that were other-regarding. Self-regarding actions affected only the interests of the individual and not those of others. In contrast, other-regarding actions have an impact on the interests of others. Mill argued that the domain of self-regarding actions, the domain of private life, sexual conduct, and personal habits, including personal vices, was a domain of freedom that was immune from legal, moral, or social sanctions. For Mill, limits on individual freedom are legitimate only in cases where harm to others is involved.[36]

The rationale behind the defense of freedom of lifestyle is Mill's belief in the importance of individuality.[37] Mill argued that individuals were like plants and that they required different conditions under which to thrive. Imposing the same conditions, or the same mold on every individual is bound to stunt human development. No one suffers more from the social pressures to conform than unique and eccentric individuals. And it was for the sake of the latter that Mill was eager to curb the power of society because in his view, unique and eccentric individuals alone insure the progress of civilization. Mill realized that his defense of a private domain free from interference for the cultivation of individuality implies the necessity of defending private vices such as alcoholism and prostitution. But he surmised that these vices could be tolerated for the sake of freedom; and he also thought that the ills that resulted from these vices would be outweighed by the benefits that accrue from the cultivation of individuality.

It is important to recognize that the liberal ethos makes a very strict distinction between those who would destroy their own lives with vice and those who would profit from destroying the lives of others—the distinction between prostitution and pimping is a case in point; but other entrepreneurial endeavors that exploit human weaknesses (such as pornography) are also included. But alas, liberal society has allowed the profit motive to go unchecked, and in so doing, it has strayed very far from the liberal ideal. Liberals who defend the free market assume that it is a neutral instrument that can only enhance the freedom, independence, and self-reliance of individuals. But the market is not as neutral as it seems. It is not simply a matter of producing the best products at the most competitive prices. It does not simply sell products; it sells lifestyles. Commercials for Pepsi or for Nike are not about tasty drinks and comfortable shoes; they are about the sort of person you should be. These products are not simply intended to quench your thirst or protect your feet, they are intended to shape your sense of self.

The third phase of the liberal revolution is typified by the work of T. H. Green, John Rawls, and the development of the social welfare state.[38] It registered a dissatisfaction with what Isaiah Berlin called *negative liberty* as opposed to *positive liberty*.[39] Negative liberty requires simply the noninterference of others (including the state). It requires that one is *not* tortured, arbitrarily arrested, threatened for expressing unpopular views (as long as he is not inciting crime or being libelous and seditious), or harassed for an eccentric lifestyle. In contrast, positive liberty is not just freedom from, but freedom to—to act, to choose, or to have the opportunity for self-actualization. This understanding of freedom requires that others (or the state) actually provide one with certain things deemed necessary for a complete and fulfilling life. If rights are liberties, then we can say that there is in theory an infinite supply of negative rights because they depend simply on the will of others not to interfere. In contrast, positive rights are finite because they are contingent on the availability of resources: education, Medicare, Social Security, a paid vacation, or a minimum income are examples. And even though Berlin denounced the concept of positive liberty, historical circumstances have made it persuasive and allowed it to triumph.

In the United States, the Great Depression was critical in this development. After all, what good was it to be free from the interference of others if one was also free to starve to death? In the context of this economic crisis, the classical liberal notion of freedom seemed inadequate. President Franklin Delano Roosevelt's New Deal came to the rescue. Reasonable folks welcomed it as an antidote to the ills of laissez-faire capitalism. Marxists and Socialists regarded the New Deal as the artificial life-support system that kept capitalism alive; they wished that capitalism had been left alone to die the natural death that history had intended for it. But this was not to be. John Rawls managed to revive the fiction of the social contract. If we can imagine social life to be a free agreement among equals, then what rational individual would choose a state of affairs in which he was simply free from interference, instead of choosing the social welfare state?

The new right in America emerged as a reaction to the social welfare state created by the New Deal. It became a political force after World War II.[40] The old right was not politically significant; it consisted mostly of conservative Southerners and Confederates who clung to the old South and its slave culture, long after the Civil War. But the old South lost the battle to Abraham Lincoln whose success established once and for all that freedom not slavery was the true spirit of America. In contrast to the old right, the new right was peopled by disenchanted liberals. They were disenchanted with social welfare liberalism and harkened back to laissez-faire economics.

The new right is a term that refers to both *libertarians* and *neoconservatives.* But there is a very important difference between these two advocates of economic liberalism: libertarians are consistent liberals, whereas neoconservatives are not. Libertarians are consistent liberals because they are advocates of a minimal state, not only where the economy is concerned, but where social life is concerned. In other words, they mean to keep government out of our pocketbooks as well as out of our bedrooms. In some cases they verge on anarchism.[41] In contrast, neoconservatism combines capitalist economics with conservative social policies. It aims to keep the government out of the economy, but not out of the bedrooms, the schools, the arts, publishing, and broadcasting. Neoconservatism is the real challenge to the reigning liberal ethos. It is the dominant form that the new right assumes in America, and it is the most powerful ideological force within the Republican party.

Irving Kristol, the intellectual leader of the movement, backed Nixon in 1972. But on the whole, the new conservatives or neoconservatives did not become a force within the Republican party until the Reagan years. It was in these years that they began to hold important positions in Washington. Jeane Kirkpatrick was appointed American ambassador to the United Nations; Norman Podhoretz (editor of *Commentary*) was appointed as an advisor in the administration's international communications apparatus; Michael Novak became ambassador to the United Nations Human Rights Commission; William Bennett served consecutively as chair of the National Endowment for the Humanities and Secretary of Education, where he was assisted by William Kristol; Gertrude Himmelfarb, neoconservative scholar, wife of Irving Kristol, and mother of William Kristol, held a presidential appointment on the Council of the National Endowment for the Humanities.[42] I will not be tracing the comings and goings of the neoconservatives in Washington. This is not a book about personalities, but about ideas. I am concerned with the extent to which the ideas of the new conservatives echo the ideas of Leo Strauss.

The 1996 presidential campaign of Bob Dole and Jack Kemp is a model of the neoconservative philosophy with all its tensions and contradictions. Dole represents the social conservatism of the movement with its nostalgia for the past, its emphasis on self-restraint and self-sacrifice, its preference for virtue over happiness, and its desire to stem the tide of selfishness and permissiveness that it perceives as the legacy of liberalism. In contrast, Kemp represents the optimism of Kristol's supply-side economics, with its faith in the market, and its desire to defend the power and privilege of large corporations as a means to the prosperity and well-being of the nation.

In chapter 5, I will focus on neoconservatism as it is expressed in the writings of its leading intellectual exponent, Irving Kristol. I will show that the major themes of neoconservatism echo the political ideas of Leo Strauss—his sense of crisis, his dread of nihilism, his antipathy to liberalism, his religiosity, his elitism, his populism, and more. And far from exerting a conserving and moderating influence on American liberalism, the Strauss-inspired neoconservatism radicalizes and destabilizes American politics. Gone are the days when conservatives in America were displaced and disinherited voices whistling in the dark; American conservatism has become a political phenomenon to be reckoned with.

CHAPTER TWO

# STRAUSS'S
# JEWISH HERITAGE

LEO STRAUSS WAS NOURISHED on Jewish as well as German ideas. He
was a biblical scholar and a medievalist who studied Maimonides,
Alfarabi, Averroës, and Abravanel. Some of those who knew him say that
Strauss had the demeanor of a medieval rabbi. But at the same time, he
was a German intellectual steeped in the ideas of Friedrich Nietzsche,
Martin Heidegger, and Carl Schmitt. I believe that the key to understanding Strauss rests in comprehending his efforts to reconcile these
two disparate sets of ideas. From Judaism, Strauss inherited a posture of
resignation in the face of the injustice and tragedy of life. From German
philosophy, he inherited a political romanticism that gave him an
aversion to liberal modernity. In what follows, I will show how Strauss
blended the Judaic and the Germanic elements of his intellectual
heritage. I will argue that Strauss's Judaism was profoundly compro-
mised, and that his politics is incongruous with any modest or moderate
account of political life.

## THE JEWISH PROBLEM DEFINED

The hatred and persecution of the Jews is for Leo Strauss the most simple
"exemplification of the human problem."[1] The problem is that human
beings are divided into groups that are pitted against one another in
mutual hatred and antagonism. Indeed, if the Jews are a chosen people,
they are chosen as a graphic illustration of the intransigence of the human
problem and living proof of the impossibility of redemption.[2]

In a moving lecture, "Why We Remain Jews," Strauss promises what he has never promised before—he promises not to "beat around the bush."[3] Strauss keeps his promise; he states flatly that "there is no solution to the Jewish problem."[4] Pogroms, crusades, and concentration camps will never disappear from the face of the earth as long as the human race lives. The Crusades were partly an "orgy of murder of Jews"; the Tsarist regime dissipated revolutionary zeal through pogroms or organized massacres of Jews, and the examples can be multiplied.[5] We are no closer to a solution today than we were in the Middle Ages. In the twentieth century, things have only gotten worse as human power has been augmented by technological development. Anyone who thinks otherwise is a dreamer, deluded by the myth of progress. Strauss has no use for progressive optimism. How could he? How could anyone after the "barbarism" we have witnessed in this century?

Strauss tells the story of Jewish refugees from Russia in his father's house when he was a boy of five or six. They were on their way to Australia. At that time, Strauss thought that it could not happen in Germany, where Jews lived in "profound peace" with their non-Jewish neighbors. But still, the incident made a "deep impression" on him and for one "unforgettable moment" he sensed that "it could happen here."[6] And of course it did.

Strauss rejects all the "solutions" to the Jewish problem—assimilation, liberal democracy, and political Zionism. He considers them all to be manifestations of modernity. Instead, he suggests that we learn to live with the human problem. For the young Jews he is addressing, that means learning to live as Jews—learning to live with persecution. Strauss also rejects the Zionist solution; instead, he advocates a full-blown Jewish nationalism.

## JEWISHNESS AS ANTIMODERN

The most distinguishing feature of the work of Leo Strauss is its invective against modernity. Strauss's radical antimodernism has its source in the conviction that modernity is to blame for the Nazi holocaust or the "barbarization we have witnessed in this century."[7]

Strauss explains the connection between modernity and the catastrophe of 1933 as follows. The Germans were not great lovers of modernity. Modernity was a French phenomenon that spelled the defeat and humiliation of the Prussian armies at the hands of Napoleon in 1806. There were no doubt Francophiles like Hegel among the Germans, but on the whole, the Germans saw modernity as the triumph of the French and the humiliation of the Germans. However, Nazi propaganda identified the Jews with modernity and therefore with the betrayal and humiliation of Germany. A dichotomy was established: the modern, secular, cosmopolitan French and Jewish, on the one hand; and the traditional, religious German, particular and nationalistic, on the other. As a result, the Jews became enemies of everything German, authentic, and unique—the harbingers of French cosmopolitanism and the destroyers of German culture.[8]

Strauss comes to the defense of the Jews not by defending modernity against German parochialism, but by denying the identification of the Jews with modernity. He insists that the Jews are a supremely antimodern people.[9] Modernity is secular, commercial, and historicist. But none of these things are true of the Jewish people, whatever the Nazi propaganda might have said. The Jewish experience flies in the face of modernity. The Jewish people are a religious people, who must cling to their faith against the secular influence of modernity. Modernity liberates commerce, but the Jewish faith does not look favorably on commerce and its concomitant laxity toward the passions. Modernity is historicist, but the Jewish people are an ahistorical people, tracing their lineage back to the "seed of Abraham." Nor can the Jewish experience be historicized. Strauss is critical of those who, like Franz Rosenzweig, try to modernize or historicize Judaism in an effort to make it fit the modern world. He insists that the Jewish people are lost and homeless in the modern world.[10]

## THE IMPOSSIBILITY OF ASSIMILATION

Assimilation has always been one of the most attractive solutions to the Jewish problem. In the past, when Christianity was socially and politically significant, the simplest way for a Jew to assimilate was to convert to Christianity. Strauss surmises that this approach to assimilation may have been successful for some individuals, but it cannot be regarded as a viable solution to Jews as a group. The Spanish experiment was a case in point. The Spanish Jews were expelled from Spain in 1492. Many of them, especially those with large possessions, decided to convert to Christianity in order to stay in Spain. The result of this mass conversion was a classic illustration of the hopelessness of assimilation as a collective solution to the Jewish problem. The new converts to Christianity were distrusted and despised. They were considered men and women who preferred their fortunes to their faith. They were certainly not regarded as sincere believers in Christianity. And the Inquisition even tried to hunt them down for "Jewish practices." But it was difficult to provide legal proof of such practices, and many of these Jews survived. However, an extralegal practice emerged at the social level. The Spaniards began to make a distinction between the old Christians and the new Jewish Christians. So, the Jews who converted to Christianity were "forced to remain Jews."[11] Another example of assimilationist failure is the story of a group of Jews in Los Angeles who decided to become Christian Scientists. As their numbers grew, they were asked to form a group of their own—which is to say a group of Jewish Christian Scientists.[12] Assimilation does not work.

So, why remain Jews? Strauss echoes Theodor Herzl by saying, "the enemy makes us a nation, whether we like it or not."[13] But this is not the whole story. Jews are not forced to remain Jews because the "enemy" will not let them. Strauss does not reject assimilation simply because it does not work. He confesses that deep down he thinks that it is dishonorable. He tells us that he could never erase the "primitive feeling" he learned from his "wet nurse" that "no Jew who ever converted to Christianity was sincere."[14] Strauss therefore rejects assimilation and councils the young Jews in his audience to "remain Jews" because this is the only noble course of action.

One cannot help feeling that Strauss thinks that it is a good thing that assimilation does not work, for otherwise the Jews would lose their identity as a people, and *that,* as we shall see, is of paramount importance to Strauss.

Liberal democracy proposes *a novel form of assimilation.* Instead of asking the Jews to become Christians, it creates a society that is neither Christian nor Jewish—a society in which religion and politics are separate and where all citizens, regardless of their religious affiliation, have equal rights before the law. Liberal democracy is the brainchild of modernity or Enlightenment. It tends to be animated by a utopian vision of universal human emancipation through the triumph of reason and truth over prejudice, suspicion, and religion. It sees religion as the source of hatred and antagonism. The solution is a secular state in which the distinction between Christian and Jew is irrelevant.

Spinoza was the first Jew to advocate liberal democracy as a solution to the Jewish question. And many Jews in Strauss's generation as in our own, believe that liberal democracy is indeed the best human solution available. But Strauss begs to differ. Liberal democracy, the "regime required by modernity," is anathema to him. He makes at least four objections to liberal democracy.

First, Strauss argues that liberal society is predicated on the distinction between a small public sphere and a large private sphere. Liberal freedom is freedom from legal interference in the private sphere. So, even though the liberal state grants all its citizens equal rights, this applies only to the small "public" sphere and not to the "private" sphere that is impervious to law. But since the inviolability of the private sphere is also *protected* by law, liberal society "permits," "protects," and even "fosters" private discrimination against Jews by groups or individuals.[15] All attempts to end "discrimination" encroach on the sanctity of the private sphere and compromise the liberal principles of freedom and limited government. Therefore, liberalism cannot be considered a solution to the Jewish problem—not even in America, where it is deeply entrenched and advanced.

As Strauss sees it, American society pretends to be a liberal society of individuals, but in reality it is made up of a strict racial hierarchy in which the Anglo-Saxons are at the top, the Negroes at the bottom, and the Jews "just above the Negroes."[16] Although there are similarities between the Jewish problem and the Negro problem, Strauss thinks that there is an important difference; he says that when we (Jews) appeal to justice, "we appeal to principles ultimately which (if I may say so) were originally our own. When the Negroes fight for justice, they have to appeal to principles which were not their own, their ancestors' in Africa, but which they learned from their oppressors. This is not an altogether negligible difference, and needs to be stated by someone who doesn't want to beat around the bush."[17] Strauss does not think that a sense of justice and fair play is a universal human attribute. According to a widely circulated story, Strauss had to escape by the back door during an interview with black American activists. On that occasion, he was not esoteric enough.

Second, Strauss objects to liberal society because it destroys community. He echoes Marx's infamous essay on "The Jewish Question."[18] In that essay, Marx launches an assault on American society that, like Strauss, he considers the manifestation of the principles of liberal modernity as concocted by Hobbes and Locke. Marx begins with Hegel's distinction between the state or political domain and civil society. He argues that the American and French revolutions are bourgeois revolutions that secured the political emancipation of man, but not his genuine (or human) emancipation.

According to Marx, these revolutions succeeded only in emancipating what Hegel referred to as "civil society," which is the domain of egoism and self-interest, and destroying the state as an independent entity. Now the state is subordinated to civil society and acts only as a vehicle to preserve the latter. The American and French revolutions destroyed not only the political character of the state, but also the political character that civil society once had. In feudal times, civil society included estates, corporations, guilds, and privileges that accounted for its political character.[19] The liberal or bourgeois revolutions eliminated the political character of civil society and left a disintegrated mass of isolated individuals. The liberty granted amounts to nothing more than the absence of external impediment intended to give free reign to the frenzied pursuit of self-interest.[20] Marx does not lament the eclipse of the political, even though he grants that the demise of the political has left individuals solitary and competitive, bereft of their truly gregarious humanity. Marx quotes Rousseau approvingly when he says that the political task par excellence is to transform each individual "who, in isolation is a complete and solitary whole, into a *part* of something greater than himself, from which in a sense he derives his life and his being."[21] But for Marx, the transformation of the solitary individual into part of a greater whole must be global. Only then will mankind be *universally* emancipated from the solitary, poor, nasty, and brutish conditions of civil society.

Strauss follows Marx and Rousseau in rejecting liberal society as nothing more than an aggregate of isolated solitary monads—a sham, and not a society in any meaningful sense. For Strauss as for Marx, American society is the epitome of liberal egoism; it is incapable of transforming solitary man into part of something greater than himself. But he rejects Marx's dream of a universal community.

In Strauss's view, there can be no *universal* community of men because a community is by its nature exclusive. A society that includes all of mankind is not a society; for the latter is by its nature a bond that unites members of a group by what distinguishes them from others.[22] And that is precisely the trouble with liberal society—it is supposedly so all-inclusive that it is a void. Liberalism allegedly binds men not by what makes them distinctive or sets them apart from others, but by what all mankind have in common—which is to say, the desire for survival, ease, and security. Strauss does not think that a sense of justice is a universal attribute of humanity; he implies that all we have in common is our animality, and that is the basis of liberal society.

Strauss warns young Jews against trying to "assimilate" into such a society—because anyone who tries will become "perplexed" when he finds that there is nothing there to be a part of.[23] Strauss agrees with Heidegger that the modern project has destroyed all "peoples" and left nothing but "lonely crowds."[24]

Third, Strauss objects to the secularism at the heart of liberal democracy because it further erodes community. For Strauss, secular societies, whether liberal or communist, do not work. Religion is necessary to cement society, although adding a bond of blood does not hurt.[25] This means that Marx, Spinoza, and all those who follow them are mistaken in thinking that religion is the source of mutual hatred and antagonism among groups. Strauss argues that religion is not the culprit, since the Nazis and the Communists were not religious.

For Strauss, religion is the opium of the people, but the people need their opium.[26] Religion gives meaning and comfort to the lives of ordinary people; in contrast, liberal individualism leaves people lost, rootless, and dispossessed; it denies the reality of human groups and the human need to belong to a group. Only such belonging can save people from the nihilistic vacuum into which they have been plunged by the logic of liberal modernity.

It may be objected that liberalism is not inherently anti-religious, but that it merely relegates religion to the private domain. But for Strauss, this will not do, because the value of religion lies in the public function it performs—and this is at the heart of Strauss's criticism of American liberalism.

Strauss sees the absence of religion from the public realm as indicating the absence of any public orthodoxy. He cannot entertain the idea that liberalism might itself act as a public orthodoxy. He sees liberalism as the absence of any public orthodoxy and hence, the absence of any authoritative truth that could act as its guiding light in the public realm. In the absence of a public orthodoxy, liberal democracy is weak, floundering, and ultimately doomed. As we have seen, Strauss thought that liberal democracy leaves us vulnerable to the perils of fascism. And this explains Strauss's perennial sense of crisis. For as long as liberal democracy prevails, Western civilization will continue to be in crisis.

In conclusion, Strauss dissents from Spinoza and Marx's belief that the solution to the Jewish question is a secular society in which the distinction between Christian and Jew is abolished. But he defends both men against the charge that they were self-hating Jews: it was out of love of the Jewish people that they arrived at their solutions.[27] But the irony is that, despite their good intentions, their "solutions" lead to the abolition of the Jews as a *people*. Strauss therefore rejects their solutions as misguided.

Strauss does not reject liberal democracy simply because it fails to "solve" the Jewish problem. He rejects liberal democracy because it destroys community, including the Jewish community. It therefore accomplishes by peaceful means what the Nazis sought to accomplish with their death factories.[28] In other words, Strauss is opposed to liberalism not just because it fails, but because it succeeds—and *that* is far worse.

## JEWISH NATIONALISM RECOMMENDED

Political Zionism emerged toward the end of the nineteenth century primarily as an attempt to stem the tide of assimilation and absorption. Its goal was to preserve the Jews as a people. It summoned Jews around the world to political action intended to end their exile and return to the promised land. Its arch-enemy was liberalism; for the latter hastened the process of dissolution.

But there is also another argument in favor of Zionism, and that is that assimilation does not work, and cannot work, save in the case of a few extraordinary families such as the Disraelis and the Ricardos. And if the Jews are to be a nation like any other, if they are to have a land of their own in which their distinctive culture can develop and flourish, then they must have a country of their own. An eloquent version of this argument was made by Isaiah Berlin.[29] Berlin compares the Jews to people who have disfiguring humps on their backs. Some of them accept their humps and bear them as a special mark of honor, despite the contempt of others. This is the attitude that Berlin attributes to the Jews of Eastern Europe. They retreated into their ghettos where they developed a rich and independent life of their own that gave birth to generous, free, and unbroken Jewish personalities.[30] In contrast, the Jews of Western Europe deluded themselves by denying the existence of their humps. They struggled hard to be more German than the Germans, more French than the French. The result was a less spontaneous, less attractive, and more forced personality. In their attempt to conceal their identity, they fooled no one but themselves. Hitler caught them totally unaware. In the end, they paid a high price for their self-deception. But for those who do not wish to fool themselves and who do not wish to live with the hump, only a surgical solution can offer relief—and that surgical solution is the creation of Israel. Only political Zionism can remove the deformity, because it would make them like other nations of the world. But that is precisely what is at issue between a political Zionist such as Berlin and someone such as Strauss who rejects political Zionism and upholds Jewish orthodoxy. For Strauss, the identity of the Jews rests in not being like other nations.

In his youth, Strauss gravitated toward political Zionism. Like the Zionists, he was eager to preserve the identity of the Jewish people against the liberal tide of assimilation. But later, he abandoned political Zionism because he thought that there was something un-Jewish about it.[31] Far from preserving the unique identity of the Jewish people, Strauss came to the conclusion that political *Zionism is itself a form of assimilationism,* for its object is ultimately to assimilate the Jewish nation to the other nations of the world. The classic statement of political Zionism is Leo Pinsker's *Autoemancipation.* The idea is to inspire the Jews to restore to themselves a political state—any state, "Uganda would have been as good as Palestine."[32]

Strauss rejects political Zionism because it is a "radical break with the principles of the Jewish tradition."[33] The heart of the Jewish tradition is trust in God and not in one's own "hardware." Strauss points out that the Jewish tradition consists in waiting for the redemption of the Lord God. The solution to the Jewish problem must be a divine solution, not a human one. Political Zionism replaces divine redemption with human redemption in the form of political activism. Zionism is not content to wait for God's messianic redemptive act. It rejects the Exile, and is prepared to remedy the situation by human efforts.[34]

While pointing to the anti-Jewish nature of political Zionism, Strauss does not wish to be too hard, for he knows just how much the Jewish people have longed for a homeland. But he is eager to point out that the Jewish *nation* is unlike any other nation. For God has not assigned to the Jews a portion of the earth as he has with other tribes. In other words, God has *chosen* the Jews for suffering at the hands of others. He has singled them out as the most vivid manifestation of the human problem; he has chosen them as the living proof that there is *no redemption.*[35]

Strauss councils the young Jews in his American audience to forget about liberalism, Zionism, and assimilation in general; he councils them to return to their Jewish faith. He tries to convince them that, far from being a misfortune, being a Jew is an opportunity: an opportunity to belong to a "nation," or to be part of a "people" rather than being lost in the lonely crowd created by American liberalism. But what is the opportunity that being part of the Jewish nation offers? Strauss tells them that it is an opportunity for "heroic suffering," which is made possible only by a nation that is dedicated to something "infinitely higher than itself."[36] This is the only noble solution. Become part of the Jewish nation, and accept its unique form of nationalism, and prepare yourself for the "heroic suffering" it demands. Unlike Hannah Arendt, Strauss is not ashamed of those Jews who went quietly to their death. On the contrary, he would regard them as a testimony to the glory of the Jewish nation, for they have born the burden of "heroic suffering" that it requires. Strauss is therefore a Jewish nationalist, but not a political Zionist.

On a superficial reading, Strauss's position resembles that of orthodox Judaism. Even friends such as Karl Löwith mistook Strauss for an orthodox Jew. But Strauss denies being an orthodox Jew.[37] Indeed, there is nothing particularly Jewish about his thought, as will become more apparent.

The trouble with Strauss's "solution" to the Jewish problem is that many of the young Americans who listened to him have not the faith of their fathers. But Strauss is candid, and for once, he does not beat around the bush. He does not pretend that the Jewish heritage is glorious because it is true. He declares openly that Judaism is a "heroic delusion" and a "noble dream." And he adds that "no nobler dream was ever dreamt." And that "it is surely nobler to be victim of the most noble dream than to profit from a sordid reality and to wallow in it."[38] In the absence of faith, he implores his young listeners to embrace their "faith" as a noble delusion. In the spirit of Nietzsche, he tells them to break themselves on a rock, for there is nothing greater than to die for the glory of a splendid illusion.

Strauss does not simply begin with the fact of mutual hatred and suspicion, he promotes an atmosphere in which such mutual suspicions can thrive. He makes persecution the basis of Jewish identity. And worse of all, he demands martyrdom for nothing. To die for truth and justice befits human dignity, but Strauss invites his young friends to sacrifice their lives for myths and illusions. It matters little how noble these are, they are, by Strauss's own admission, lies.

Strauss's heroic conception of Jewish nationalism is reminiscent of German romanticism. There is no doubt that German romanticism contributed to the pathological nationalism of the German people and fueled the murderous hatred of the Jews. But Strauss is soft on romanticism because he shares the romantic aversion to liberal individualism, rationalism, and universalism. He regards romanticism as a fellow traveler, and praises it as the strongest German protest against liberal modernity.[39]

Strauss's Jewish nationalism echoes the classic nationalism of Giuseppe Mazzini and his slogans: "nationality is a mission," the "nation means sacrifice."[40] And like Mazzini, Strauss embraces nationalism and its ethic of sacrifice as a remedy for the natural human propensity for selfishness and self-indulgence. But the trouble with this remedy for human failing is that it often relies too heavily on the presence of an enemy, and the magnification of the threat of the other. In order to sustain itself, nationalism must exaggerate the differences between groups and cultivate the eccentricities and uniqueness of each as if it were the highest end. In so doing, nationalism tends to undermine the humanity we share in common.

Nationalism divides humanity into nations, identified by their linguistic, cultural, racial, and religious characteristics. It assumes that these groups are the natural units of political life. Individuals become fully human only to the extent that they are members of these groups. It is the duty of the state to preserve the uniqueness of the people within its borders, even if this means persecuting and expelling foreign elements that pollute the purity of the nation.[41] Prior to the establishment of the state of Israel in 1948, the Jews of the modern world had no territory of their own, they had to inhabit other states as foreigners and outsiders. And if this nationalist philosophy is to hold true, then it is inevitable that the Jews are persecuted. But Strauss's point is not that their persecution is inevitable, but that it is good and wholesome, because it keeps them from assimilating with the peoples of the nations they inhabit; it preserves their identity as a unique people.

This is also the task that Strauss expects the state of Israel to accomplish, and it explains his explicit support for the state of Israel, despite all his objections to political Zionism. In a letter to *Commentary*, Strauss complains that despite the otherwise excellent points of view expressed in this magazine, he has detected a certain animus toward Israel in some of the articles.[42] He was particularly irked by a reference to Israel as a "racist state." He surmises that it is a reference to the absence of all civil marriages in the state of Israel—all marriages must be either Jewish, Christian, or Moslem. This means that there can be no intermarriage among these groups. Strauss then proceeds to defend this policy, saying that civil marriages (and hence, mixed marriages) are not an unmitigated blessing. In fact, he argues, this policy is at the very heart of what Strauss calls the "conservatism" of the state of Israel, as well as of political Zionism itself. Strauss explains that political Zionism saved the Jews from "complete dissolution"—he is not referring to Hitler's death camps, but to assimilation. Political Zionism "fulfilled a conservative function" by stemming the "tide of 'progressive' leveling of venerable ancestral differences."[43] The prohibition of mixed marriages is therefore at the very heart of what Strauss sees as the special value of political Zionism.

From the point of view of Strauss's nationalist philosophy, liberalism is a special threat to the uniqueness of peoples. By bringing a diversity of European peoples to live in America, American liberalism threatens to rob them of their distinctiveness. It threatens to make them merely human, which is to say, little more than beasts. For its politics is coarse and crude, concerned with material wealth and creature comforts. Strauss abhors liberalism not because he thinks that it does not work, but because he fears that it might. The totality of Strauss's rejection of assimilation is a measure of his rejection of American liberalism and the American melting pot. It does not occur to him that the "peoples" of Europe are not some mystical purebreds that have sprung from rock and oak, but are themselves products of other melting pots. It does not occur to him that the assimilation of different peoples in America will result in the emergence of yet another distinctive people.

It seems to me that the very things that Strauss dislikes about American liberalism are the things that recommend it. Liberalism regards politics as a practical and prosaic affair—not the stuff of poetry and martyrdom. Liberalism is the enemy of Strauss (and of romantics and nationalists as a whole) because it is rooted in rationalist and Enlightenment thought. But one need not be a liberal or a rationalist to take a modest view of politics as the domain of material interests rather than of high-minded principles. Politics is the domain of the cold and mundane. It is not the business of politics to intensify life, to give it meaning, mystery, and magic. For that, art, love, religion, science, sport, and other beguilements of culture are necessary.


## THE WISDOM OF LESSING REJECTED

It is instructive to compare Strauss's nationalist thinking with the views expressed by Gotthold Ephraim Lessing (1729-81) in his play *Nathan the Wise*.[44] Lessing was a dramatist, art critic, theologian, and the leading representative of Enlightenment thought in Germany. Like other intellectuals of his generation, Strauss was familiar with Lessing's play, but he obviously had little sympathy for its teachings. Lessing's play is set in the late twelfth century. It features Saladin as the Sultan, Sittah as his sister, Nathan as a rich Jew, Rachel as his adopted daughter, and a Templar or Christian Crusader who fought on the side of England's Richard the Lionhearted (who failed to recapture the Holy City from Saladin). The play is a comedy in which Lessing sets out to mock conventional bigotry and prejudice. His point is that beneath diverse cultural veneers, Moslems, Christians, and Jews are very much alike. And if people would only use their intelligence, they would realize that a good man is a good man in any culture, creed, or religion; and that treachery, fraud, violence, intemperance, cowardice, and vulgarity are despised by all.

Lessing's play also warns about too great an emphasis on religion because its singularity, or its conviction that it is the only true route to salvation, tends to lead to fanaticism. It is difficult for those who believe that their religion is the only way to God to stand by while their friends take what seems to them like the wrong course. In the play, Rachel's Christian nurse Daya is an example. But her vices pale in comparison to those of the Patriarch of Jerusalem, who is a first-class scoundrel. "The Jew must burn!" he says of Nathan. And what is Nathan's crime? He has taken an orphaned Christian child and raised her as his own; he has showered her with love and affection, provided her with an education, a home, and a Christian nurse. But in the Patriarch's eyes, Nathan has snatched an innocent child from the bosom of the church in which she was baptized, and condemned her to eternal damnation. In truth, Nathan must burn for his kindness, his goodwill, and his fatherliness. His wife and seven sons were burned by Christians, and he had every reason to harden his heart against Christian people, but he does not. Instead, he accepts his fate as the will of God and thanks the Lord for the daughter He has given him in compensation for the loss of his sons.

Lessing's play could very well have ended tragically, but tragedy is averted only because Lessing's characters are noble men and women who manage to transcend the parochial prejudices that their respective religions have inculcated. This is not an easy task, even for enlightened characters, because superstitions can continue to have a hold on us even after we recognize them as the falsehoods that they are.

In an unpublished essay on Sigmund Freud, Strauss describes Freud as a great man, but a bad Jew. The distinction might appear to mirror Aristotle's distinction between the good man and the good citizen, but this is not so. In Aristotle's view, being a good citizen is relative to the particular constitution or polis at hand, but being a good man is not a relative matter. Moreover, the good man and the good citizen are the same only in the best or ideal constitution. But since every constitution is flawed, there will always be a distinction between the good man and the good citizen.

In contrast to Aristotle, Strauss thinks that goodness is relative to politics, and religion is the handmaid of the political. In nature there can be great men, but not good men. Being a good Christian will differ considerably from being a good Jew or a good Moslem. And for Strauss, human beings must be Christians, Moslems, or Jews, otherwise they are gods or beasts. Strauss thinks that great men are godlike because they are not tied to the conventions of any particular city, but live according to nature. And since morality is a matter of convention (not nature), the philosopher is beyond good and evil. This is precisely why Strauss suggests that gods and beasts have a certain affinity with one another.[45]

Strauss's understanding has the effect of undermining morality and trivializing the great monotheistic religions. Strauss betrays the universalistic spirit of these religions. In contrast, Lessing sees them all as differing roads toward the same eternal truth, the same everlasting God. When asked to choose which of the three religions is best, Lessing puts his own twist on the old fable of the three rings. Based on an ancient tale in Boccaccio's *Decameron,* the story is about a magical ring that makes its wearer beloved of God and men alike. The ring was passed on from father to favorite son for generations, until one father was unable to carry on the tradition: he was unable to choose between his three sons because they were all equally deserving of the ring. When he was alone with his eldest son, he promised him the ring; but he did this also with his second and third son. In every case, he was earnest and had no intention of deluding them. But when his death neared, he realized that he had to do something. So, he called a jeweler and asked him to make two more rings identical to the original. When the skilled jeweler returned with the rings, the father could not tell which was the original. So, on different occasions, he gave each son a ring—each thinking it was *the* ring. When the father died, the brothers discovered that they each had a ring. They quarreled with one another, each insisting that his ring was authentic while the others were imposters. To end their dispute, they went to see a judge to adjudicate on the matter. The judge responded that they should all go away and wear their rings, each believing himself to be the bearer of the true ring; for the magic of the ring springs from the faith of the wearer. Inspired by the ring to behave in ways that make him beloved of God and men, he will prove that his ring is the genuine article. In Lessing's account, the three rings are the three religions. Lessing's tale implies that the truth of these religions depends on the deportment of their believers; and if all deport themselves honorably, then all are true. The tale blurs the distinction between the counterfeit and the authentic, a distinction that religions tend to insist on vis-à-vis one another. Just as all the rings came from the same loving father, so the great monotheistic religions came from the one and only God the father.

Lessing's play is powerful, and it underscores the shortcomings of Strauss's position. But instead of meeting the challenge of Lessing head on, Strauss proceeds to defang the opposition. Using vintage Straussian tactics, he argues that Lessing had a "conversion" that revealed to him the error of Enlightenment ideas and led him to embrace the esoteric philosophy of the ancients.[46] As proof of this, Strauss refers to Lessing's "Ernst and Falk, Dialogues for Freemasons," which he regards as a critical work in his own discovery of esotericism.[47] A brief look at this dialogue explains why it was of such interest to Strauss.

In the late eighteenth century, Germany was gripped by a passion for secret societies. The lodges of the Freemasons were among the most preeminent. The dialogue is partly autobiographical, since Lessing became a member of a Masonic lodge in Hamburg in 1771 (after several aborted attempts). In the dialogue, Ernst wonders if his friend really belongs to a secret society. But his friend responds with the most evasive answers. Ernst is eager to know all about the secret teaching that one must know to be admitted. Falk tells him that the truths of the brotherhood cannot be uttered because some truths are better left unsaid. Ernst rightly wonders how they manage to spread their beliefs so far and wide without ever uttering them. Falk suspects that those who admit others to the brotherhood have no idea what the secret teaching is. Meanwhile, the initiates are kindled with fantastic hopes. But mostly, everyone is attracted to the secrecy and the brotherhood—because the brothers support one another and promote one another's welfare. The dialogue is a comic account of the childish absurdities of secret societies. The general picture that emerges is not unlike the picture that Stanley Rosen, a renegade Straussian, paints of Strauss's own secret society.[48]

Despite its satirical qualities, the dialogue has a very serious side. Falk, the Freemason, explains to his friend what he thinks the secret teaching is all about and why secrecy is necessary. What follows is a discourse on political theory that was obviously a source of much inspiration for Strauss. As the Freemason explains, human beings will always be divided into societies characterized by their diverse cultures, religions, and interests. These shared values keep the group together, but they also make the group vicious toward outsiders. In this atmosphere, an enlightened, cosmopolitan attitude, an attitude that transcends the details and dogmas of religious belief, is likely to be regarded with suspicion by one's neighbors and fellow citizens. In the infancy of mankind, those who are not zealots are likely to be considered traitors. But those who know the truth, know that it is often bad to be patriotic. So they create a secret brotherhood that is superior to any other brotherhood because its members respect one another's dignity and humanity regardless of the superficial outward forms of religion, class, or nationality. In every country, these secret societies busy themselves with good works that attract attention and undermine suspicion. But the real advantage to humanity is the cultivation of a generous disposition of mind.

Ernst is so enchanted by the whole matter that he becomes a Freemason. But he is sorely disappointed and blames his friend for leading him astray. All he finds is nincompoops thinking that they will discover how to make gold, conjure up spirits, recover the order of the Knights Templars, or distribute "juicy sinecures among themselves and their friends."[49] He also discovers that the egalitarianism of the brotherhood has severe limitations; neither Jews nor shoemakers are admitted to this select society. Falk is forced to concede that the whole project is doomed to failure and that Freemasonry is like any other religion—it deteriorates as soon as it is institutionalized. This insight dovetails with Lessing's distinction between Christianity on one hand and the religion of Christ on the other.[50] Lessing was neither a friend nor an enemy of religion; he was in search of the genuinely noble spirit that was at the heart of every religion.

In *Nathan the Wise,* Lessing describes religion as the "sweet delusion" that gives way to an even "sweeter truth."[51] The latter is the true heart of every religion. In his "Education of the Human Race," Lessing maintains (in Thomistic fashion) that the Scripture is the story of God's education of mankind. There is really no conflict between the Old and the New Testament: each is appropriate for the stage of human development for which it is intended. The hope is that mankind may learn to obey the law out of love of God, or the pleasure of doing the right thing, without any expectations of rewards and punishments (either in this world or in the next). Clearly, this sort of enlightened morality was Lessing's ideal. However, the dialogue between Ernst and Falk reveals that Lessing was not a blind optimist about the inevitability of human progress toward moral perfection. By the same token, it provides no evidence that a "conversion" is at stake.

In view of his interest in secrecy, Strauss's fascination with Lessing is understandable. But the similarities between Strauss and Lessing are altogether superficial. Lessing is eager to promote a cosmopolitan spirit that transcends the narrow and parochial, but Strauss thinks that cosmopolitanism is misguided because human beings are too evil to be expected to behave honorably unless they are in the grip of some noble lie or pious fraud about rewards and punishments in the afterlife. Strauss takes Lessing literally when he says that religion is a "sweet delusion." But Lessing thinks that the delusion highlights the beauty and goodness of the truth. In contrast, Strauss juxtaposes the sweet delusion with the "sordid truth."[52] Lessing is a rationalist who believes in the goodness of nature and in reason's ability to provide a foundation for moral life and conduct. Strauss wrote his doctoral dissertation on F. H. Jacobi, who was Lessing's contemporary, and who was convinced that reason is destructive of morality and religion alike.[53] Strauss shares Jacobi's convictions and rejects the wisdom of Lessing.

## MAIMONIDES REINTERPRETED

Strauss is a highly regarded scholar of Jewish thought, and it is often difficult for young Jewish scholars who were taught to look up to him to discover that his reverence for Judaism, as for any religion, is little more than a veneer adopted for political purposes.[54] In view of the fact that Strauss divides the history of thought into the wise ancients and the vulgar moderns, it is quite legitimate to attribute to him the ideas he attributes to his wise ancients. Maimonides is a classic case in point; an examination of Strauss's study of Maimonides is therefore bound to reveal a great deal not only about Strauss's view of Judaism, but also about Strauss's political philosophy as a whole.

Moses Maimonides (1135-1204) was a philosopher and physician who lived in the times in which Lessing's play took place. Maimonides was the physician to Saladin or his viceroy in Egypt. And his reputation was such that he was sought after by Richard the Lionhearted.[55] He is reputed to be the greatest Jewish philosopher of the Middle Ages. He is the author of the *Mishneh Torah* (written in Hebrew), a work on Jewish law, and *The Guide of the Perplexed* (written in Arabic), a philosophical work giving an account of the relation between faith and reason, the nature of God, creation, free will, natural law, and the problem of evil. This work exerted a notable influence on Christian philosophers such as St. Thomas Aquinas and Albertus Magnus.

Despite his accomplishments, his fame, and his contribution to Judaism, Maimonides is the subject of great controversy within the Judaic tradition. On one hand, he is admired as Judaism's greatest philosopher, the "second Moses," and the Thomas Aquinas of Judaism who managed to reconcile the Bible with Greek philosophy. On the other hand, he is reviled and repudiated as a heretic, an atheist, and a traitor to the faith.[56]

Strauss's interpretation of Maimonides combines the two opposite accounts in a uniquely Straussian reading in which Maimonides emerges as a Straussian. Whenever Strauss examines the work of a great thinker, he invariably uncovers himself. Strauss's interpretations of Plato, Aristotle, Xenophon, Alfarabi, Averroës, Maimonides, and the other greats, tells us more about Strauss than about the thinkers in question. The point that Strauss wishes to impress upon us is that there can never be any disagreements among the wise on any matters of substance. And since his own teaching accords perfectly with ancient wisdom, its truth cannot be questioned, and anyone who dares to question it must be a fool. One thing for which Strauss deserves credit is his masterful use of the old argument from authority—something is true because the divine Plato says so. This is the subtle process of intimidation that is integral to a Straussian education.

The substance of the ancient wisdom that Strauss "discovers" is clearly illustrated in his reading of Maimonides. Strauss begins in the usual way, warning us that Maimonides, like the other greats, is an esoteric writer who imparts the truth darkly and briefly in riddles, parables, hints, and intimations that can be decoded only by initiated readers such as Strauss, who knows just when a philosopher is telling the truth and when he is dissembling, when he is serious and when he is kidding. Strauss tries to write obliquely, elliptically, and esoterically himself, but to no avail. His message is loud and clear to anyone who is patient enough to read carefully and to the end.

Strauss tells us that Maimonides is preoccupied above all else with the conflict between reason and revelation, Athens and Jerusalem, philosophy and the city, Enlightenment and orthodoxy, atheism and religion. For Strauss, this conflict is unremitting and insurmountable. It has its source in two antagonistic and irreconcilable worldviews. The orthodox view asserts the truth of creation, miracles, and revelation. In this view, man is not lord and master of the earth, but is subject to an unfathomable God and to a hostile nature.[57] Man needs revelation for the guidance of life. In contrast to orthodoxy, Enlightenment posits a world in which man is lord and master of nature and of his own life. It seeks to protect man from the "grasp of the omnipotent God."[58] It regards religion as the oppressive invention of greedy priests who are bent on depriving mankind of happiness in this world by making them believe that there is another world.[59] It assumes that religion fills man with fears and superstitions and deprives him of the earthy goods, which are the only ones available. As a result, Enlightenment sets out to refute and destroy orthodoxy.

Strauss warns us not to confuse the conflict between orthodoxy and Enlightenment with the controversy between *ancients* and *moderns*—another central theme of Strauss's writings. What is at issue between ancients and moderns is *how* to resolve the conflict between Athens (Enlightenment) and Jerusalem (orthodoxy), and how to assess the social importance of religion. Convinced of the social utility of religion, the ancients try to preserve it; they do their best to shield it from the corrosive effects of their own philosophizing. In contrast, the moderns embrace Enlightenment without reserve, and set out to refute religion and ground society on philosophy alone. Strauss makes it clear that neither he nor his wise ancients have any intention of relinquishing Enlightenment or rationalism altogether.[60]

Strauss is at his most eloquent when he explains that his objection to modernity has its source in the latter's unabashed devotion to Enlightenment. Strauss thinks that the world that modernity has created is a failure because no civilization can destroy the "terror and hopelessness of life." Religion is not so much the source of terror and torment as of consolation.[61] But modernity recognized its own failure and assumed a new posture—that of heroic probity. It rejected religion, not because it was the source of fear and prejudice, but because it decided to reject all consolation and "endure the fearful truth" in the name of "probity and hardness." It rejected the human inclination to escape from existence and deceive oneself.[62] In other words, modernity started out with the Enlightenment rationalism of Voltaire and ended with the existentialism of Heidegger.

In contrast to the moderns, the ancients understood that reason and philosophy cannot supply all the truths necessary for life. This is to say that philosophy recognized its own limitations and yielded to the truths of revelation.[63] Of course, there are truths for philosophers alone that are distinct from the "truths necessary for life."[64] Strauss repeats again and again that reason recognizes its own limits and yields to revelation. But he makes it clear that reason does not yield to revelation as something truly grand, or as something that supplements the truths of reason, or as something that contains a higher morality, but simply as something absolutely necessary for the lives of the vulgar many. Indeed, he says explicitly that medieval philosophers such as Maimonides, "did not believe in Revelation properly speaking. They were philosophers in the classical sense of the word: men who would hearken to reason, and to reason only."[65]

Strauss understands Maimonides as part of an Islamic medieval tradition of Falsifa that includes Alfarabi and Averroës. For Strauss, Averroës provides the definitive account of what "rationalism" in medieval Judaism is all about. In Strauss's view, Maimonides and Rabbi Levi ben Gerson are Averroists.[66] This means that they agree with Averroës on the following: First, the law itself commands those "suited to philosophize" to do so, because the purpose of philosophy and the purpose of the law are the same—namely the "bliss" of man.[67] Second, when a conflict between reason and the law is encountered in the process of philosophizing, then philosophers are authorized to interpret the law. They are free to reject the literal interpretation as being "merely valid for the many," and to give the law their own "figurative" account.[68] Third, philosophers are "commanded" to keep their interpretations "secret" from the unchosen multitude.[69] The reason is that the "inner" meaning of the law is different from its literal meaning. In other words, there are two truths, one for philosophers and another for the rest of humanity. Philosophers are totally free from the law that binds the rest of humanity, on the condition that they do not publicly undermine the faith. For example, they are forbidden to publicly deny the existence and unity of God, the truth of the creation, or the hope in a future life. They are also forbidden from introducing "innovations" into the faith.[70] The freedom of philosophy rests on its bondage—its commitment to secrecy and its efforts to publicly uphold the law.[71] This is what Strauss means when he says that Averroës is not the Voltaire of the twelfth century.[72]

For Strauss, Maimonides is an Averroist, and not the St. Thomas Aquinas of Judaism. Maimonides is under no illusion that philosophy can provide rational foundations for faith. According to Strauss, Maimonides does not even think that philosophy can prove the creation as opposed to the eternity of the world. And since creation is the basis of Judaism, philosophy can provide no support whatsoever for Judaism.[73] Faith and reason cannot be reconciled. Philosophy can provide a solution to the conflict, but it cannot resolve it. Letting philosophy loose on Judaism is not the right solution—it is irresponsible, sinful, and prohibited by the law to which philosophy is in "bondage." But this bondage notwithstanding, Strauss explains that Maimonides is a thoroughgoing rationalist, who gives primacy to reason, and this is why he has been accused of heresy, apostasy, and atheism. Strauss does not deny the truth of these accusations, but he defends Maimonides against the charge that he was a traitor to the faith, saying that Maimonides was a very esoteric writer who was mindful of his social responsibilities and therefore did not spread his rationalism too liberally.[74] Maimonides expressed himself in "parables and in riddles," and when he spoke of God, his speech was "dark and brief" because a philosopher cannot know God.[75] This darkness of speech is intended to make his thought incomprehensible to the unchosen many.[76] Although he was as much of a rationalist as Voltaire, Maimonides was no fool; he was wise enough to know that the world needed protection from rationalism. Unlike modern rationalism, ancient rationalism is rooted in a wisdom about the nature of man and society that has been lost to the moderns. Maimonides was thoroughly steeped in this ancient wisdom; he was fully cognizant of the corrosive effects that philosophy had on faith; and he was fully aware of the indispensability of faith for social order. In contrast, the moderns thought that they could found society on reason alone—on rational self-interest. But this view was no part of ancient rationalism. In short, "the medieval Enlightenment was fundamentally esoteric, while the modern Enlightenment was fundamentally exoteric."[77]

For Strauss, there is a gulf that separates the truths of reason from those of revelation—the truths of revelation and the truths of reason are not the same. Reason can know only the sensible world, the lower world, the world in which we dwell. It cannot know anything about God or the upper world—that is the domain of revelation. It is impossible for reason to *refute* revelation since they are not operating in the same domains. Reason has no access to the Heavens; and revelation does not play by reason's rules.[78] In Strauss's view, it is not even accurate to say that the truths of reason and those of revelation come into conflict, because revelation does not provide truths, it provides *law.*[79] There is however one point of contact between reason and revelation—the *prophet.* Indeed, revelation is not "merely God's miraculous act," it can be accomplished only through the prophet, and prophecy is natural, not miraculous.[80] Since the prophet is a lawgiver, he "must also be a philosopher" who knows what sorts of truths are necessary for life.[81] But he is also a philosopher of the highest rank because he is characterized not only by the perfection of the intellect, but also of imagination, divination, and inventiveness.[82] Strauss implies that because the philosopher cannot *know* God, he must invent him.

Strauss explains that *politics* is the key to the "meaning and purpose of prophecy."[83] The prophet is a "teacher and leader, philosopher and lawgiver in one" and that prophecy has a "political mission."[84] When Strauss talks of man being a "political animal," he does not mean, as Aristotle did, that man is naturally gregarious, rather, he means that man needs politics for his very survival. Strauss believes that for no other animal is socialization "so necessary and so difficult."[85] The function of politics is to ward off conflict by forging an agreement to abide by law.[86] Strauss's view of human nature is closer to Hobbes's than to Aristotle's But unlike Hobbes, Strauss does not think that individuals can be induced to regulate their actions according to law simply by appealing to their rational self-interest. Strauss does not think that arguments from rational self-interest can succeed; and this applies to the narrow understanding of self-interest found in Hobbes, as well as the deeper understanding of self-interest found in Plato.[87] This is why very special leaders are necessary—leaders whose superiority is so evident to others that they will be induced to follow them. Luckily, Strauss tells us that "in no species other than the human is there so great a difference, even oppositeness, in the character of individuals."[88] Strauss is not referring to moral character, but to the qualities of the prophet-philosopher-leader—the qualities of intellect, imagination, and divination.[89] The evident superiority of the prophet—his imaginative capacity to communicate in images, and his inventive ability to give God all the credit for his wisdom—is precisely what will inspire others to follow him. Strauss claims that the historical appearance of the prophet solves Plato's dilemma, which is how to get people to submit to the rule of the wise. In Strauss's view, the appearance of the prophet has "fulfilled" what Plato had only "demanded"—namely the rule of the philosopher-king. Prophecy therefore solves the obstacles to the realization of Plato's ideal city.[90]

Strauss's interpretation of Maimonides manages to reconcile the two opposite conceptions of Maimonides—as an atheist, a heretic, and an apostate on one hand, and as the second Moses on the other. Thanks to Strauss's ingenuity, Maimonides emerges as an atheist and a heretic who was devoted to the care and protection of Judaism for political reasons. In short, Strauss rescues Maimonides from infamy by turning him into a Straussian.

## CRITIQUE OF STRAUSS

In what follows, I will make three objections to Strauss's thought as illustrated in his reading of Maimonides.

### 1. THE RABBINIC AND MYSTICAL TRADITIONS

Strauss is quite right to point to the esoteric nature of Maimonides's writing. Maimonides himself calls attention to the secretive nature of his work. In the introduction to *The Guide of the Perplexed,* he warns his readers that his book is filled with hints, equivocations, and even contradictions; he insists that nothing in it is haphazard, and all of his diction is chosen with "great exactness and exceeding precision."[91] He explains that there are seven reasons why contradictory statements can be found in a text, and after listing all of them, he tells us that the contradictions in his own treatise are due to the fifth and seventh causes.[92] The fifth reason has its source in the difficulty and obscurity of the subject matter. But in the course of explaining a simple matter, one is often compelled to refer to the difficult subject in a lax fashion that is more useful than accurate. Later, one returns to the difficult matter and gives a more complete account in more exact terms. But the early or casual account will not be totally compatible with the later and more complete account.

Maimonides explains that the seventh reason why there are contradictions in his text is the desire to reveal some things and to conceal others. In particular, where discussion of law is concerned, "the vulgar must in no way be aware of the contradiction."[93] These statements fuel Strauss's imagination and confirm his view that Maimonides is an esoteric writer. But Strauss's explanation of why he was secretive and what kinds of secrets he was concealing are not necessarily plausible for the following reasons.

There are two main currents in the history of Judaism—the rabbinic and the mystical. The former is rooted in the Talmud and its laws, and the latter has its source in the Zohar. The tension between these two traditions is primarily theological. By its nature, mysticism is the desire for a spiritual union with God; it aspires to an intimate relation with the creator. This desire is necessarily viewed with a certain suspicion by a religion that depicts God as so great and mighty that human beings are hardly fit to utter his name, let alone establish any degree of intimacy with him. The mystery and obscurantism in which the Jewish mystical tradition is shrouded is largely due to its heretical flavor.

The Jewish mystical tradition is referred to as the Kabbalah, denoting a secret wisdom that is orally transmitted and received.[94] This intimacy with the Almighty threatened rabbinical authority by encouraging a degree of liberty that was incompatible with the theocratic self-government that characterized the Jewish communities in the Diaspora or dispersion. And because many mystics were also Talmudists who were eager to preserve the rabbinic tradition, their esotericism was often self-imposed—it had its origins in self-censorship, and not just in fear of persecution. Mystics insisted that they were not trying to destroy or transform the Jewish community or its form of worship. They emphasized that they were advocating this secret wisdom only for the very few who could see God without losing their mind, as the famous story of the four rabbis has it. Of the four rabbis who entered paradise and gazed upon the Godhead, one died instantly, the other lost his mind, the third became an apostate and seduced the young, only the fourth entered and emerged in peace.[95] The story emphasizes the dangers involved in revealing the secrets of the Torah indiscriminately. Maimonides mentions the rabbinic prohibition against delving into mysteries such as Ezekiel's chariot to heaven, saying: "the Account of the Chariot ought not to be taught even to one man, except that he be wise and able to understand by himself, in which case only the chapter headings may be transmitted to him."[96] Maimonides assures us that he has no intention of offending against this rabbinic prohibition. Strauss suggests that Maimonides was the first Jewish mystic. But how can he be a mystic and an atheist who thinks that he is a god among men and the real lawgiver? The idea seems obscenely narcissistic, but typical of Straussian self-congratulation.

Strauss admires a mystic such as Maimonides because he does not threaten the rabbinic tradition. Strauss's Judaism is rabbinic in the worst sense. He is interested only in the political advantages of religion. He values only its capacity to create order by investing authority with superhuman sanctification. Strauss has little or no appreciation of the inner dimension of faith that is at the heart of religious experience. He reduces religion to irrational prejudice, fear, and superstition. He ignores the miracle of the direct relation with the infinite. This explains his rejection of Franz Rosenzweig's existential brand of Judaism.[97]

Rosenzweig was skeptical of Herman Cohen's reconciliation of reason and revelation. He thought that traditional philosophy was too abstract and impotent to be a reliable guide to truth. Instead, he posited the primacy of the concrete individual—his anxiety, his fear of death, his loneliness, and his longing for God. In contrast, Strauss clings to distant and supposedly authoritative traditions. Rosenzweig fused philosophy and theology because they both have their source in the wonder of the finite in the face of the infinite. Strauss insists on the mutual incompatibility of philosophy and theology. Rosenzweig spoke of love as the first commandment, and the secret to overcoming our isolation. Strauss speaks only of obedience and mindless conformity to inherited traditions. The six-point "star of redemption" consists of God, World, and Man on one side, and Creation, Revelation, and Redemption on the other. God created the world, and revealed himself to man, and this revelation is the beginning of redemption. Rosenzweig is interested in constantly renewing the revelation granted to Adam. Strauss regards revelation as a great historical swindle accomplished by the philosopher-prophets whose law and authority are our only redemption from a state of endless strife.

Strauss cannot appreciate Rosenzweig because his own understanding of religion does not spring from the same inner need. Besides, the more intimate relation with God that is at the heart of Rosenzweig's religiosity is a threat to the harsh authoritarianism of Strauss's rabbinic understanding of Judaism.

Strauss does not realize that the religion of rote and ritual is not a religion of the heart and mind and that such a religion is bound to decay and atrophy from the very weight of its own meaninglessness. Nor is this peculiar to Judaism; every religion eventually deteriorates into meaningless rituals. Religion is an experience, an adventure, and a risk. There is no telling that it will yield politically salutary results. History does not necessarily bear out Strauss's view of religion. Even though it has been a source of love, order, justice, and harmony, religion has also been a source of hate, war, and revolution. Nor can religion be reduced to a political tool without being thoroughly corrupted.

## 2. Hard and Soft Averroists

It is important to distinguish between two different versions of Averroës's famous doctrine of the two truths—the hard and the soft versions. On the hard view, there are two truths whose contents differ widely; one truth for the few, the other for the many. The truths of philosophers are secular and well founded in reason, but the truths for the multitude are religious, filled with magic and miracles, divine revelations and other superstitions that have no rational foundations whatsoever. On the soft view, the two views differ only in form, not in content. One set of truths is a rational and sophisticated account, while the other is a simple and mythical account of the same truth and the same ethic.[98] The soft Averroist thinks that only the few can penetrate the rational ground of religious truth, whereas the rest must be satisfied with the authority of divine law, and with simple or mythical accounts of the truth. As a philosopher and a Jew, the soft Averroist can live harmoniously inside the same skin, because he is one and the same person—a person who lives according to a single reality, a single truth, and a single ethic. There is therefore no reason for the philosopher who is also a Jew to live a divided life—inwardly denying the Scriptures, but outwardly adhering to their commands in order not to undermine the political life of the community. But Strauss is a hard Averroist. He acknowledges the divine law outwardly while denying it inwardly. His obligation to the city is grounded in his self-interest, in his desire to pursue the pleasures of the philosophical life unhampered. This means that there will be no reason for him to adhere to the divine law when there is no chance of being found out. The philosopher-prophet must live a divided and duplicitous life, a life filled with deception, duplicity, and subterfuge. It is no wonder that Strauss undermines Maimonides's insistence that the prophet must be morally perfect.[99] Far from being morally perfect, he must be morally depraved not to suffer from inner turmoil and conflict.

Strauss's philosopher-prophet does not suffer from inner torment or conflict. His lofty imagination comes to the rescue. He falls prey to his own bodyguard of lies; he begins to believe that he is in truth the humanly perfect manifestation of the divine mind; in fact, the only divinity available. After all, he is the author of the law. And does the law not have a divine author? The philosopher-prophet runs the risk of self-delusion on a grand scale. He is like a sorcerer's apprentice who is taken in by his own tricks.

Strauss is under the impression that his philosopher-prophet is the incarnation of Plato's philosopher-king. But this suggestion is rather difficult to support. Plato makes a point of distinguishing between the *verbal lie,* the *noble lie,* and the *lie in the soul.*[100] The verbal lie is the ordinary lie that is told by someone who knows the truth, but wishes to conceal it. The noble lie is a version of the verbal lie, but it is justified on two counts. It is justified on utilitarian grounds as useful to the city, but also on moral grounds because it contains a moral truth about humanity. In other words, the noble lie is not properly speaking false since it contains an important truth, albeit expressed in mythical form. The noble lie is not literally true—human beings did not spring full grown out of the bowels of the earth; their earth mother did not literally mix gold, silver, and bronze respectively in their souls. However, the truth is that there are men with different characters, some are more virtuous, less likely to be corrupted by power, and therefore more fit to rule than others. In contrast to the ordinary lie or the noble lie, Plato judges the lie in the soul to be the worst kind of lie. He explains that the lie in the soul is told by one who does not even know the truth; it is a reflection of the deep ignorance and self-deception of the one telling the lie. Far from being a noble liar, Strauss's philosopher-prophet is suffering from a serious case of self-delusion or the lie in the soul that Plato rightly identifies as a profound deformity of character.

Strauss's deprecation of morality explains his rejection of the neo-Kantian philosophy of Herman Cohen.[101] It is not just that Cohen was an egalitarian who cared about the working class and their interests, or that Cohen believed in progress. The real difference between Strauss and Cohen is that Cohen believed that the moral life is at the heart of the highest understanding of religion.[102] And like Kant, he believed that the moral law has its source in the autonomous will. But this idea came into conflict with his Jewish faith. Cohen resolved the dilemma by claiming that religious morality is a mythical version of rational or philosophical morality. He distinguished between mythic time and cosmic time. Myth is tribal, but reason and ethics are universal. The true ideal of religion is the cosmic or universal, not the tribal. Nevertheless, Cohen did not deprecate religion for he believed that it accounted for the only glimmer of good that can be perceived in the world. As things stand, Judaism is indispensable in the life of man because he does not fully comprehend the commandments, and is not fully capable of carrying them out. Judaism is symbolic of man's moral training, and it provides the only hope that someday man will become a fully moral being. In contrast to Cohen, morality does not play a significant role in Strauss's thought, as he himself acknowledges.[103]

## 3. KABBALISM REVISITED

Strauss is often described as a Kabbalist because of the secretive nature of his work. And even though Strauss is not a religious mystic in any sense of that term, it can be argued that Strauss's thought is a secularized version of Jewish mysticism.

First, Strauss shares the Kabbalistic method of interpretation and the esotericism and secrecy that has always been the hallmark of the mystical or Kabbalistic tradition. This tradition gained ascendancy in times of terrible persecution; when the Jews were expelled from Spain in 1492, and when the Eastern European Jews suffered the terrible atrocities inflicted on them by the Cossacks in 1648. The orthodox or rabbinic explanation of these dreadful times was that the Jews were being punished because they had defected from the law. The proper response was to redouble the individual and collective effort to obey every letter of the Torah. The mystics also agreed that persecution was a punishment from God for having broken the Covenant or agreement with God to obey His commandments in exchange for His protection. However, they explained that the reason for the failure was not so much ill-will, but lack of understanding. The mystics believed that the Torah was but an outer shell that contained a deeper meaning. They thought that God intended something deeper and more meaningful than external compliance with established rituals. Consequently, they proceeded to study the Torah's every letter and even the whites around the letters in search for its hidden meaning. The Zohar, the fundamental work of Jewish mysticism, is a commentary on the Torah. Its assumption is that the surface teaching is but the outer garment that conceals the body beneath. To know a person is not to know their garments or even the body beneath the garments, but the soul that dwells within. It is the hidden inner soul of the Torah that the mystical exegete is in search of.

Strauss studies the works of political philosophers in the same way that the Kabbalists studied the Torah—looking for clues, in nuances, allusions, apparent contradictions, and even in trivial details. For Strauss as for the Kabbalists, numerology became one of the most important clues in deciphering the secret meaning of the text. Numerology has its origin in the fact that every Hebrew letter has a numerical value. By adding up the numerical values of the letters, it is possible to discover the numerical equivalent of any word or thing. For example, the first words that God spoke to Abraham have the numerical value of one hundred, and this is taken to be a clue that he will have a child when he is a hundred years old.[104] By the same token, the name of the serpent, Nahash happens to have the same numerical value as the word Messiah. For reasons that will become clearer shortly, the Kabbalists did not think this was a coincidence; on the contrary, they gave it great interpretive significance. Likewise, Strauss is notorious for attributing significance to the number of the chapters in Machiavelli's *Prince* and to Locke's habit of numbering the paragraphs of his *Two Treatises*.

Second, Strauss shares the Kabbalistic view of knowledge as both *dangerous* and *erotic*. The Kabbalists believed that the secrets of the Torah were dangerous in a double sense: they were dangerous to the Kabbalists themselves because the heretical quality of the teaching could lead to excommunication, *and* because the truth itself is not fit for all. Knowledge is typically associated with the tree of knowledge, with sin, guilt, the fall, and the devil. Knowledge is dangerous while ignorance is innocence and bliss. Secrecy was therefore of the essence. It had its source not only in fear of persecution, and the desire not to threaten the rabbinic order, but also in the desire not to harm the world with a truth that is too dangerous and too easily misunderstood by the uninitiated. In the Kabbalistic tradition, the secret teachings were to be orally transmitted to one person at a time, and only to a special breed of those who will be able to understand it, and then only by hints and allusions.[105] The motto of the Kabbalists was: "The best of what you know you may not tell to boys."[106]

Strauss's *Persecution and the Art of Writing* insists that all the great authors of the Western tradition are esoteric writers for exactly the same reasons as those enumerated by the Kabbalists. Strauss's book is often read superficially as an expression of the simple thesis that political philosophers had to write cautiously if they were to avoid the wrath of repressive and illiberal regimes. And while this is true, Strauss's thesis is far more interesting. It is not just fear of political persecution that makes esotericism necessary, but also the necessity of "considering one's social responsibilities."[107] And like the Kabbalists, Strauss associates the tree of knowledge with philosophy, with sin, the fall, and the devil.[108] And this explains why he insists that philosophy must keep itself hidden.

By using a religious model for disseminating his philosophy, Strauss did a great disservice to the philosophical life. The latter is by its nature open, and relies on debate and persuasion, not inculcation of secret doctrines to the initiated. Secrecy has the effect of emasculating reason, which leads to surrender, not to God, but to the professor who poses as the organ for the dissemination of divine wisdom. Nor was Strauss as esoteric as he thought he was. Forgetting the Kabbalistic motto, he may have spread his dangerous teachings too liberally.

Strauss also shares the Kabbalist view that knowledge is not only dangerous, but erotic. Sexual asceticism was never part of the Jewish tradition; nor was Jewish mysticism ascetic in character. On the contrary, the mystical desire for union with God was generally expressed in sexual terms. Moreover, the Kabbalistic view of God diverged significantly from the orthodox view because it gave God a feminine as well as a masculine persona. Much of the mystery of the Kabbalah revolves around the Shekinah or God's feminine dimension.[109] She is a complex figure that is both identical with God and yet separate enough to be his divine spouse. In giving an account of the divine as masculine and feminine simultaneously and of seeing the source of all life and vitality in the relation between God and the Shekinah, the Kabbalistic tradition makes the erotic the heart of Being. Knowledge of reality— metaphysical and theological—is therefore highly erotic. The fact that the Bible uses the same word for knowledge as for sexual relations further reinforces the Kabbalistic inclination to identify knowledge with eros. Besides, the paradigm for knowledge as for sex is penetration beneath the surface.

Likewise, Strauss often tells us that philosophy is a manifestation of eros. The explanation is that eros is identified with nature as opposed to convention, and philosophy is the quest to understand the raw and unadulterated nature that is hidden beneath the conventional, the traditional, the ancestral. Philosophy, as Strauss understands it, drives a wedge between the good and the ancestral. Every society tries to blur the distinction; it insists that the ancestral is identical with the good. Indeed, Strauss believes that the identity of the two is essential to the stability of the social order—a stability that is upset by philosophy. Eros, like nature, is the enemy of society, marriage, order, and stability.[110] For the Kabbalists, eros is what is hidden behind the official conception of the Godhead, and is the secret foundation of all life and vitality.[111] For Strauss, eros is also the secret foundation of all things, yet it is hidden behind the conventions of society. It is the dangerous as well as the erotic task of philosophy to uncover this hidden secret.

This explains why Strauss thinks that philosophy is itself the highest manifestation of eros. After all, philosophy is *phil sophia,* or love of wisdom. Strauss associates wisdom with Metis, Zeus's first spouse. Love of wisdom is therefore not love of God, but of the erotic Metis. In the Greek tradition philosophy is a competition with Zeus for the possession of Metis. This may explain why Straussians believe that women cannot be philosophers. The lesbian imagery is more than they can stomach. Although it must be added that they have no objection to pederasty. Strauss points out that the greatest philosophers, those who manage to rise above convention altogether, are pederasts.[112] But all this is not altogether consistent with Strauss's interpretation of Genesis, where he recognizes Eve as the first to eat of the tree of knowledge, the first philosopher, the first lover of wisdom, the first rebel against God, tradition, and the ancestral.[113]

Third, there is an uncanny resemblance between Strauss's view of the philosopher-prophet and the Sabbatian conception of the Messiah. Sabbatianism was a popularization of Kabbalistic ideas. It is named after Sabbatai Zevi, who is also called the "false Messiah." But in the middle of the seventeenth century, he was believed by many Jews to be the real Messiah. He was a charismatic figure who traveled widely, and declared himself to be the Messiah. Wherever he went, people fell before him in ecstasy. Gershom Scholem describes Zevi as a man pursued by demons who alternated between euphoria and melancholy. His psychic exuberance led him to violations of the moral law. In times of normal lucidity, he was deeply troubled by his transgressions.[114] His disciple, Nathan of Gaza, convinced him that these transgressions were part and parcel of his messianic mission. According to Nathan, there is a connection between the Messiah and the forces of darkness. As we have noted earlier, there are numerological clues for this connection. Nathan explained that from the beginning of time, the soul of the Messiah was held captive in the realm of darkness. The Messiah must therefore descend into the crucible of sin to wrench his soul from the darkness that holds him captive.[115] In this way, Nathan gave Zevi's transgressions a millenarian significance. He convinced him that the law does not apply to him. Evil was sanctified as having a significant role in the process of redemption. In this way, the doctrine of the *holy sin* was born. As Scholem explains, this doctrine is connected to the idea that "the elect are fundamentally different from the crowd and not to be judged by its standards. Standing under a new spiritual law and representing as it were a new kind of reality, they are beyond good and evil."[116] Strauss's philosopher-prophet is a secularized version of the same conceit. The standards of the law that apply to all humanity cannot apply to the noble liar. The philosopher-prophet is the secular messiah who descends to the depths of nihilism and bears the yoke of the terrible truth for the sake of humanity. He represents a reality that transcends the law, a reality that is beyond good and evil. From the abyss of nihilism he brings forth God and his law. In so doing, he provides a political and this-worldly solution to man's infirmities. He is the savior of humanity, the only messiah we can rationally expect. His lies are sanctified by the law because they are necessary to the bliss of humanity, and his sins are absolved by the law because they are holy sins. Strauss accepts the Machiavellian doctrine according to which moral considerations have no place in politics and power. This explains why he was compelled to undermine Maimonides's insistence on the moral perfection of the philosopher-prophet.[117]

Strauss's political ideal is a nightmare that leaves us entirely at the mercy of cunning and ambitious priests, who are more terrifying than Dostoevsky's Grand Inquisitor.

## CHAPTER THREE

# STRAUSS'S GERMAN CONNECTION

## HEIDEGGER AND SCHMITT

THERE ARE TWO GERMAN CONTEMPORARIES whose work had a lasting influence on the political thought of Leo Strauss: Martin Heidegger and Carl Schmitt. Both writers besmirched their reputations by their enthusiastic alliance with the Nazis. In this chapter, I will discuss each of these writers in turn, emphasizing the ideas that made a lasting impression on Strauss. First, I will argue that even though Strauss personally abhorred Heidegger, he shared his view of modernity—a view that is central to Strauss's understanding of America. Second, I will show that Strauss's fundamental political concepts as well as his critique of American liberal democracy are borrowed from the brilliant but disturbing work of Carl Schmitt.[1]

## NIETZSCHE, HEIDEGGER, AND THE NAZIS

The centrality of the holocaust in the thinking of all the German émigrés cannot be overestimated. This is true of Strauss as of all the others, even though he did not write any treatises on totalitarianism as Hannah Arendt did, or on the authoritarian personality as Theodor Adorno did. Nor would it be an exaggeration to say that political philosophy and the social sciences in the second half of the twentieth century have been preoccupied above all else with the questions: How did it happen? How could it have happened in the West? Why did it happen in the twentieth century? Can it happen again? and How can it be prevented? These are also the questions at the heart of Strauss's political thought.

Although Strauss does not express it so starkly, his view on the connection between Nazism and modernity can be expressed briefly as follows. The Nazis were not a freakish accident of history, but a logical manifestation of the spirit of modernity. Modernity has given birth to two dangerous doctrines—nihilism and technological mastery. And taken together, they are a lethal combination. Nihilism is the view of the world as a formless chaos in which God and all His moral restraints are absent. Nihilism may be passive and resign itself to the meaningless chaos of the world; but it is more likely to be active and resolve to impose order and meaning on the void. Nazism is an active nihilism whose power has become augmented by modern technology.

Strauss believes that there is no foundation for morality except belief in "active gods" who busy themselves with man's affairs, punishing the wicked and rewarding the righteous. The ancients understood this and therefore concealed their philosophical skepticism out of a sense of social responsibility. But this ancient wisdom has disappeared, and classical rationalism has been replaced with Enlightenment rationalism, which is the hapless belief that knowledge of the truth is good for man and is bound to improve society. But in Strauss's eyes, the holocaust was ample proof that the faith in Enlightenment was altogether misplaced. It was a costly mistake, and it behooves us to return, if such a return is possible, to classical rationalism. Strauss is therefore not an antirationalist. He is deeply committed to reason and to truth despite the fact that he thinks that they undermine everything sacred. But he would like to restrict access to the world of thought to the few who can be trusted not to abuse the privilege. The Nazis were untrustworthy people; having discovered that the world was void, they took it upon themselves to re-create it according to their own specifications. In the absence of God, force, brute strength, and resoluteness filled the void and shaped the world. This is the danger of nihilism. And this danger is further augmented by the degree of technological mastery that modernity makes possible.

In his analysis of nihilism, Strauss relies on Nietzsche and Heidegger. For Strauss, the difference between these two thinkers is critical. Strauss repudiates Heidegger (as someone whose philosophy led him directly to nazism) while endorsing Nietzsche as a reincarnation of classical wisdom. Strauss's claim against Heidegger is not well substantiated, although Strauss's case can be made. Before summarizing Strauss's view of the critical difference between Heidegger and Nietzsche, I will explain why Strauss, like many others, believes that Heidegger's philosophy has a special affinity with nazism.

In view of the influence of Heidegger on the powerful postmodern movement in academe, the controversy over his connections with the Nazis has become more than academic. Since the publication of Victor Farias's book, *Heidegger and Nazism,* no one dares to deny the extent of Heidegger's involvement with the party and his willingness to do its bidding as rector of the University of Freiburg.[2] But Heidegger's many disciples and defenders claim that there is no logical connection between his politics and his philosophy, even though they are fully aware of the fact that Heidegger himself made the connection.

It may be argued that Heidegger's political speeches are a betrayal of the radically individualistic message of his existential philosophy in the first part of *Being and Time.*[3] The existential ethic of authenticity bids the individual to be true to himself, rather than living as "they" expect, and silencing the voice within, as Ivan Ilych did most of his life. Leo Tolstoy's *Death of Ivan Ilych* is often considered a more vivid account of Heidegger's view of living unauthentically, but this is not altogether accurate.[4] Ivan lives all his life with the decorum and propriety that is expected of a man in his station. But when he faces death, he realizes that his whole life has been nothing but a web of lies; he realizes that the inner voice that he suppressed was the voice of truth, love, and forgiveness. Tolstoy's story is a Christian story because the inner voice that Ivan discovers just before his death is the voice of God and of conscience. In contrast to the Christian ethic, the existential ethic tells us simply to be true to our unique individuality, to listen to our inner voice, not because it is the voice of God or conscience, but simply because it is ours. But what does it mean to be true to oneself, to be authentic? What is the self to which we should be true?

It does not help matters to tell us that we can live authentically if we accept who we are and affirm our destiny in the spirit of Nietzsche's *amor fati*—the injunction to love our fate, to affirm our life, and to choose it energetically. This is a strange ethic indeed. Is it not more honorable to resist or rebel against a disgraceful fate, no matter how inexorable? Is that not why we admire Oedipus? He did not say: "I was destined to kill my father and marry my mother, hurrah!"

Telling us to be true to ourselves and our inner voice tells us very little about how we should live; because in truth, our inner voice is not singular, but plural, and has many conflicting messages. The question is: How do we choose among the conflicting voices within? The existential ethic leaves us lost if not totally paralyzed and unable to choose. But it also teaches that not choosing is the most unauthentic thing of all. As difficult as it is, we must be resolved to choose and must be totally committed to our choice, no matter what it is. Because of its contentless emphasis on commitment, the existential ethic can lead to the valorization of monstrous criminals as heroic nonconformists who are true to themselves. They are supposedly admired for having freely chosen their life of crime, being wholeheartedly committed to it, and heroically refusing to conform to the values shared by the rest of humanity. In short, they refuse to live as "they" expect. It seems that the road to authenticity may require turning our backs on the rules of human decency that human beings share in common. This explains why Jean-Paul Sartre valorized Jean Genet who was a pimp, a pederast, a homosexual prostitute, a thief, and a paid informer for the Nazis.[5] From the point of view of the existential ethic, Genet lived authentically because he chose his life energetically, and put his whole heart into his vices. The same reasoning could explain why Heidegger supported Germany's snubbing the League of Nations.

Long before Heidegger, Ralph Waldo Emerson made this radically individualistic and nonconformist ethic fashionable in America. In his essay "Self-Reliance," he condemned conformity to tradition as the worst evil and celebrated faithfulness to one's inner voice as the highest virtue. Then he raised the obvious objection that neither Heidegger nor Sartre were candid enough to confront: what if the inner voice is the voice of base impulses rather than high principles? His answer contained the sort of flippancy that is at the core of the existential ethic. He bluntly stated that he did not care; if he was the child of the devil, then so be it. The inner voice was sacred, whether it was the voice of God or the devil.[6]

The best that can be said for Heidegger's existential ethic is that it is individualistic and nonconformist, and therefore it forces people to think for themselves and not just to go along with the crowd. But Heidegger betrays the individualistic core of his existential ethic in his political speeches. When the desire for authenticity is socialized, it is transformed from an individualistic into a collectivist ethic. Accordingly,

Heidegger called on the German students to surrender themselves to their führer and to embrace their destiny.[7] When it is socialized, when it is applied to groups and not to individuals, the existential ethic becomes more disastrous for being on a grand scale.

Those who think that Heidegger's philosophy is incompatible with nazism must argue that the socialization of the existential ethic is a betrayal, and that it is a flagrant contradiction of his earlier position. But those who think that Heidegger's philosophy is compatible with nazism must argue that the existential ethic of authenticity is equally appropriate for groups, and that Heidegger's political stance is therefore compatible with his existentialism. Ironically, Heidegger's critics side with Heidegger and accept the intimate connection between his thought and his politics. This is the position accepted by Strauss—a position that was developed by a fellow émigré and a student of Heidegger, Karl Löwith.[8]

Strauss's essay on Heidegger is a mixture of admiration and contempt.[9] Strauss is convinced that it was not an accident or a failure of judgment that led Heidegger to nazism; the logic of his thought required it. As Strauss points out, Heidegger's enthusiasm for the Nazis was not brief. As late as 1953, in his *Introduction to Metaphysics*, Heidegger spoke of the "inner truth and greatness of National Socialism." Strauss points out that the book has been whitewashed, with "errors" removed, including Heidegger's reference to the "cleansing" of the German universities—a reference to Jewish intellectuals such as Strauss and Löwith.[10] Strauss surmises that by 1953, Heidegger must have known the nature of the political party he supported, yet his enthusiasm was not dampened by its atrocities.

In light of this, how could Strauss describe Heidegger as the greatest philosopher of our time? And how could such a great philosopher be captivated by the likes of Hitler? What could explain such a dreadful error of judgment? Where did Heidegger go wrong?

Strauss's answer is that Heidegger was the greatest philosopher of our time because he understood the magnitude of the crisis of the modern world. He was the only philosopher to fully comprehend the impending decadence engulfing Europe. For Strauss, Heidegger was a great diagnostician of the modern malaise, but he did not have a cure. Strauss suggests that the key to understanding the root of Heidegger's mistake is to compare him with Nietzsche. In contrast to Heidegger, Nietzsche understood the cure as well as the disease. The difference between them is instructive. Strauss uses Nietzsche's image of the Blond Beast to make his point.

Before giving Strauss's account, it is significant to recall that the Nazis portrayed themselves as the liberators of the Blond Beast, which they took to be the symbol of the strong, natural, and healthy Nordic or Teutonic man. On one of their campaign posters, the Nazis portrayed the Blond Beast breaking the chains that hold him captive—the Jews, the capitalists, the bankers, and the Communists. Of course, the Nazis were hard-pressed to explain how the Jews could be the bankers and the Communists at the same time. But logic was not their strong suit. They portrayed themselves as the party whose goal was to liberate the noble beast from the servility that ill becomes him. The Blond Beast is portrayed as wild, strong, and beautiful; and now that his powers have been unleashed, he looks resolute and invincible. His beauty and grandeur make him look as if he is destined to triumph in the Darwinian struggle against hostile forces.[11] But somehow, the triumph of the strong, which is the natural order of things, has been foiled by inferior races. The success of the latter, unlike the success of the Nordic beast, is not a sign of nobility, strength, beauty, goodness, superiority, or intelligence. It is simply a function of clever but cheap tricks. However, racial justice is destined to be done; nature will have her way. The Nazis therefore portrayed themselves as the political party of both Nature and Destiny. It is somewhat paradoxical that Nature and Destiny would need a political party to champion their cause; but the Nazis were not the first or the last political party to be guilty of illogic.

Strauss rejects the Nazis' use of Nietzsche's image. Instead he proposes the following view. The Blond Beast represents Western man. Once biblical morality is exploded by nihilism, Western man becomes a beast. Biblical morality was responsible for humanizing and civilizing Western humanity; in its absence, man reverts to barbarism. Once the chains have been loosed, mercy, compassion, altruism, and brotherly love must necessarily give way to "cruelty and its kin."[12] Strauss argues that Nietzsche would never have capitulated to the Nazis as Heidegger did, because his analysis did not end with the Blond Beast, but proceeded to the Overman, which is the answer to the Blond Beast.[13]

According to Strauss, Nietzsche's Overman is none other than the philosopher of the future. Nietzsche saw the twentieth century as an age of world wars leading up to "planetary rule" exercised by a united Europe.

In this new "iron age," democratic government would give way to a new aristocracy with a "new nobility" and a "new ideal."[14] The new aristocracy would consist of invisible ruling philosophers.[15] This elite of supermen will rule the world society that is at hand. To accomplish his monumental task, the Overman must transcend "man as hitherto known at his highest."[16] For "all previous notions of human greatness would not enable man to face the infinitely increased responsibility of the planetary age."[17]

For all its newness, Strauss observes that the idea of invisible ruling philosophers is reminiscent of Plato's philosopher-king. But Strauss thinks that Nietzsche's philosophers will be more concerned with "the holy" and their "philosophizing will be intrinsically religious."[18] For they are heirs to the Bible and the deepening of the soul, which was the effect of biblical faith.[19] This is why the Overman must be a Caesar with the heart of Christ.[20] But for all their apparent religiosity, the philosophers of the future will not believe in God. They will be "atheists" who are "fully loyal to the earth."[21] The duplicitousness of the new ruling class is understood by Strauss as a paternalistic necessity intended to save the world from the corrosive effects of nihilism.

Strauss thinks that some of Nietzsche's predictions have turned out to be true. The twentieth century has indeed been an age of world wars ending in a struggle for planetary rule. The struggle was among the Fascists, the Communists, and the liberals. After the defeat of the Fascists, the Communists or Soviets and the liberals or Americans continued the struggle for dominance. Strauss characterizes that struggle as a competition between "iron compulsion" and "soapy advertising."[22] We have since Strauss's death witnessed the triumph of soapy advertising.

For Strauss, as for Heidegger, the difference between Moscow and Washington is not of great moment, for the two are "metaphysically the same."[23] This is not to underestimate the importance of means, and Strauss has on several occasions praised the American way of colonizing the world as more humane. But the outcome is the same. A world society ruled by Washington or Moscow is the same since they are both wedded to the same egalitarianism, democracy, and technological mastery.

Strauss praises Heidegger because he understood the horrors of the world society. He recognized the magnitude of the crisis in which we live, and he rightly referred to it as the "night of the world."[24] The victory of the technological West over the whole planet, the social leveling, the uniformity, the disappearance of peoples, the prevalence of lonely crowds, all seemed to Strauss, as to Heidegger, as a hitherto unsurpassed catastrophe. Strauss could not have been more sympathetic to Heidegger's despair in the face of the modern predicament. In the modern world human life is "nothing but work and recreation" and "complete emptiness!"[25] Strauss shares Heidegger's negativity toward modernity.

Strauss explains that it was in the face of such utter hopelessness that Heidegger grabbed at straws. It was the bleakness of modernity that made him do it. Strauss sounds almost sympathetic when he writes, "one had to be inhuman to leave it at Spengler's prognosis. Is there no hope for Europe? And therewith for mankind? It was in the spirit of such hope that Heidegger perversely welcomed 1933."[26] In the midst of this "night of the world," Heidegger needed hope; he therefore mistook the Nazis for Nietzsche's new planetary aristocracy. Nevertheless, Heidegger made a terrible mistake. The Nazis were not the Overman but the Blond Beast. Heidegger thought that the Nazis were a solution to the night of the world, instead of a manifestation of the darkness. He failed to understand the importance of Nietzsche's distinction. Unlike the Overman, the Nazis were altogether devoid of religiosity; instead, they radiated with the spirit of nihilism, which was also the spirit of Heidegger. And this is precisely why there is an affinity of spirit between Heidegger and the Nazis.

Like the Nazis, Heidegger did not shrink from nihilism. He made the mistake of trying to eke an ethic out of the void—the existential ethic of authenticity and resoluteness. His ethic of authenticity consisted in despising all sham certainties and living in the face of the abyss without any comforting illusions or "artificial netting" to conceal the horror.[27] Strauss is not too keen on authenticity. He thinks that an "artificial netting" is exactly what is needed for mankind to live a genuinely human life. Nietzsche recognized that Western civilization's devotion to truth led to its demise. Biblical faith reinforced the love of truth by insisting on probity at all costs. But Nietzsche returned to the mendacity of the ancients. He overthrew the yoke of truth. He restored "the Platonic notion of the noble delusion."[28] He renounced probity in favor of the noble lie. But Heidegger would deprive man of all comforting delusions and then wonder why he had become a beast.

For Strauss, the holocaust has its source in the fact that the "artificial netting" that kept the abyss at bay had been dismantled. Nietzsche understood the corrosive effects of truth but Heidegger did not. When he finally recognized that the devotion to knowledge had turned Western civilization into a technological nightmare of barbarous mastery, Heidegger abandoned the Western tradition altogether in favor of Eastern mysticism.

In what follows, I will make two objections to Strauss's intriguing account. First, I will show that Strauss's critique of Heidegger is very problematic because Strauss shares more with Heidegger than he cares to admit. Second, I will reject Strauss's attempt to hide behind the authority of Plato and Nietzsche. I will argue that Strauss's position differs from Plato's as well as Nietzsche's, and is inferior to both.

## WHY STRAUSS'S CRITIQUE
## OF HEIDEGGER IS PROBLEMATIC

Strauss is critical of Heidegger's "resoluteness" and suggests that the proper philosophical attitude is not resoluteness but resignation.[29] Strauss distinguishes between ancient and modern skepticism. He thinks that philosophy properly understood is *zetetic* or skeptic in the ancient sense of the term.[30] Strauss's defenders often describe him as a *zetetic* in order to distinguish him from modern nihilists such as Heidegger.[31] The suggestion is that ancient skepticism was reclusive and conservative, whereas modern skeptics, such as Heidegger and his postmodern followers, are politically radical and engaged.

Ancient skeptics such as Pyrrho and Sextus Empiricus claimed to be followers of Socrates.[32] Like Socrates, they thought that the unexamined life is not worth living. So they examined their lives philosophically. But after questioning everything, they found, as Socrates had before them, that they did not have knowledge. And they ended up where they started—stuck with the conventions of their time; because in the absence of knowing the truth, they had no reason to abandon the local pieties. In one sense, ancient skepticism was both futile and conservative because it left the world unchanged. But the skeptics thought that even though philosophy yields no truths on which to act or to change the world, it changes the philosopher. Philosophy leaves the world and everything in it as it was before; but the philosopher is changed by the process of philosophizing. The philosopher is still in the world, but he is not of the world. He has new spectacles with which to see the world and its conventions. The philosophical journey makes the philosopher aware that the world and its conventions are not as solidly grounded in truth as he once thought. He begins to realize that social norms and conventions are totally arbitrary and groundless. But at the same time, he realizes that the conventions work, that they are useful, and allow people to live together in relative harmony. In the absence of knowledge that would yield a higher truth, skeptical philosophers are prepared to go along with the status quo. Terence Penelhum illustrates the similarity between these ideas and those of modern skeptics such as David Hume, Ludwig Wittgenstein, and Richard Rorty. And he concludes that the results of skeptical philosophy are conservative.[33] Is this the case? And can the same be said for Leo Strauss?

It does not seem to me that skepticism necessarily leads to political conservatism. It could equally well lead to political radicalism, as it has in the case of Michel Foucault, Jacques Derrida, and other postmoderns. It is equally logical for the skeptics who discover the total groundlessness of the conventions and norms of their society to launch an all-out war against normalization, and to take pleasure in the process of deconstructing the conventions of their world, not just for themselves, but for everyone else. This is all the more likely if they are in love with the process by which normalized individuals become conscious of the total arbitrariness and groundlessness of the social norms that they had for so long considered eternal and immutable truths. Does Strauss belong with the ancient skeptics and their modern counterparts—Hume, Wittgenstein, and Rorty? Is his skepticism resigned and conservative? Or is it radical and activist like the skepticism of Foucault, Derrida, and Heidegger?

The answer depends on the conventions in which the philosopher finds himself. In a tolerably good society, Strauss would advise the philosopher to retire to his garden, enjoy the company of his friends, and uphold the status quo. But in a seriously flawed regime, the philosopher has an obligation to undermine it, to deconstruct it, to uncover its groundlessness, and to expose its shortcomings.[34] This is possible precisely because knowledge is power; the liberation that philosophy makes possible allows those who have been liberated from the shackles of their time to make and unmake the illusions that hold everyone else captive. But Strauss warns against becoming too intoxicated, although it is not always clear that he follows his own advice.[35]

If the fundamental insight of skepticism is that all regimes are equally groundless, then how is the philosopher to know when to leave well enough alone and when to ferment the revolutionary cause? The explanation is that Strauss's skepticism, like most others, has limits. Strauss's skepticism does not just lead to a knowledge of one's ignorance. It also leads to insights about which ideas, norms, and myths are useful and which are not. Strauss sometimes speaks as if the modernity in which he lived was an intolerable state of affairs that must be destroyed for the sake of man's humanity.[36] But mostly he speaks of a crisis of impending doom. In either case, his position is not that of a reclusive withdrawing into his garden and enjoying the fruits of the philosophical life. His position is politically activist; it begs for action on behalf of those alone who can rescue humanity from the impending catastrophe. Strauss is therefore not as politically conservative or as resigned as the ancient skeptics tended to be.

Strauss criticizes Heidegger for his "resolve" and his political activism. Heidegger wanted to be the führer of the führer, the éminence grise—the power behind the throne. But despite all his overtures to the importance of resignation, it must be admitted that Strauss shares the same view of the relation of philosophy to political power. He associates this view with Plato's philosopher-king, and Nietzsche's Superman, and it exercises a significant hold on him and his disciples.[37] Certainly, the Straussians that have flocked to the political arena, especially during the Reagan and Bush administrations, took the matter very seriously.[38] After all, unless there is an intimate connection between politics and philosophy, the latter cannot work its magic, and Western civilization is robbed of philosophy's redeeming properties.

Strauss also shares Heidegger's understanding of modernity as the night of the world; he shares Heidegger's dark apocalyptic premonitions and his pretentious negativity; he talks constantly in terms of crisis; he blames modernity for the impending doom. Like Heidegger, he holds modernity responsible for the propagation of the cosmopolitan spirit that accounts for the disappearance of peoples, and the homelessness of man. Like Heidegger, he associates modernity with liberalism, and he abhors its universalistic spirit, and blames it for undermining the vitality of human groups. Strauss's Jewish nationalism echoes the tribal, *volkisch*, and nationalistic ideas of Heidegger. It is not the case that Strauss merely shares Heidegger's diagnosis of the problem. He also shares a great deal of Heidegger's solutions.

In his search for the solution to the crisis of modernity, Strauss mirrors Heidegger's style, temper, and motifs. Like Heidegger, he believes that the West is a victim of amnesia. Like Heidegger, he treats the great texts of Western civilization as a psychoanalyst treats a victim of amnesia, bringing before him words from a forgotten past in the hope of jogging his memory. Heidegger usually begins with a fragment from Heraclitus and focusing on phrases, even syllables, he attempts to excavate the lost meanings. The idea is that the forgetfulness of the original meaning has debilitated the development of Western civilization, and that the recovery of the long-buried meaning will miraculously revitalize the West and bring forth a renaissance. By the same token, Strauss believes that the original meaning of the classics has been lost, even totally perverted; and like Heidegger, he believes that this loss is at the heart of the crisis of the West. His study of the classics is not just an academic exercise; it is a therapeutic work intended to recover the vitality of the West. So understood, scholarship becomes a heroic activity that is the key to saving civilization from impending doom.

The spirit, style, and temper of Strauss's approach to philosophy bears a remarkable similarity to Heidegger's. Heidegger presents his philosophical project as the complete overthrow of the thoughtless and mindless history of philosophy. In the same way, Strauss sweeps away the history of scholarly understanding of the classics as nothing more than a thoughtless misunderstanding. Like Heidegger, he also resolves to start anew. And though they say it will not be easy, this approach is attractive precisely because it frees their students from the burden of the past, the weight of the history of philosophy, and the history of scholarship about the great philosophers.

The whole point of sweeping away the past is to start anew, and this time to take the right steps, embark on the real journey, and not get lost in the woods. Heidegger promises illumination, a clearing, or just a "lit darkness." Like Heidegger, Strauss also promises illumination; he regards philosophy as a dangerous activity that reveals a secret teaching. Both men present philosophy as a project of unconcealing. The attraction is no doubt erotic. And Strauss never tires of repeating that philosophy is the highest eros.

When Heidegger approaches a text, a text that promises the desired illumination, he invariably finds himself. His study of Parmenides is a case in point.[39] The same is true of Strauss's approach to the wise ancients whose texts contain the requisite illumination. If Strauss is not convinced by Plato's argument that justice leads to happiness, he dismisses it as a salutary teaching for the masses.[40] If he does not like Plato's argument about the equality of the sexes, he surmises that Plato was joking.[41] And when it comes to the courses offered at universities, the Straussians and Heideggerians are characterized by the same self-referential quality. The only books recommended for reading in these courses are books by other Heideggerians or Straussians as the case may be. When all the authorities point in the same direction, the student is caught in a circle from which it is difficult to escape, even if one had the will. But most do not aspire to freedom; they are desperate for illumination; they are hungry for truth. It does not occur to them that the wise may disagree, and that philosophy is far more exciting than their limited education allows. Unfortunately, it is more comfortable to remain within the charmed circle, but it can hardly be illuminating.

Nothing made a greater impact on Strauss than Heidegger's manner of studying a text. He was totally struck by Heidegger's analysis of Aristotle's *Metaphysics*; he thought that Heidegger's approach laid bare the intellectual sinews of a text; and it was unlike anything else he had ever seen or heard.[42] Strauss's reaction is not unusual; Heidegger's style of teaching was reputed to have a totally mesmerizing effect. He has been accused of a certain "mystical bullying."[43] The goal was not so much understanding as initiation in a mystical cult. This is precisely why Karl Jaspers's letter to the Denazification Commission advised against Heidegger's return to teaching after the war.[44] The gist of Jaspers's letter was that Heidegger's style was profoundly unfree, and that the students were not strong enough to withstand his sorcery. The youth are not safe with Heidegger until they can think for themselves, and Heidegger is no help where that is concerned. On a much smaller scale, the same can be said for Strauss. Except for the odd renegade, his students invariably discover what he has taught them to find in the texts.

Strauss's account of modernity, his abhorrence of liberalism, his *volkisch* proclivities, his authoritarianism, his philosophical mystique, his knack for amassing disciples, and his ability to eke an ethic out of nihilism, all bear an uncanny resemblance to the style as well as the substance of Heidegger's thought. For all these reasons, Strauss's critique of Heidegger is disingenuous.

## STRAUSS'S BOGUS AUTHORITIES: PLATO AND NIETZSCHE

Strauss may reply to this criticism by pointing to the fact that, unlike Heidegger, he has kept his nihilism secret and has not allowed it to contaminate the city. Instead, he followed Plato and Nietzsche in offering the city a concoction of noble lies and pious frauds.

Strauss invariably imparts his wisdom by relying on the authority of the great philosophers of the past. But those who read for themselves need not fall prey to Strauss's bogus authorities. Neither Plato nor Nietzsche endorsed lies and deception on a mass scale as a political ploy necessary to save civilization from the horrors of truth and the abyss of nihilism.[45]

Plato made a distinction between the deliberate lie and the lie in the soul.[46] The deliberate liar knows the truth but the lie in the soul is a profound self-deception. There is another equally important distinction to be made among deliberate lies: that is the distinction between the noble and ignoble lie. Plato thought of his own myths as true myths or noble lies and regarded Homer's myths as false and ignoble. The difference is not in the literal truth of the myth, but in its moral. Homer's myths were lies because they promoted a false image of ourselves; they taught that all our vices can be blamed on the gods. If someone lost his temper and did something rash and violent, then Zeus made him do it; if someone committed adultery, then Aphrodite must have got hold of his mind. These myths are pernicious lies because they allow us to deceive ourselves about our nature; they allow us to live a lie and to pretend that we are not responsible for our actions.[47] That is the lie in the soul that Plato abhorred. In contrast, he believed that all sorts of myths and stories may convey a true moral even though they are not literally true. He thought that the myth of metals was a noble lie.[48] But he did not justify the lie simply on the basis of the salutary effects it may have, nor did he think that lying was necessary because the truth is intolerable and must be kept hidden from the multitude. Plato intended his myths to be a fanciful account of the truth—the myth of the cave, the myth of metals, the story of Gyges, the story of Leontius, and the parable of the ship are all intended as fictions depicting profound truths about political life and the human condition. The magical ring that made Gyges, the shepherd in the service of the king of Lydia, invisible, is a good example. With this ring, Gyges seduced the queen and with her help murdered the king and took over the kingdom.[49] The moral of the story is that hardly any of us could withstand the acid test of Gyges and escape with our characters intact. Only men and women of real mettle can withstand the ordeal of Gyges. Just as only men and women with golden souls can withstand the temptations of politics, because politics is like the ring of Gyges—it presents opportunities to do wrong with impunity. This is precisely why Plato thought that the political problem par excellence was moral.

Plato's myths are not a set of lies intended to dupe the multitude and secure power for a special elite, especially one that is convinced that its destiny is to rescue civilization from impending doom.

Nietzsche's position on the role of myths and illusions differs significantly from Plato's. But it is equally instructive. Unlike Plato, he did not associate the truth with the light but with darkness. Fearing that the truth was a void that would lead to nihilism, despair, and despondency, Nietzsche praised the life-giving illusion.[50] But this was not a license for indiscriminate lying intended to manipulate others and gain power. It was intended to impose on life a meaning that would give it vitality and significance. Feast your eyes on Plutarch, Nietzsche advised, and dare to believe in his heroes. Nietzsche cared little that these heroes were fictions. His only worry was that the fictions could become so grandiose and so ridiculous that instead of inspiring life and action, they may paralyze it.[51] After all, what could possibly compare to Pythagoras's golden hips, or Plato's virgin birth? If the past becomes too grand, life in the present may look paltry and worthless. Nietzsche's myths and illusions are not so much lies as ideals.

Nietzsche celebrated the lie because he wanted the philosophers of the future to be brave enough not to despair in the face of the truth of nihilism; he wanted them to be great artists who would consider the void as an opportunity to create beautiful myths and illusions of their own— illusions that would humanize and beautify an otherwise cold and heartless world.[52] Nor would these free spirits despise their creations any less for not being true; unlike Socrates, they would not be captivated by truth; on the contrary, they would love their illusions like artists love their creations. Nietzsche's Supermen are bewitched by their illusions, and this is a far cry from Strauss's liars who fancy themselves gods playing pranks on mere mortals. Nietzsche's lies are more like ideals than deliberate falsifications of reality—ideals that the free spirits are eager to live by. In contrast, the heartless liar lives by a standard other than the one he imposes on others.

Strauss's position is a tasteless mixture of Plato and Nietzsche that is inferior to both. Contrary to Plato's sunny disposition, Strauss finds the truth dark, even sordid, and threatening to political order and stability. But even though Strauss begins with Nietzsche's assumptions about the darkness of truth, he ends with Plato's conclusions. Instead of descending into the cave with knowledge of the sunny truth, he believes that the role of the philosopher is to manipulate the images in the cave. He teaches that philosophers must fabricate lies for the many while embracing the darkness for themselves. Unwittingly, Strauss cultivates an unprincipled elite whose lies are intended for others and not for themselves. It is the sort of elite that would be regarded with contempt by Nietzsche and Plato alike.

## LYING AND POLITICS

Hannah Arendt described totalitarianism as the triumph of politics over truth.[53] She thought that propaganda or the systematic attempt to conceal the truth was the fundamental ploy of totalitarian politics. But she could not have dreamed that these totalitarian tactics would be rehabilitated, made respectable, and considered politics as usual.

There has always been a tension between politics and truth-telling. No one who undertakes the special obligation of caring for the community can afford the luxury of perfect honesty. Anyone who is not willing to tell a petty lie to save his state from annihilation is not fit for a political career. And in very extreme cases, Machiavelli may have been right when he said that a prince must love his country more than his soul; as someone who is entrusted with the care and preservation of his community, he may have to do things that in the Christian faith are punishable by eternal damnation.

The problem with our postmodern world is that politics is no longer seen as the domain of judicious lying. Politics has become an arena of creative lying. Lying has become synonymous with politics; it is now considered an art. This state of affairs could not have come to be without the rehabilitation and transfiguration of lying into the supreme virtue of the postmodern world. Believing that it is following Nietzsche's lead, the postmodern world has dispensed with truth. But in a world devoid of truth, can we call the fabrication of reality a lie? No, that is impossible when the lie is all the truth there is. In the postmodern world, there are interpretations without texts, illusions without reality, and conventions without nature. In a world where reality is a void, the creative art rules supreme. In such a world, what could be more creative than lying? After all, a great lie, one that is believed, gives form to the void, imposes order on chaos, and creates the world ex nihilo. In such a world, one must dispense with the concept of lies as well as the concept of ideology, because they contain a hint of moral contempt, a certain self-righteousness, and a smug belief that there is a truth beneath the lie, a truth that transcends ideologies. The electronic media and its capacity for instant mass communication lend themselves to this state of affairs.

Strauss has unwittingly allied himself with the postmodern tradition that has rehabilitated totalitarian tactics in politics. He has dispensed with truth in the political arena and endorsed systematic lying—supposedly out of love for humanity. But far from saving civilization, Straussian political wisdom aggravates the problems of modern politics—contempt for politicians, lack of trust in the political process, and rampant cynicism. Besides, an elite that identifies its own pursuit of power with the necessary means of preserving Western civilization and preempting catastrophe is bound to be an unprincipled elite, unfit for political power. The loftiness of their enterprise, coupled with their sense of crisis, may lead them to sweep aside moral limits as applicable only to other people. The tragedy is that Strauss unwittingly prepares the way for the Blond Beast. And like Heidegger, he confuses the bestial and the noble.

## CARL SCHMITT DENOUNCES
## LIBERAL DEMOCRACY

Carl Schmitt is famous for three ideas about politics that are central to Strauss's political thought in general and to his understanding and critique of American liberal democracy in particular. First is the idea that liberalism is a terrible blight on European history that has extinguished the glory of politics and replaced it with the banality of economics. Second is the idea that liberalism and democracy are incompatible, and that the latter is preferable to the former. Third is the idea that politics is a glorious affair that has been eclipsed by the triumph of liberal democracy. I will discuss each of these in turn.

Schmitt's critique of liberalism is part of a grand tale about the history of European civilization. The story is one of decline and degeneration, deception and chicanery. It all begins with royal absolutism, which Schmitt regards as the pinnacle of European civilization. In his view, royal absolutism was a state of affairs that reflected the elegance of the cosmos—hierarchy and order, discipline and vitality. Just as the world was ruled by a supreme lawgiver, so the state was ruled by a supreme sovereign. Just as God was not himself bound by his own laws, so the sovereign was above the law. Nor was this a harsh, mechanical, or tiresome state of affairs; on the contrary, it was a universe full of pardons, amnesties, contingencies, exceptions, and emergencies—all the things that require the direct interference of God. Like God, the sovereign was free to pardon; and in an emergency that threatened the life of the state, the sovereign was free to act without the restraint of law. Schmitt compares the sovereign's capacity to come to the rescue of the state with God's miracles.[54]

For Schmitt, the state has its source in will, or what he calls "decisionism." Following Joseph de Maistre, Schmitt reduces the state to "the moment of decision, to a pure decision not based on reason and discussion and not justifying itself, that is, to an absolute decision created out of nothingness."[55] Like God, the sovereign creates ex nihilo; and like God, he has no obligation to be rational. Schmitt's politics is based on an existential theology—a willful and inscrutable God.

Unhappily, this exhilarating state of affairs has been eclipsed by an utterly drab and mechanical view of things. The Enlightenment philosophers led an assault on royal absolutism in the name of reason, law, and justice. They replaced the traditional God with a deist God. In the deist universe, God creates the world but he does not interfere with it. His relation to the world is like that of the watchmaker to his clock. The deist universe is orderly, mechanistic, and predictable—it is a universe in which pardons as well as miracles have disappeared. The constitutional state is the mirror image of the deist universe. And far from thinking that the new order magnifies liberty, Schmitt laments it as a "tyranny of reason."[56] The expression exemplifies the postmodern view of modernity.[57]

In Schmitt's view, the history of European civilization since the French Revolution of 1789 has been characterized by the "triumphal march of democracy."[58] Democracy replaces the sovereignty of the king with the sovereignty of the people. But as a mere *form* of government, democracy is vacuous and has little appeal. It can only be defended if it is made substantive, or if the will of the people is given a definite content. But unfortunately, the people cannot be relied on to know their own true will; someone must educate and lead them. Rousseau, the founder of democratic thought, suggests a lawgiver with the power to transform human nature and to shape the will of the people. Democracy flounders on just how the people's will is to be formed.[59] And until the time comes when the people know their true will, a vanguard party or a single dictator may be the true bearer of the people's will. This is the "Jacobin logic" of Rousseau that makes democracy compatible with Bolshevism, Caesarism, and dictatorship.[60] Even though democracy is self-refuting, it has remained the most irresistible political force in European history. Every political movement that hopes to succeed must present itself in democratic guise—liberalism, Marxism, and socialism have done just that.

Schmitt regards the rise of liberalism in the nineteenth century as a far greater calamity than the triumphal march of democracy. In Schmitt's view, the historical alliance of liberalism and democracy against absolute monarchy has camouflaged the deep conflict between them. Schmitt drives a wedge between liberalism and democracy. Liberalism is individualistic, apolitical, and radically egalitarian. It is predicated on the equal worth of every adult person, simply for being a person. Its respect for the human worth of the individual leads it to demand political and economic equality on a global scale. Schmitt defines liberalism as a "democracy of mankind" where every person is equally entitled to citizenship.[61] In contrast, democracy advocates a much more limited equality—the equality of citizens who are equal in virtue of their physical, linguistic, cultural, moral, or religious sameness. Democracy therefore presupposes homogeneity, and the exclusion of the heterogeneous. Democracy understands the concept of the foreign, the outsider, or the other.[62] Democracy is not indiscriminately egalitarian.

Even colonies like Australia have immigration policies that admit only "the right type of settler." It is quite consistent with the logic of democracy to exclude slaves, aristocrats, atheists, or barbarians. This was as true of Athens as of the British Empire. Democracy is political, whereas liberalism is global and apolitical. Democracy requires homogeneity, but liberalism protects individuality. This is why liberalism and democracy are incompatible, and why any regime in which they exist simultaneously must choose between them. Schmitt's own choice is clear. He denounces liberalism because it upholds the equality of individuals—all men are created equal. In Schmitt's view, the global character of liberal equality makes it meaningless. Where everyone is equally privileged, no one has any privileges. Politics is about distinctions and inequality; and in destroying the latter, liberalism also destroys politics. And since politics is linked to man's humanity, the triumph of liberalism is a greater calamity than the success of democracy.

There is something cosmic and apocalyptic about Schmitt's critique of liberalism. Liberalism depoliticizes the world, it trivializes it, robs it of all its seriousness, and turns it into entertainment. By the same token, it transforms political problems into organizational, economic, technical, and sociological "tasks." It turns the state into a "huge industrial plant."[63] Liberalism is the borification of the world. Schmitt associates it with the state of affairs that Max Weber anticipated with horror—the world of "specialists without spirit and sensualists without heart."

Schmitt's critique of liberalism is ambiguous. On one hand, he laments the liberal depoliticization of the world; on the other, he accuses liberalism of having forged a new and more deadly friend-enemy grouping. Schmitt sets out to unmask the apolitical character of liberalism as a fraud. Liberalism may pretend to establish a world that transcends the filthy and rapacious world of politics, it may look like it is replacing war and politics with reason and commerce, but far from abolishing the political, liberalism introduces a more intense and unclean politics that is as lethal as the religious politics of old. It introduces a covert global politics.

For all its egalitarianism, Schmitt does not for a moment believe that liberalism has banished inequality. Barred from the political sphere, inequality is confined to the economic domain, where it rules with a vengeance. Liberalism has inaugurated a world of economic imperialism that is even more exploitative than the old political mode of domination. All that has been accomplished by the liberal revolution is the replacement of the overt repression of the political with the covert repression of the economic.[64] Schmitt's complaint about the clandestine nature of modern politics is echoed in Michel Foucault's complaint about the nature of post-Enlightenment power in general. What is wrong with the new modes of power is that they are covert and clandestine, as opposed to the old modes that were overt and conspicuous.[65] In the post-Enlightenment era, power is masked by moralistic conceptions of justice, truth, goodness, humanity, and rationality, which pretend to universal validity.

Schmitt admires the genius of Marx, who understood that liberalism can only be fought in its own economic domain with its own quasi-religious weapons. But he regards Marxism as a hybrid of liberalism. Like the latter, it denounces the political while forging a friend/enemy grouping that encompasses the whole world.[66]

The last aspect of liberal hypocrisy that Schmitt sets out to expose is parliament—the liberal institution par excellence. It represents the liberal belief in endless talk—freedom of speech, freedom of the press, freedom of assembly. At the root of this liberal faith in speech is the belief that through open discussion truth and justice will come to the fore. Schmitt balks at this faith in openness and discussion, which he associates with impotence and effeminacy. In his *Political Romanticism* he links liberalism with the romanticism of Adam Müller, whom he depicts as incapable of being manly and decisive.[67] Given a choice between Christ and Barabbas, liberals suggest that a committee should examine the matter.[68] In Schmitt's view, liberal society is crippled by indecisiveness and is doomed to perish in an emergency. Liberalism has absolutely no understanding of politics and no capacity for decision. For Schmitt, politics is about decisions and choices that are not grounded in reason, and therefore cannot be the result of parliamentary debate and discussion.

Schmitt denies that the "crisis of parliamentary democracy" has its source in the external threats of fascism or socialism; rather, it has its source in liberalism itself. It has its source in the fact that liberalism no longer believes in its own principles.[69] Parliament presupposes individuals who are free to convince and be convinced by others of the truth or rightness of certain positions. This assumes that they are not hampered by party loyalty. But this is no longer the case. Instead of setting out to discover what is rationally correct, parliamentary government has become a contest of competing interests. Open debate has become an "empty formality" appealing to the passions in an effort to manipulate public opinion. The idea is to win a majority and use it to govern absolutely. There is no longer any meaningful distinction between a constitutional regime based on persuasion, and an absolute regime based on command. Instead of open debate, parliament now resorts to a multiplicity of committees that make decisions in secret and behind closed doors. Parliament is but a front for the "committees of invisible rulers."[70]

As we shall see, Schmitt's critique of liberalism is echoed in the Straussian critique of American liberalism. Schmitt's critique of liberalism is threefold. First, liberalism is hypocritical; it has its roots in the faith that open debate will allow truth and justice to emerge. But instead, parliament has given way to endless committees and secret decisions behind closed doors. Although there is an undeniable validity to this critique, it is an internal critique, a critique that a liberal would make of the failures of liberal society to actualize liberal ideals.

Second, liberalism replaces the closed societies of old with an insipid and meaningless global egalitarianism. This picture of liberalism as a democracy of the world, where every person is entitled to equal citizenship by virtue of being a person, is in my view, a preposterous fiction. To the extent that liberalism allies itself with capitalism, insists on free trade, and subordinates the political to the economic, it does indeed generate global forces with their own logic of economic domination. But by the same token, there is nothing inconsistent about liberalism in one country.

The idea that liberalism is a democracy of the world is a caricature of liberalism presented by Schmitt and echoed by Strauss and his American followers. But in truth, liberalism is not by nature egalitarian, but meritocratic. It tries to replace an inequality based on birth with one based on talents. In aristocratic or class societies, a person's status is determined by birth or luck. But the liberal ideology of equal opportunity declares the status of individuals to be a function of their own talents and abilities, or lack thereof. Those who are at the bottom of the social scale have only themselves to blame—they are either stupid, lazy, or both. This is precisely what makes liberal inequality so hard to bear.

It also explains why liberal society must perpetually work to make equality of opportunity a reality, even though the latter can never be achieved. The critique of liberalism as an indiscriminate egalitarianism that banishes all inequality is an attack on a straw man. In truth, liberalism is not only inegalitarian, it provides a harsh rationale for inequality. But even though Schmitt's account of liberalism has not a shred of support in liberal theory, it has played a large role in the Straussian critique of American liberalism.

Third, Schmitt fears that the nascent globalism at the heart of liberalism will mean the eclipse of the political—and that would be the greatest catastrophe of all, since it would drain the world of everything meaningful, magnificent, and glorious—namely, the political. Again, this criticism plays a significant role in the Straussian critique of American liberalism.

As we shall see, Schmitt's critique of liberalism is central to the Straussian understanding of America. Like Schmitt, Strauss's American followers drive a wedge between liberalism and democracy. They affirm democracy because, like Schmitt, they think that democracy is vacuous and depends on who will shape the will of the people. Following Schmitt, they repudiate American liberalism because they regard it as a leveling and homogenizing brand of imperialism.

## SCHMITT CELEBRATES POLITICS

In his *Concept of the Political,* Carl Schmitt romanticizes the political. He argues that politics is an autonomous and unique domain of life that is distinct from the moral, religious, economic, and aesthetic dimensions of existence. According to Schmitt, each domain of existence has its own peculiar dualism: morality is about good and evil, economics is about profits and liabilities, and aesthetics is about beauty and ugliness. What is true of all these domains of life, is equally true of the political, which has its own peculiar dualism—the *friend* and the *foe*.[71] Schmitt goes to great length to show that this peculiarly political distinction is not identical to any of these other distinctions, nor does it overlap with any of them. The political enemy "need not be morally evil or aesthetically ugly;" he need not even be an "economic competitor."[72] It suffices that the political enemy is "the other, the stranger, . . . something different and alien."[73] The foe is one who threatens one's own existence and way of life. To be political is to recognize the foe and to keep him at bay.

Schmitt fancies himself a latter-day Hobbes. Like Hobbes, he believes that the supreme political problem in his day, as in Hobbes's, is the absence of an absolute sovereign whose political authority is incontrovertible. What is needed is an absolute power with a jurisdiction over life and death. Like Hobbes, he thinks that only such a sovereign can ward off chaos and secure peace. But Schmitt demands not just peace, but "total peace."[74] This requires the absolute unity, singularity, and cohesiveness of the state. To secure this total peace, the state must be free to define the foe as it sees fit. This means that the foe need not simply be an external foe. In "critical situations" the state can declare a "domestic enemy."[75]

Schmitt was first and foremost a political realist concerned with the survival of the state. Schmitt was critical of the Weimar Republic because its liberal constitution was antithetical to what he considered an intelligent understanding of the political. If Weimar was to survive, Schmitt thought that it should eliminate the two extremist parties—the Communists and the Nazis—because they threatened the very being of the regime. Schmitt wrote a letter to President Paul von Hindenburg advising him to do just that.[76] Needless to say, his advice was not heeded and Weimar was destroyed. In Schmitt's eyes, as in the eyes of many other German writers, including Leo Strauss, Weimar became the paradigm of liberalism—weak, spineless, and stupid.

It is not difficult to understand why Schmitt embraced Hitler and the Nazis with enthusiasm—he became their leading jurist and intellectual ornament. He wrote wildly anti-Semitic articles blaming Jews (from Spinoza to Marx) for the intellectual paralysis of Leviathan; he also wrote articles legally justifying the Nazi purges. Unlike the liberal-minded Hindenburg (operating in a vacuum of legalistic doctrines), Hitler understood politics—that is, he grasped the fundamental idea of the foe, and proceeded to eliminate it with a deadly efficiency. But unfortunately for Schmitt, the Nazis discovered the letter he had written to Hindenburg and had him expelled from the party. This misfortune served him well in 1945 when he appeared before the Allied War Crimes Tribunal at Nuremberg.[77]

Schmitt's defenders have argued that Schmitt made an effort to purify the enemy from all moralistic contamination, and in so doing, posited a "clean enemy." This, they believe, is a very good idea, because it has the effect of moderating politics, and undermining the venomous hatred that is often heaped on political enemies when morality and religion are confused with politics. The idea is that when political enemies are not regarded as the incarnation of evil, then there is little reason to destroy them; it suffices that they be made innocuous. Morality and religion have the effect of intensifying the inhumanity of the political. They make the enemy unclean, and hence make politics more savage than it has to be. A war against an enemy who is considered evil is the most intense and inhuman of wars because it is not satisfied with defeating the enemy but will not rest until the enemy is totally destroyed.[78]

This interpretation of Schmitt is partially confirmed by his text. But it remains the case that politics consists of "the most intense and extreme antagonism."[79] And this antagonism naturally results in war, which Schmitt understands as the "*existential negation* of the enemy."[80] The point of purifying the enemy is not just an effort to moderate the excessive inhumanity of war, it is intended to underscore the supremacy of the political in its own totally unchallenged domain. To isolate the political domain from all other human endeavors and to make it autonomous and self-sufficient is intended to insure that the political is subservient to no other domain of existence. In other words, political enmity is a self-sufficient reason to kill the other for the simple reason that he is other, different, or alien. It suffices that he is defined as the *foe*. It is political authority that defines the foe; and this definition cannot be challenged by considerations of religion, morality, or aesthetics. The political is the domain of life and death, killing and being killed. Political enmity is a sufficient reason to kill. In Schmitt's view, there is no ethical principle necessary or possible that can justify war and killing, which is why he rejects the whole idea of a just war.[81] The point of making politics autonomous is to make it into a domain that is exempt from providing any justification for killing—a domain of life that is not subject to reason.[82] It matters not at all whether the enemy is ugly or beautiful, wicked or innocent, an infidel or a believer. Schmitt's enemy may be clean, but there is absolutely no reason for thinking that the clean enemy makes politics more humane.

There is no doubt that the Nazis must have appeared to Schmitt as paradigms of the political. They not only defined the foe, they also confronted a pure political enemy. Indeed, Hannah Arendt's description of Adolph Eichmann can be seen as a variation on the theme of the pure political enemy. In her *Eichmann in Jerusalem,* she reveals the extent to which Eichmann went about conducting his business of exterminating the Jews without animus or hatred. He can indeed be said to have confronted a clean enemy. He never hated them; he never thought that they were evil, ugly, or economically threatening; they deserved extermination because they were *other.* It seems to me that this is the logic of Schmitt's political— it provides human life with a domain of violence free of guilt.

What is troublesome about Schmitt's efforts to purify the political is that such purification is likely to make politics more rather than less inhuman than it generally is. But one wonders if the cleanliness with which Eichmann confronted his enemies was not the reason for the efficiency he displayed in their extermination. If Arendt's portrait of Eichmann reveals anything, it reveals that the political as understood by Schmitt and Eichmann is nothing but an alibi for thoughtlessness and vulgarity.[83]

It is important to note that there is a certain ambiguity in Schmitt's account of politics. Schmitt's conception of the political has two dimensions that are not altogether compatible with one another. On one hand, Schmitt writes as if the political is a datum, a fact of life, an irreducible reality that only the self-deluded can deny. On the other hand, Schmitt speaks as if the political is something honorific and glorious, which has been obscured and forgotten in a world dominated by the economic or vulgar. He romanticizes the political, and regrets that it has been undermined by the success of liberalism. It is not that liberalism has simply obscured or hidden the truth from view; it has eclipsed a superior world that was more real, more serious, and more manly. There is a tension between these two accounts.

If the political is indeed a fundamental and irreducible reality, then one need not fear that it will be eclipsed by liberalism or any other development. This is the sense in which he uses the term when he says that liberalism may have camouflaged the political but it has not succeeded in exterminating it, and that far from transcending it, has intensified it. If the political is indeed an eternal and irreducible fact of life, then there is no sense lamenting its loss.

In a fascinating essay, Schmitt describes the history of Europe in the last four centuries as an unsuccessful movement in the direction of neutralization and depoliticization. He claims that Europeans have been searching for a neutral ground that transcends politics but every time they find one it becomes politicized.[84] This implies that there is no escaping from the political; there is no neutral ground where peace and agreement are possible. In fact, all attempts to escape from politics only succeed in intensifying it; we are now standing on the threshold of a grand political conflagration. In the sixteenth century, theological war led Europe to search for a neutral ground outside the theological. But no sooner is such a neutral ground found then it becomes politicized, and a new domain of neutrality is sought. The theological age gave way to the metaphysical age (seventeenth century), which in turn gave way to the humanitarian or moral age (eighteenth century), which in turn gave way to the economic age (nineteenth century). In every case, the neutral zone that is discovered loses its objectivity and is politicized. The latest zone of neutrality to be discovered is technology. The new religion of technicity is characterized by the belief that this is a genuinely neutral zone. Schmitt believes that technology is in fact neutral between the revolutionary and the reactionary, war and peace, centralism and decentralism. But to say that a genuine neutral domain has been discovered is not to say that the world has been permanently depoliticized. On the contrary, as Schmitt himself recognizes, the very neutrality of technology and the hitherto unsurpassed power it provides those who can wield it are bound to inaugurate a new age of terrible wars. What remains to be seen is what forces will emerge, what new friend-enemy groupings will wield its power.[85] If this is the case, then politics is an ineradicable component of existence, and it makes no sense to lament its eclipse.

## STRAUSS RADICALIZES SCHMITT

In his commentary on Schmitt's book, Strauss reveals the extent to which Schmitt's concept of the political proved irresistible. Strauss is unable to liberate himself from the conception of the political by which his people were so tragically victimized. He shares Schmitt's demonization of liberalism; he accepts Schmitt's characterization of the political as the organization of men into fighting units; he accepts Schmitt's analysis of politics in terms of the distinction between friend and foe, *we* and *they*. All this is clear not only in his commentary on Schmitt, but in his analysis of the Jewish problem, and even in his commentaries on Plato.[86] The similarities between Strauss and Schmitt notwithstanding, there is an important difference between them.

Strauss is aware of the ambiguity in Schmitt's conception of the political; and his commentary amounts to telling Schmitt how to be more consistent. Strauss rightly argues that the political cannot simply be affirmed on the basis of its reality, or because it exists. It must be affirmed because it is superior to a depoliticized world. What is wrong with liberalism is that it depoliticizes the world; and this is a phenomenon that Strauss appears to take more seriously than Schmitt. The latter always seems confident about the irreducible fact of politics. But Strauss genuinely worries that the political will be totally eclipsed from the world. For Strauss, the political is not an inescapable destiny of man, for there are powerful (liberal) forces that are pacifying and depoliticizing the world. And if they succeed, the world will become less human. The depoliticization of the world would be a catastrophe because Strauss thinks of politics as a humanizing force. He therefore regards liberalism as a threat to man's humanity.[87] Strauss's view of the political and his demonization of liberalism are more consistent and more radical than Schmitt's.

Strauss believes that the root of Schmitt's error was in his admiration of Hobbes. Strauss totally disagrees with Schmitt that Hobbes's understanding of politics was luminous. On the contrary, Hobbes lays the foundations of the liberal tradition that Schmitt hoped to escape. Strauss points out that even though Hobbes's state of nature was a state of war of all against all, it was not political—it was not the enmity of organized groups, which presupposes friendship within the group.[88] Hobbes begins with a condition of war and enmity only to transcend it. Strauss reminds Schmitt that for Hobbes, life and security are the ultimate ends—ends that are deeply at odds with the political, which requires men to kill and die.[89]

Strauss rightly claims that Schmitt's position assumes the goodness of the political and its intimate connection with man's humanity. He agrees with Schmitt that politics needs to be defended against its modern negation. But if politics is to make human life serious again, if it is to rescue humanity from the triviality of liberalism, then it must be wedded to the most serious questions about right and wrong, good and evil, truth and falsehood. In short, Schmitt's insistence on the autonomy of politics prevents politics from playing a serious role in human life, and in so doing, frustrates Schmitt's own purpose.

The solution that Strauss proposes is to re-theologize the political. Strauss rejects Schmitt's insistence on the autonomy of politics because he believes that politics needs all the help it can get from other domains of life. Deprived of its alliance with religion and morality, Strauss argues that politics cannot succeed in accomplishing its task of uniting people and making them willing to lay down their lives for the collective.[90] Strauss argues that despite his praise for Hobbes, Schmitt just does not take the evil and selfishness of humanity seriously enough. The function of the state is to humanize man or to cultivate his social nature. This is no mean task, and it cannot be accomplished simply by commanding men to fight for material gains—for territory, wealth, or a higher standard of living. The secular state cannot inspire men to fight and die. Something more is necessary—something magnificent and majestic, something splendid and sublime, something like Judaism, Christianity, or Islam.

It is not a question of believing that religion and morality are superior to politics and should govern it. On the contrary, Strauss sees religion and morality as subservient to politics and ministering to its needs. His reinterpretation of Maimonides makes it clear that religion is a pious fraud perpetrated by prophets and wise men who knew just what people needed to make them into a single fighting force ready to lay down their selfish interests and sacrifice their lives for the group. Strauss regards justice itself to be a political invention—a matter of doing good to friends and evil to enemies.

In the final analysis, Strauss's view of politics is much harsher and more radical than Schmitt's. By linking faith and politics, Strauss makes the latter more dangerous and more bloody. And Strauss's critique of Schmitt amounts to saying that Schmitt just does not go far enough.[91]

In conclusion, there is a certain sense in which political realism is irrefutable. Schmitt and Strauss are absolutely right in pointing to the fact that human beings have always lived in societies characterized by mutual hostility and antagonism. And there is no reason to think that this will ever change. But Schmitt and Strauss are not simply bringing this reality to our attention; their aim is to glorify and romanticize the political.

I think that Schmitt is right in thinking that the *other* need not be evil, but not because politics is a domain of life beyond good and evil, but because political conflicts are likely to be conflicts between mutually incompatible goods. Political communities may represent incommensurable goods that come into conflict. But to acknowledge this is not to valorize it. On the contrary, it is a human tragedy of great proportions. It means that human life cannot escape injustice. And the political domain is assigned the task of imposing our conception of the good against others. In other words, politics must shoulder the dirty tasks that make the pursuit of the good life possible. But there is no reason to valorize politics as Strauss and Schmitt do. Nor is there any reason to pretend, as Strauss does, that the violence of politics against foreigners and outsiders is "political justice." Such obfuscations conceal the ugly truth of politics and encourage people to feel morally self-righteous in their iniquities.

By insisting on the moral autonomy of politics, Schmitt hoped to rob it of moral and religious support. And while I would applaud this position as less radical than Strauss's, it could hardly be considered moderate. Schmitt wanted people to confront a pure political enemy, without considering whether the foe was good or evil, innocent or guilty. Unfortunately, the goodness or innocence of the foe is not irrelevant. On the contrary, an innocent foe cannot be treated with excessive force without casting a dark shadow over all our endeavors, no matter how good they are when considered in abstraction. To pretend that the innocence of the foe is irrelevant is self-delusionary. Politics cannot be an autonomous domain. And even if the strict principles of morality cannot apply to politics, it can never be free of moral and religious censure. Even the Nazis understood this, and it explains why they went to such great lengths and invented so many euphemisms to conceal their iniquities. They knew that their grandest plans are bound to be paltry if not utterly repellent once the evils they thought necessary to accomplish their dreams were discovered. By the same token, the Allies did not fight an altogether just war—they used tactics such as the bombing of Dresden and other German cities for the purpose of terrorizing and demoralizing unarmed civilians. Cynics may argue that the Allies went unpunished because only the vanquished are ever punished for their crimes. And those who are even more cynical may argue that history is written by the victors, and hence the war fought by the Allies was deemed to be a just war. But in truth, the best wars cannot bear too much moral scrutiny. Nor is it ignorance of Allied transgressions that accounts for the view that they fought a just war. It is precisely the magnitude of the foe's iniquity that excuses the Allies, and crowns their efforts with approval.

Schmitt's defenders deny that Schmitt intends to romanticize war and politics. They believe that he is not so much lamenting the absence of politics, as its global proportions, which make it more lethal than it has to be. On this view, Schmitt is simply a political realist who is making the best of a bad situation. He is a champion of the "pluriverse"—a globe populated by a plurality of diverse societies that are internally homogeneous. On this view, the pluriverse is the antidote to the homogenizing forces of global capitalism, liberal freedom, and human rights.[92]

It seems to me that the appeal of Hitler for men such as Heidegger and Schmitt had its source in the fact that Hitler appeared to be a champion of the pluriverse against the global forces of liberalism.[93] Of course, this turned out to be false, since Hitler had imperialist aspirations that were as global as they were homogenizing—he aspired to world dominance for the superior race. Nevertheless, in a world where nazism has been defeated militarily, communism has collapsed, and liberal capitalism is sweeping the globe, these sentiments are as germane today as ever. Many feel that the triumph of global capitalism has homogenized the globe and drained the world of uniqueness and eccentricities. By the same token, the fear of this global threat has fueled an opposite reaction—toward tribalism, nationalism, and provincialism. But heaping abuse on everything global and universal has become the fashionable hallmark of postmodernism. Strauss and Schmitt are classic examples. The trouble with this way of thinking is that it is hostile to *everything* universal. So much so that it confuses morality with imperialism, universal moral norms with normalization, and human rights with homogenization. In rejecting the global homogenization of capitalism, they reject the moral law that human beings share in common. It is therefore no surprise that Schmitt railed against the ideas of natural law as anarchical, fanatical, and destructive of the political.[94] Nor was Strauss a champion of natural law, despite his reputation to the contrary.[95] If human beings from different cultures do not share the most elementary moral principles, then diplomacy is impossible, and all disputes must be settled through war.

As we shall see in the following chapter, the American followers of Leo Strauss such as Allan Bloom and Willmoore Kendall echo the ideas expressed by Heidegger and Schmitt. Like Heidegger, they identify American liberalism with modernity, the homelessness of man, and the disintegration of peoples; and like Schmitt, they drive a wedge between liberalism and democracy and affirm the latter while denouncing the former. They abhor the liberal demotion of politics to a mere instrument; they consider a political society healthy only when the state is at the center of life and elicits the love, devotion, and total surrender of its citizens. They detest the pluralism of American society, and long for the cohesiveness of Schmitt's total state.

CHAPTER FOUR

# AMERICAN APPLICATIONS OF STRAUSSIAN PHILOSOPHY

IN THE YEAR OF THE BICENTENNIAL of the American Constitution, Gordon S. Wood wondered why the Straussians dominated nearly all of the academic conferences devoted to the study of the American founding.[1] Part of the answer is that American Straussians are generally conservative, and for conservatives, history is the truest guide to the correct political policies. This is not to say that they are historicists. On the contrary, Straussian conservatives differ from classic or conventional conservatives precisely because they deny that history is the source of truth. Unlike traditional conservatives, they know that every tradition has an origin in the art and inventiveness of great men. Traditions are therefore not as mystical as traditional conservatives generally believe. But this is no reason not to privilege the ancestral, which in this case is the American founding.

There is also another answer to Wood's question, and that has to do with the guilt involved in being conservative in America. There is an assumption, which is not without foundation, that being conservative is somehow un-American.[2] And if that is so, then nothing could do more to diminish the guilt of being conservative than a scholarly literature intended to show the conservatism of the American Founding Fathers. If conservative policies and ideas can be traced to the Founding Fathers, then being American and being conservative can no longer be regarded as mutually exclusive.

Armed with Strauss's distinction between the wise ancients and the vulgar moderns, Strauss's students set out to discover vestiges of ancient wisdom in their own heritage. Some of them believed that the American founding had its roots in the great tradition of the ancients as defined by Strauss.[3] Others surmised that America had small vestiges of ancient wisdom, but they have for the most part been overpowered by her enchantment with modernity. Yet others thought that the American founding was so hopelessly mired in modernity that America was almost beyond redemption. These diverse assessments of the American founding have been the source of much of the internecine debates between Strauss's American students. But however much they disagree about the fundamental nature of the American heritage, they are all united in thinking that America is on the verge of some crisis that will devastate her, and maybe even the world, and that the impending doom can be allayed only if she is made to accept, willy-nilly, a kernel of ancient wisdom that would halt the deadly march of liberalism.

In this chapter, I will identify at least three different American reactions to Strauss's political thought. Although these reactions are distinct, they are not mutually exclusive, and may overlap. I will define the three different reactions to Strauss with the words: *denial, despair,* and *pragmatism.* The first reaction is a denial that America is modern; a denial that is predicated on a reinterpretation of the American founding as an ancient polity rooted in the great tradition in general, and the classical ideas of the Greeks and the Romans in particular. Harry V. Jaffa is the leading representative of this view. The second reaction begins with an awareness that America is the embodiment of modernity and that her triumph is the death knell of classical wisdom. On this view, the principles on which America is founded are hopelessly modern and tragically flawed. This reaction is understandably filled with despair and foreboding. The gloom of Allan Bloom's *The Closing of the American Mind* is particularly representative of this view. The third reaction acknowledges the truth of Bloom's vision, but refuses to despair. Instead, it takes a pragmatic approach and sets out to make the most of a bad situation. Willmoore Kendall is the best example of this approach, although it can be argued that Joseph Cropsey, Martin Diamond, and Thomas Pangle provide variations on this theme. This pragmatic approach lays the foundations of neoconservatism discussed in the next chapter.

## HARRY JAFFA: AMERICA'S ANCIENT LINEAGE

Many of Strauss's students and admirers are blind to the depth of Strauss's antipathy to America. They cannot believe that Strauss was not an admirer of American freedom, nor a lover of American equality. They cannot imagine that a refugee of Nazi Germany would be critical of a society in which the civil rights of every citizen are guaranteed by the Constitution. This is a natural reaction. After all, Nazi Germany was a hellish place for Jews such as Strauss precisely because Jews had no rights. But in America, everyone has rights that are recognizable and enforceable by law. Supposedly, what happened in Germany cannot happen in America, where the rights of citizens are enshrined in a Constitution that Americans fought and died for.

This is the reaction of Harry Jaffa. In his view, America is everything that Strauss could possibly have hoped for. America is the Zion that will light up all the world. She is a nation founded on eternal and immutable principles of right; her history is a testimony to the triumph of classical wisdom. Strauss's indictment of modernity is therefore not an indictment of America, because the latter has its roots in ancient wisdom. Strauss's critique of modernity must be understood merely as a warning to America, who had better remain true to her roots if she does not wish to court disaster. What are these ancient roots? And how can they be discovered?

In *Crisis of the House Divided,* Jaffa argues that the Lincoln-Douglas debates are the American version of what is at issue between Socrates and Thrasymachus in Plato's *Republic.*[4] Lincoln's position was Socratic—he believed that popular government must depend on a standard of right and wrong independent of mere opinion. In contrast, Douglas was an advocate of popular sovereignty unhampered by independent principles of right; for him as for Thrasymachus, justice was the interest of the stronger, and in a democracy, the majority is the strongest. The triumph of Lincoln over Douglas is therefore the triumph of Socrates over Thrasymachus, freedom over slavery, natural right over majority rule, immutable principles over relativism and nihilism.

Jaffa is quite oblivious to the fact that Strauss regards Thrasymachus and not Socrates as the true spokesman for Plato.[5] For Strauss, Thrasymachus is the one telling the truth; the harsh and savage truth, that there is no such thing as natural right or justice, and that what we call justice is but a set of rules made by those in power to serve their own interests. Strauss believes that Socrates never did succeed in refuting Thrasymachus, but only in silencing him.[6] Apparently, Socrates tells him (off-stage) that his views are true but too dangerous for public dissemination. In fact, the whole Socratic notion that justice is natural, accessible to reason, and independent of human convention (the fundamental assumption of the doctrines of natural law and natural rights) is itself a Socratic noble lie intended to promote social order and harmony. For Strauss, Socrates is the dissembler, while Thrasymachus is the truth-teller. Jaffa mistakes Socrates's noble lies for the truth.

Jaffa takes Strauss at face value, as many others have done.[7] He assumes that Strauss understands the classics in the conventional fashion, and that the classical philosophers are moral objectivists, and that Plato is not Nietzsche in disguise. But even if we begin from the conventional account of the classics, it does not follow that the American founding extends back from Jefferson and Locke to Aristotle and Plato. I will show later that there is good reason to doubt that there is any line that extends from Aristotle directly to Locke. Suffice it to say that Jaffa's own insistence on equality flies in the face of Aristotelian ideas.

## EQUALITY AND THE DECLARATION

For all his talk about the classics, Jaffa is first and foremost a Lockean.[8] Like Locke, he believes that consent is the foundation of government; and like Locke, he insists on a natural law and a natural right that antedate all government, including government by consent. In other words, Jaffa follows Locke in championing limited constitutional government. This is why Jaffa is opposed to the populist and majoritarian tendencies of modern American conservatives. In contrast to Willmoore Kendall and others, Jaffa affirms a set of absolute and inviolable principles that sets limits on what majorities can decide.

For Jaffa, the Declaration of Independence is an expression of the proper relation of natural right and government by consent. Accordingly, Jaffa idealizes Jefferson, and glosses over the contradictory nature of this slave-holding, freedom-loving Founder.[9] Like Jefferson, Jaffa thinks of America as an unprecedented human experiment and not as a repetition of the old world. Like Jefferson, his political philosophy is based on nature rather than tradition, natural rights and not the rights of Englishmen. And like Jefferson, he is opposed to those who regard the Constitution as a national shrine fit only to be worshiped and otherwise left untouched. For Jaffa, the Constitution can only be understood as a temporary compromise by its authors. But once the times are favorable, then the full measure of the Declaration must be made manifest in the Constitution. Abraham Lincoln is Jaffa's hero precisely because he set America on the road to the actualization of her true principles.[10] Lincoln realized that slavery was a cancer in the American nation that contradicted her very being. Southern efforts to extend slavery into the territories had to be stopped.

Clearly Jaffa regards the American Declaration of Independence as the definitive document in America's founding.[11] This is a most unusual position among American conservatives who are inclined to dismiss the radical and egalitarian Declaration in favor of the conservative and aristocratic Constitution. The Declaration is a revolutionary document that appeals to God and nature, and not to venerable traditions; it breaks with British Parliament and the British heritage, and it resolves to make a new start, to build a society based on the self-evident truths that all men are created equal and endowed by their creator with the inalienable rights to life, liberty, and the pursuit of happiness. Nothing is more antithetical to conservative taste than the resolution to start anew, to break with the past, and to assert the equality of men. In contrast to the Declaration, the Constitution is a product of compromise that accepts inequality, even slavery.

Jaffa is a maverick among conservatives in general, and Straussians in particular, for he insists on the equality enshrined in the Declaration. Strauss and his followers balk at the idea that all men are created equal. As Jaffa points out, his fellow Straussians and conservatives are inclined to agree with John C. Calhoun that only two people were ever created— Adam and Eve—and one was subordinate to the other; the rest of humanity was not created at all, but born, and not born equal.[12] But Jaffa relies on Locke to make his case, and he makes it eloquently. The equality in question is not an equality of talents, wealth, wisdom, or physical strength. The point is that whatever inequalities there may be among men, they cannot justify making some the beasts of burden for others. It is simply not the case that some men are born to rule and others to be subjects. Nothing in the nature of things justifies this state of affairs. And because being subject is not the natural human condition, the existence of government itself requires the consent of the governed.[13] This is the Lockean argument that leads to the conclusion (which Jaffa shares) that government by popular consent is the only legitimate form of government.

## THE CONSERVATIVE BETRAYAL OF AMERICA

Jaffa castigates his fellow conservatives for being historicists and relativists without principles. He denounces their unprincipled attachment to the past. He tells them that they are no better than liberals and leftists, and that they share the latter's sordid view of the American founding. Like their liberal and leftist opponents, the conservatives regard America's past as rooted in racism, slavery, inequality, and injustice. The only difference is that the leftists reject the past while the conservatives embrace it.[14]

Jaffa's distraught polemics against his fellow Straussians and conservatives are connected to what he rightly sees as their betrayal of the American Revolution.[15] He criticizes conservatives such as Russell Kirk, Irving Kristol, Jeane Kirkpatrick, Martin Diamond, Walter Berns, and Willmoore Kendall for rejecting natural right in favor of rights rooted in history and tradition. He reveals the extent to which the idea of equality in the Declaration is anathema to those who long for social hierarchy and who are nostalgic for the slavery of the South. He accuses American conservatives of being propagandists for the Confederacy, and ignoring James Madison, Thomas Jefferson, and Abraham Lincoln in favor of John C. Calhoun and Stephen Douglas. No one proves better than Jaffa the truth of John Stuart Mill's claim that conservatism is the stupid party. When conservatives speak of a "better guide than reason," they are referring to the superstitions and prejudices of the past, no matter how unjust and decrepit.[16]

Nor is Jaffa exaggerating. Conservative and fellow Straussian Willmoore Kendall is a case in point. Kendall vilifies Lincoln as the traitor who betrayed the great tradition and derailed the American founding.[17] He regards Lincoln as the spiritual father of the New Deal, the expanded presidency, and the welfare state. Kendall surmises that there is a direct line that leads from Lincoln to the demands for equality of contemporary liberals to totalitarianism! Natural right is anathema to him. Kendall is an apologist for the Confederacy and longs for the good old days of Southern slavery. He is also a defender of Senator Joseph McCarthy and his Communist witch-hunt. Kendall is convinced that liberal elites have distorted the true principles of the great tradition, but the latter can still be found in the "hips of the people." Nor is Kendall an insignificant figure; he was the teacher of William F. Buckley, who is no doubt the best-known conservative in America.[18] And Kendall's star continues to shine, for he is much adored at the University of Dallas where T-shirts can still be found that read: KENDALL FOR GOD.

In light of Kendall's beliefs, it may seem puzzling that Jaffa insists on thinking of himself as a conservative rather than a liberal. Part of the answer is that Jaffa's liberalism does not extend beyond the seventeenth century. Jaffa is a Lockean liberal—an advocate of constitutional government and civil rights. But he is not sympathetic with the rest of the liberal revolution. Jaffa has no sympathy with the economic freedom championed by Adam Smith and his modern libertarian and neoconservative followers. Nor is Jaffa in favor of personal freedom or freedom of lifestyle as represented by John Stuart Mill. He is opposed to the liberal distinction between the public and the private realms. He does not recognize a domain of absolute freedom in the private realm. He believes, much like Mill's critics, that the distinction leads to private debauchery that in the long run undermines the polity because the latter depends on the virtue of its citizens.[19]

The battle between Jaffa and his fellow conservatives and fellow Straussians focuses on issues in American history, with each justifying their claims by appealing to the past. Jaffa focuses on the Declaration, while other conservatives focus of the Constitution. But Jaffa does not wish to ignore the Constitution altogether, and he joins fellow conservatives in advocating that the Constitution be interpreted according to the "original intent" of its authors. In Jaffa's view, the "original intent" of the authors of the Constitution is nothing short of the full realization of the ideals of the Declaration. This idea is very important to Justice Clarence Thomas, whose writings are influenced by Harry Jaffa.

## ORIGINAL INTENT

The battle over the original intent of the authors of the Constitution is first and foremost a debate between liberals and conservatives. Liberals argue that the Constitution is a "living document" that has different meanings in different times and circumstances. Chief Justice Earl Warren and Justice William J. Brennan are representatives of this view. In contrast, conservative jurists such as Judge Robert Bork, Chief Justice William H. Rehnquist, and Attorney General Edwin Meese are all advocates of original intent. They regard the Constitution as a sacred document containing time-honored principles that should be preserved. They believe that the courts must interpret the law in light of the historical Constitution and its original meaning, rather that relying on a Constitution of their dreams, or a "living" Constitution that changes with the times. In other words, judges must uphold the law, not their own personal and political preferences. Otherwise, we will end up with judge-made law, which means that judges will usurp the legislative power of Congress.

Conservatives complain that liberal judges have little regard for precedent. They are inclined to ask: Is this right? But the conservative advocates of original intent insist that it is not the place of judges to determine the rightness of law. Instead, they must ask: Is it legal? Or, is it constitutional? Or, was it deemed right by the original framers of the Constitution? Whether the Supreme Court judges approve of the law or not is irrelevant. The idea is not to keep the Constitution in tune with the times, but the times in tune with the Constitution. Of course, the Constitution can be changed, not by judges, but by Congress or the legislative branch of government.

The doctrine of original intent insists that judges stick to the letter of the law and not get too creative in their interpretations. But to say that the judge must stick to the original intent of the law does not resolve the difficulties involved. Judges have to apply laws in situations that could not have been anticipated by the original makers of the law. Besides, the Constitution of the United States does not have a single author with a single intention. It has a multiplicity of authors with diverse intentions, and is in the final analysis a product of compromise. The doctrine of original intent is intellectually fraught with difficulties.[20]

Chief Justice Roger B. Taney, who presided over the famous decision in the *Dred Scott* case (argued in the Supreme Court 1856-57) can be regarded as the most eloquent representative of the doctrine of original intent. Judge Taney argued that the Constitution regarded slaves as property and that the right to property in a slave was to be protected in the same way as the right to any other article of merchandise. And since the Constitution had not been amended, he as judge was not in a position to invent something that was not there. He surmised that as a judge, he had to abide by the letter of the law where this "unfortunate race" was involved. The decision in the *Dred Scott* case brought the conflict between the North and the South over the extension of slavery into the western territories to a head, and this in turn precipitated the Civil War.

Jaffa disagrees with Justice Taney's decision, saying that he was wrong to deny that the descendants of African slaves are not included in the word "citizen" as used in the Constitution. But instead of abandoning the doctrine of original intent, Jaffa insists that it must be reinterpreted. He insists that the intent of the framers is that the Constitution must be understood in light of the Declaration. And since Taney's interpretation of the law is contrary to the Declaration, then it is contrary to the doctrine of original intent properly understood. Jaffa's reinterpretation of original intent is questionable, and it is not surprising that many conservatives reject it.[21] But Justice Clarence Thomas shares Jaffa's view of original intent.[22]

The doctrine of original intent is positivistic in its tenor—it says that law is valid and must be upheld whether it is just or not, whether judges approve of it or not. But Jaffa is an advocate of natural law and natural right and these are concepts that are not always compatible with the conservative reverence for law. It seems to me that an advocate of natural law cannot wed his views with original intent without creating a strange and contradictory hybrid. Jaffa uses the doctrine of original intent to bridge the gap between what is right and what is legal. In essence, his position is that what is legal is right—at least deep down in the hearts and minds and intentions of the authors of the law, if not in the letter of the law itself. But this idea undermines the conservative and positivistic character of original intent.

Jaffa's version of original intent explains the importance of prudence and statesmanship in his thought. Prudent judges must interpret the law in the most charitable light, the light of the natural law (Justice Roger B. Taney did not display this sort of nobility in the Dred Scott case).[23] The same is true of great statesmen such as Lincoln; he knew what was right and he did his utmost to move his people and their laws closer to the philosophic ideal of right. Jaffa also thinks that the same standard applies to lower officials such as Oliver North who was at the heart of the Iran-Contra affair. North was involved in a covert operation to sell arms to Iran and use the profits to provide military aid to the Contras who were conducting a guerrilla war against the Sandinista government in Nicaragua. The operation was illegal because it was contrary to legislation enacted by Congress. The executive branch was opposed to the legislation and may have turned a blind eye to the operation. The extent of the involvement of President Ronald Reagan and Vice-President George Bush was never clearly determined. Jaffa regards Oliver North as a hero and condemns the president for not having supported him vigorously and openly. Jaffa's position is puzzling because condoning Machiavellian tactics in the administrative branch goes contrary to his own insistence on government by consent. Of course, Jaffa believes that the people don't always know what is right or what is good for them, and this is why leadership is of the essence. However, there is a difference between leading people openly through persuasion, and using devious methods to circumvent the law, supposedly for the people's own good. This is the difference between great statesmen and Machiavellian scoundrels.

Jaffa clearly believes that devious and illegal methods are justified when those in power are convinced of the rightness of their ends. In this way, Jaffa combines the anarchic risks of the natural law doctrine and its high-minded moral appeal with more than a dash of political Machiavellianism. In responding to my claim that Strauss's conception of natural right was consequentialist and Machiavellian, Jaffa revealed his own sympathies to Machiavelli.[24] But Jaffa does not think that devious and duplicitous tactics are Machiavellian when they are used by those on the side of the good, the right, and the national interest. The trouble is that if great statesmen use the same tactics as tyrants, then it becomes difficult to distinguish them. Jaffa thinks that this is a politically naive point of view. And I would grant him that the greatest statesman cannot afford a policy of total honesty if he hopes to care for the welfare of his people. But by the same token, there must be sacrifices that he is willing to make for the sake of doing what is right. The great statesman must set limits on what he is prepared to do to pursue the most felicific course of action. It is precisely the absence of this moderate spirit that is disturbing about the famous dictum that Jaffa coined for Senator Barry Goldwater's campaign for the presidency in 1964: "Extremism in defense of liberty is no vice. Moderation in pursuit of justice is no virtue."

Jaffa can be understood as a quintessential modern from the Straussian point of view. For Strauss, modernity contains tyrannical proclivities that are global, precisely because it is founded in a universal and rationally justifiable set of absolute and inviolable moral principles. When this faith is healthy, it invites global tyranny and totalitarianism; when it falters, it ushers in nihilism and despair. So, whether healthy or not, modernity is undesirable. From this point of view, Jaffa's modernity is robust but disastrous. It leads him to confuse the good with American interests around the globe.[25] Although I am sympathetic to Jaffa's liberal rationalism, I think that Strauss and other postmodern writers have good reason for thinking that rationalism often has despotic tendencies.[26]

## CRITIQUE OF JAFFA

In conclusion, I would like to return to Jaffa's insistence that America is heir to classical ideals. It seems to me that there is a profound and fundamental difference between the American and classical traditions that Jaffa overlooks, largely because of his Straussian education. Strauss's Manichaean dichotomy between the wise ancients and the vulgar moderns obscures the significant divide between the pagan and the Christian traditions. Locke and Jefferson belong to the Christian rather than the pagan tradition. The doctrines of natural law and natural rights are not classical in origin. They have their source in the Christian belief in the inviolability of individuals because the latter are the property of God, made in His image. This means that no amount of social benefits or advantages to the society as a whole can justify the violation of the life or liberty of individuals. This emphasis on the sanctity of individual life explains the prohibitions on infanticide and abortion. But pagans like Aristotle thought that infanticide and abortion were legitimate means of controlling the size of the population.[27] Aristotle's rationale was that the state exists to promote human happiness, understood as the life in which the highest human faculties are cultivated. There is a clear sense in which individuals are responsible for their own happiness, because it is up to them to take the initiative to cultivate themselves. Nevertheless, it is also the case that they need certain external goods that would provide them with the opportunity for self-cultivation. The function of the state is to provide the conditions under which this optimum self-development of individuals is possible. Wealth, leisure, friendship, and even an opportunity to exercise one's rational and deliberative faculties in the political arena are among the conditions of the good life. The state is justified in doing whatever is necessary to make the good life possible. It is this consequential reasoning that led Aristotle to justify slavery as a necessary means to the leisure needed for the good life, and to regard infanticide and abortion as equally necessary and justifiable.

Another reason that the American Founders are not heirs to the classics has to do with the question of equality. The classical thinkers were not egalitarians. They did not believe that human beings were born equal.[28] They thought that people had radically different potentialities and this meant that they were not entitled to the same privileges and the same consideration, or even formal equality before the law. Jaffa is quite mistaken in thinking that there is a line that extends directly from Aristotle to Locke. After all, Aristotle defended slavery, while Locke argued for equal rights because he thought that whatever differences there were among people, they were all the property of God and cannot be abused or destroyed without offending Him.[29]

There is absolutely nothing Aristotelian about the American founding. Aristotle is a eudiamonistic and consequential thinker. To use John Rawls's expression, he believes that the good is prior to the right; in other words, he posits a certain good, then he declares that the right is what best promotes the good in view. In contrast to Aristotle, the rights of the Declaration (which are enshrined in the amendments to the Constitution) are fundamental. They are prior to the pursuit of any given good.

Another important difference between American liberal assumptions and the classics has to do with the pursuit of happiness. Contrary to the assumptions of the classics, American liberalism as enshrined in the Declaration regards the pursuit of happiness as plural rather than singular.[30] The function of the state is not to promote a particular understanding of the good, but to protect individual rights and freedoms so that citizens can pursue their own visions of the good life without interference as long as they do not violate the rights of others to the same.

This liberal aspect of the American pursuit of happiness is not endorsed by Jaffa. Jaffa shares with conservatives and fellow Straussians from Willmoore Kendall to Allan Bloom the view that America is too liberal and pluralistic and that what it needs is a single orthodoxy that governs the public and private lives of its citizens.

There is yet another reason that the American Founders are not first and foremost heirs to the classics, and that is the question of virtue. As Jaffa makes clear, the Founders were lovers of liberty; but he also thinks that they were equally lovers of virtue. And it is their love of virtue that brings them closer to the classics, because the latter were not partial to liberty. I believe that Jaffa is right in thinking that the Founders were lovers of liberty as much as lovers of virtue. This is not surprising since freedom and virtue are both genuine goods of equal worth that enhance human life. However, the tragedy of political life is that it is impossible to choose both of these goods in full measure. A society must choose which one will be fundamental; it must order them hierarchically. If we value virtue above all else, then we must be willing to forgo a great deal of the freedoms we now take for granted. If we choose freedom, as liberal societies do, then we must be willing to put up with a certain degree of vice. It is impossible to have both perfect freedom and perfect virtue at the same time.

Liberals have always defended private vice, not because they are drawn to it, but because they are compelled to defend a domain of liberty that is free from government interference, even when this liberty is badly used. Liberals know that the cost of liberty is a certain tolerance of vice. And it may well be that their love of liberty is so immoderate that they are willing to accept more vice than a society can withstand and still thrive. The question that liberals are reluctant to ask is: at what point does private vice infect public order and decency? But even if they are reluctant to ask that question, liberals are cognizant of the fact that liberal society is premised on a certain degree of self-restraint. The question is: has this self-restraint been sufficiently eroded as to make a free society no longer viable? And if this is the case, then we should not be surprised to lose some or all of our cherished freedoms; because we are likely to get the government we deserve.

There is little indication that the Founders were very clear on these issues. In fact, they were often attracted to the most foolhardy aspects of liberal doctrine. I am referring to the intoxicating idea that the proliferation of private vice contributes to the maximization of public benefits. Private vices, such as greed and the love of wealth, unwittingly contribute to the commonwealth by increasing productivity. Adam Smith popularized the doctrine with his concept of the "invisible hand" that insures that everything works out for the common good, even though individuals pursue their own interests with little regard to the welfare of others. The idea is as enticing as the advertisements that promise a sleek and fit physique without diet or exercise. It implies that we can have excellence without effort. This view was satirized by Bernard Mandeville in his poem *Fable of the Bees* that was subtitled "private vices, public benefits." Mandeville laughed at a society in which every part is full of vice, yet the whole mass a paradise![31]

This is the sort of doctrine that one finds in the writings of James Madison, side by side with overtures to virtue. Madison echoes Kant's view that if men were angels, then government would be unnecessary.[32] The implication is that well-crafted institutions where interest checks interest would make good government possible even in a nation of devils. But this seductive doctrine is totally antithetical to the sobriety of ancient philosophers who taught a hard truth about politics—namely, that our government is only as good as ourselves and that without self-restraint we cannot hope to have justice. Plato taught that the state was a microcosm of the individual and that the character of the state will always resemble the dominant character of the citizens, especially those in power.[33]

The doctrine of the separation of powers that has played such a significant role in American politics is a procedural technique by which power will check power. This device may limit the abuse of power, but it cannot secure justice unless it is endowed (as it often is) with magical charms. Institutions alone cannot guarantee justice. Corrupt individuals will always find ways to circumvent the system; they will manage to discover loopholes in the law. This is why Plato banned lawyers from his ideal regime. He thought that a society that depended on law alone and not on the virtue of its citizens would be perpetually making laws to fill the loopholes discovered in the previous ones. He compared the efforts to secure justice in such a litigious society with the hopeless enterprise of cutting off a hydra's head (twelve more grow in its place). To the extent that America's Founders believed that liberty and justice can be secured by an ingenious Constitution, by the separation of powers, or by any other legal and institutional devices, they have fallen prey to an intoxicating doctrine that is no part of the sobriety of the ancients.[34] For all these reasons, Jaffa's claim that the American Founders were heirs of the classics is highly questionable.

## ALLAN BLOOM:
## AMERICA'S INCURABLE MODERNITY

Allan Bloom's *The Closing of the American Mind* is the most successful popularization and application of Strauss's ideas to America. Bloom's view of the American founding is diametrically opposed to the view expressed by Harry Jaffa. Bloom portrays America as a polity grounded in the ill-conceived ideas of modernity, ideas that are engulfing the globe and shattering the glorious heritage of Western civilization.[35]

According to Bloom, America's Founding Fathers were the heirs of early modern philosophers such as Hobbes and Locke. These moderns were not privy to the sublime insights of the classics or their recent heirs—Rousseau and Nietzsche. Instead, they looked at man in his brutishness: untamed, uncultivated, and self-centered. And, incredible as it may seem, the early moderns set out to create a society made up of these selfish creatures. The result was a society of individuals whose natural tendencies for self-seeking and self-satisfaction were not suppressed by culture, but simply rechanneled into commerce. In this way, man's natural egoism assumed a form that was not altogether destructive of social life. The result was a bourgeois society that is paradigmatic of American life.

Bloom portrays American society as a collection of solitary individuals with nothing to live or die for. American society offers man a sterile vehicle for self-preservation, self-aggrandizement, and the pursuit of wealth. Such a society cannot become the object of love and devotion. It cannot elicit the sort of passion that is equal to the strength and violence of sexual passion. This is the meaning of Bloom's notorious complaint that there is no mention of sex in the American founding.[36] "Why should there be?" reviewers like Harry Jaffa have scoffed.[37] Bloom's apparently outrageous remark is meant to indicate the absence of a culture whose charms can transfigure sexual energy into love of motherland.[38] As a result, Bloom believes that America fails to provide a culture that can be embraced, loved, and appropriated by its citizens. She offers them only an opportunity to devote themselves to the satisfaction of their brutish nature. Far from teaching them to have contempt for themselves and their brutishness, it teaches them smugness and self-satisfaction.[39] America provides her people with nothing splendid and sublime to bow before. All this is due to the fact that her roots are hopelessly mired in modernity. And this leads her to believe that a society can be built on truth, philosophy, and enlightened self-interest. But the wise know that society needs myths, religion, and self-sacrifice, otherwise it is little more than an animal farm.

## AMERICAN LIBERALISM

Bloom heaps abuse on American liberalism and its open society. He complains that America mistakes her supreme vice, the greatest threat to her well-being, and the source of all her troubles, for her supreme virtue. Bloom makes three distinct objections to openness. First, he provides what appears to be a typical conservative indictment of liberalism. This criticism amounts to saying that a healthy society is one in which citizens are united by a single orthodoxy or a set of shared values that are believed to be superior to those of every other culture. In contrast to this unitary and cohesive model, American liberalism is open to a plurality of values, lifestyles, and cultures, and this supposedly makes America little more than a collection of isolated, alienated, and disoriented individuals lost in a morass of cultural relativism and meaninglessness.

It would be a mistake to suppose that Bloom objects to openness tout court. On the contrary, Bloom regards openness to be appropriate for philosophy, but not for society. Philosophy must be open to the truth that transcends convention. Like Strauss, Bloom thinks that the truth discovered by philosophy is relativistic, nay even nihilistic because philosophy can provide no rational justification for the morality necessary for convention—any convention. Philosophical openness is appropriate for the few who can live in the absence of dogmas and conventions, but it is not appropriate for society. Society needs its dogmas.

For Bloom, as for Strauss, society cannot be modeled on philosophy without courting disaster. An open society encourages citizens to think that all cultures are equal, and that their own culture has no special status in the world, or mission in history. This leads to relativism and its concomitant results—indifference, nihilism, and political annihilation.

In response to this objection, it is important to point out that for all its devotion to openness, liberalism is not itself nihilistic or relativistic. The liberal devotion to openness does not have its source in skepticism or relativism. Liberalism is not born out of the belief that there is no such thing as truth, or that everyone has their own truth. On the contrary, the liberal devotion to freedom of thought, speech, and discussion is rooted in the liberal love of truth, and the hope that the truth will best be served by open discussion and debate. John Stuart Mill argued eloquently for freedom of thought and speech on the ground that no one has a monopoly on truth. To assume that the conventional opinions are true, and that dissenting opinions should be silenced, is to rob mankind of the opportunity to exchange error for truth.[40] It was on account of truth that liberals put their faith in openness. But Bloom has no faith in the salutary effects of truth. And this is the real source of his objection to openness. Anticipating Straussian objections, Mill argued that in an age "destitute of faith, but terrified at skepticism," men will insist on the protection of public orthodoxies not because they are true, but because they are useful to society. But the usefulness of an opinion is itself a matter of debate.[41]

One of the pervasive problems with Bloom's critique of American liberalism is that it confuses liberal reality with liberal ideals. In criticizing American liberal society, Bloom is under the mistaken impression that he is also criticizing liberal theories, ideas, and ideals. This confusion has its source in the assumption that American liberal society is the actualization of liberal ideals, or the logical and inescapable consequence of these ideas. Listlessness, indifference, promiscuity, and nihilism are assumed to be phenomena that belong only to liberal societies. Liberalism is assumed to be bereft of all moral fiber; only conservatives have principles. But in truth, many of Bloom's criticisms of American liberalism are made by liberals such as Ronald Dworkin. Dworkin uses liberal arguments to oppose rampant commercialism and its attendant pornographic excesses.[42] He feels that it does not provide the neutral public space that liberal society needs to make freedom in the private realm possible. He worries about how those with traditional attitudes to sexuality can live freely and pass their convictions and traditions to their children in an atmosphere so charged with sexual libertinism. It is therefore not the case that American liberal society is the manifestation of liberal principles and ideals.

Bloom's second objection to openness is that it contributes to the weakness of society by allowing it to embrace within itself a multiplicity of cultures and ways of life. In so doing, openness prevents the development of a "collective consciousness."[43] Bloom points out that in America, majorities have always been suspect, and as a result, American politics is dominated by minorities, or what the Founders called "factions." Bloom remarks that the Founders were wise enough to be wary of factions.[44] By the same token, it must be added that the American Founders were not so wary of factions as to try to eliminate them altogether. On the contrary, Madison thought that it is impossible to eliminate factions without also destroying freedom.[45] He therefore tried to create a system that would mitigate the effects of factions, without actually prohibiting them. To eliminate factions is to give priority to collective consciousness over individual freedom, and to abandon Locke in favor of Rousseau— and this is precisely the position Bloom takes.

Bloom is suspicious of factions because he follows Strauss in thinking that Weimar is the prototype of liberalism. He therefore transposes the Weimar experience onto the American setting. As a result, his book is full of vague and formless premonitions of disaster. One of the most pervasive themes of his book is the uncanny coincidence of American popular culture with that of Weimar and Nazi Germany. For Bloom, America is the ghost of Nazi Germany. He would dearly love to save America from the catastrophes of Europe, but America's love affair with her own liberal modernity fills him with unmitigated gloom.

For Bloom, liberalism sets the stage on which the conflict between irreconcilable factions takes place. These conflicts are bound to erupt into violent confrontations, which could end only with the dominance of the triumphant faction. This is what happened in Weimar, and it will very likely happen in America. In order to convince his readers of the aptness of the comparison between America and Weimar, Bloom spends a great deal of energy documenting the subliminal similarities between America and Weimar. Americans are unconsciously using the same words ("hang loose" is really a translation of Heidegger's *Gelassenheit*), the same music (Louis Armstrong's "Mack the Knife" was Marlene Dietrich's song), and the same social science (values, charisma, and gestalt are all German in origin).[46]

It is worth noting that Bloom's second criticism contradicts the first. The description of America as threatened by the possibility of violent conflict between groups contradicts his claim that openness reduces America to a collection of atomized, isolated, unconnected individuals. It is possible to argue, as Hannah Arendt does, that the isolation and atomization of individuals makes them vulnerable to becoming a "mass" blindly led by self-proclaimed supermen.[47] But Bloom cannot use this argument against liberalism precisely because his conception of social health is intimately connected to the idea of a mass blindly led by a philosopher-superman. This is the source of Bloom's admiration for Rousseau, whose democratic ideas are shot through with the towering image of the great lawgiver—the architect of the will of the people. If openness really makes people into atomized, isolated, passive monads who are easily led and manipulated by demagogues, then Bloom should praise openness as a necessary stage on the way to a truly united, cohesive, and meaningful social order.

Bloom's third objection to openness is that it is a fiction and a sham—it is impossible for a society to be open. In reality, American openness is a fraud that camouflages her imperialistic inclinations. When Americans set out to learn about other cultures, they find that they are closed, each thinking that it is the best. For example, Herodotus reports that the Persians thought of themselves as the best, and the nations bordering them as second best, and the nations bordering the nations bordering them as third best, and so on.[48] The Persians considered themselves as the model of civilized humanity, and judged everyone in terms of their proximity to themselves. Americans are supposedly repelled by this closedness, which they reject in favor of their own openness. In other words, Americans reject every other culture in favor of their own. This is the import of Bloom's claim that the great opening is really a closing and a "disguised form of a new imperialism."[49] Bloom implies that Americans are just as overbearing as the Persians were. In short, American society is, in spite of itself, a closed society, and to the extent that it is determined to divest every other society of its closedness, American society becomes imperialistic. Unwittingly, Americans behave much like the Persians (whom Bloom considers strong and healthy). But even if Bloom is right in thinking that America's openness is hypocritical, it does not follow from his own criteria that this hypocrisy makes her weak and vulnerable.

Bloom's claim that America is weak and in danger of dissolution is not consistent with his observations and assumptions. Openness is the form that American culture assumes; it operates like other successful cultures in history—overbearing, self-righteous, and imperialistic. It may be worth recalling that after the Gulf War of 1991, American bumper stickers read: "we're number one and don't you forget it." It seems to me that American boorishness is not to be outdone—not even by the Persians. Far from being atomistic, nihilistic, and indifferent, Americans often seem menacingly patriotic. There may be all sorts of things wrong with America, but on Bloom's criteria she must be deemed very healthy indeed.

Bloom's criticism of American openness is contradictory. Either America is open, and hence weak and vulnerable, or she is closed, and hence strong and imperialistic. Bloom begins by objecting to openness because it threatens America with "decomposition," and ends by denouncing openness as a new form of imperialism.[50] I contend that it is not America's weakness to which he objects but her strength. Bloom is fully aware of the ease with which America is quickly remaking the world in her own image, and is worried that her brand of imperialism might prove irresistible. But he does not admire her strength.

The explanation has its source in the fact that Bloom finds American culture repellent.[51] Nothing exclusively American counts as culture. He is blind to American art forms such as jazz and blues. He is not capable of appreciating, as Nietzsche would, the triumph involved in turning the pain of slavery into art. His objection to American liberalism has everything to do with its strength and its seductive appeal, not its weakness.

In summary, Bloom's objections to American liberalism are three-fold. First, liberalism fosters atomized, nihilistic individuals. Second, liberalism endangers America by making her into a stage on which the conflict among cohesive groups takes place. Third, liberalism is hypocritical because it is just as imperialistic and bombastic as any closed society. These criticisms are paradigmatic of the futility of the Straussian critique of American liberalism. Like Strauss, Bloom cannot endorse either pluralism or the unity of the American melting pot. Pluralism is divisive and reminiscent of Weimar; while the all-American melting pot robs Europeans of their identities in favor of the meaningless individuality of liberal society. Bloom longs for the clannish brotherhoods that existed before the melting pot had a chance to do any damage. In short, the liberal creed and its love of freedom cannot be the foundation of a new community; true community has its source in blood, soil, and religion.

It is clear that Bloom's Straussian philosophy cannot provide America with a meaningful critique of her liberal tradition. Straussian conservatism can neither ennoble nor inspire American liberalism, it can only reject it. Strauss has taught his students to despise America's liberal heritage, not just because it can fail, but because it might succeed.

## EDUCATION

When William J. Bennett, former secretary of education and chairman of the National Endowment for the Humanities, published a report on the state of the humanities in higher education, it sparked a controversy that has not abated.[52] Bennett's report was damning; it maintained that students graduate from colleges and universities ignorant of the great works of Western civilization; as a result, they live as aliens in their own culture. Higher education has failed these students because it has not enriched their lives as it was meant to do. The source of the problem is the universities themselves. In particular, the professors have retreated behind the cloak of expertise, professionalism, jargon, and pedantry. Bennett reprimands the academics for losing their nerve, and drowning in the quagmire of relativism. Bennett is right, but that's not the whole story.

Bennett implies that there is a single, coherent set of ideals and principles contained in the great books of Western civilization, and that it is the function of the university to inculcate these values. Based on this belief, Bennett was grouped with Allan Bloom and Saul Bellows as conservatives and dubbed by their opponents as the three killer Bs.

The most ardent opponents to this conservative view of education are the fashionable postmoderns in the academy. But in my view, the Straussian outlook on education is not that different from the postmodern position. On the postmodern view, all ideals are but excuses for domination. All claims to knowledge are but disguised manifestations of the will to power. The canonical works of the Western tradition are nothing more than subtle and seductive tools by which the West inculcates its values and insures its supremacy. In the eyes of the postmodernists and deconstructionists who follow Michel Foucault and Jacques Derrida, the values of the West are the values of domination—

the colonial domination of the Western over the non-Western world, of whites over all other races, and of men over women. Postmodernists reject the pedagogical emphasis on the great works of Western civilization because the latter is imperialistic and oppressive, and its art and literature are simply ornaments intended to justify or camouflage its "white mythology."[53]

To undermine this subjugation, literature penned by the subjugated, the downtrodden, and the colonized must take the place of books penned by the dead white males of the Western tradition. Postmoderns do not pretend that these new books will replace the old regime of power with a new regime of truth; they will simply replace one regime of power with another. In this struggle for power, the humanities are the architectonic activity—the makers of civilization, and the shapers of minds and souls.

The trouble with this view is that it leaves us completely at sea. It replaces the search for truth with the quest for domination. It dismisses all ideals as lies and subterfuges. But in truth, ideals always look like lies to those who are disenchanted with the realities of their own civilization. And it is also the case that every civilization falls short of its ideals. There is always a gap between the realities of a civilization and its ideals; the size of the gap is a measure of a civilization's success or failure. It is indeed the case that Western civilization has not lived up to its ideals. But there is no better way to shame a civilization than to compare its actions with its own ideals and principles. Asking it to abandon those principles altogether can only augment its crimes and pave the way for its complete demise.

The debate between the conservative and the leftist views of education is often mistaken for a debate between radical relativists and moral objectivists in search of timeless truths.[54] But it is important to recognize that Bloom does not condemn the universities for failing to inculcate the truth. On the contrary, he regards the truth as too dangerous to be spread liberally by universities intended for mass education. His point is that the universities, because of their commitment to openness, have failed American society on two counts. They have failed to educate either the many or the few. First, they have failed to impart to the many what Strauss calls noble lies or salutary myths; the myth of openness is destructive, not salutary, because it fails to cement individuals into a single whole with a single identity.

Second, the universities have failed to provide the few with what Bloom regards as an education in the real sense: a capacity to transcend the myths of the cave and see the truth. To do this, philosophy must dismantle culture, and Bloom warns that this is a "dangerous business."[55] Philosophy breaks the spell of culture. It liberates man from the charms by which culture holds him captive. It is therefore a threat to civil society. American universities are heirs of the modern belief that philosophy is not dangerous to political life and that it can be unleashed on the many without cost. Bloom has no intention of replacing philosophy with indoctrination into the myths of culture. He would simply like to reserve philosophy for the few. But how can this be done in universities designed for mass education?

Strauss comes to the rescue. The great books of Western civilization contain a dual teaching as Strauss tirelessly illustrates. They can therefore be adapted to the needs of education in a mass society. They can teach the many to weep and worship while fashioning the supermen who will be the architects of the lores and legends of society. In this way, philosophy, understood as the brutish return to nature, is preserved without wreaking havoc on sacred culture. Bloom's central objection to American culture and American universities is that they spread nihilism about too liberally.

In the past, the debate between the right and the left proceeded on objectivist premises. At the heart of the debate was a discourse on justice, or what a just and good political order requires. But in the contemporary version of the debate, the two antagonists agree that justice and truth are fictions intended to conceal the arbitrariness of traditions and their attending customs, powers, and conventions. The left sets out to uncover the fiction, while the right upholds it. Since there are no legitimate grounds for authority, the left defends the new order simply on the grounds that it is the turn of the downtrodden to wield power, while the right tries to hold on to the power it has against the intrusion of the rabble.

Both parties to the dispute share the postmodern preoccupation with power and the postmodern belief that knowledge is power. The debate is intractable because it begins from the same premises. Indeed, it is not an intellectual debate at all, but a political conflict about who should be given the liberty or privilege of shaping reality.

Contrary to the assumptions of the postmoderns on both the right and the left, the greatest books produced by the West are not a homogeneous lot with a uniform set of values. They are neither morally abhorrent (as the left maintains) nor are they flawless founts of wisdom to be disseminated with uncritical reverence (as the right assumes). The great books are neither evil incarnate nor goodness personified. They are not a pernicious quest for domination. Nor are they a value-free and apolitical account of a single, objective truth. They are a dispute and a conversation about the right and the good—a conversation that is the heart and soul of the Western tradition.

The university has always been political, and a liberal arts education is a political education because it is an education in the best political alternatives that have been proposed or thought by the writers and thinkers of the West. Plato, Locke, and Marx are not apolitical writers. Their works are not value-free, nor do they pretend to be. The writers of the Western tradition, even if they are all male and white (there are exceptions) do not speak with the same voice, which is to say that their sex and their race do not altogether determine their thoughts.

At the heart of Bloom's conception of higher education is the Straussian assumption that a tradition is like a house of cards; it cannot afford to be too closely scrutinized. This is why philosophy must retreat or be kept secret. Traditional conservatives have always distrusted reason. But it was only individual, isolated, ahistorical reason that they distrusted. They still believed that their traditions were grounded in the wisdom of the ages, or the reason of humanity. This is why they warned against sweeping away the past and replacing it with newfangled ideas and institutions. No matter how reasonable the latter may seem, conservatives caution that their rationality has not been fully established because they have not withstood the test of time. In contrast to traditional conservatives, Bloom, like Strauss, regards traditions as the rationally groundless inventions of philosophers, sages, and prophets who pretend that their inventions have their source in divine inspiration. Supposedly, Moses, Jesus, Mohammed, and Buddha were creative geniuses who invented Judaism, Christianity, Islam, and Buddhism. These traditions are founded neither in reason, God, nor nature. What makes a people what it is, what lifts it out of the brutishness of nature, is the adoption of a way of life that involves sacrifice and hardship.[56] It matters little what that hardship is for. It is no wonder that so arbitrary a burden cannot withstand rational scrutiny.

It may well be that Strauss and Bloom are wrong. Far from destroying a tradition, rational discourse serves to strengthen it. A tradition that is unexamined, a tradition whose rational justifications have been forgotten, a traditional that is never challenged, is bound to atrophy into what John Stuart Mill called the "dull and torpid assent" that is generally accorded to dead dogma, and what A. N. Whitehead called "mental dry rot."[57] More recently, Alasdair MacIntyre, who is not himself a liberal, has brilliantly defended this conception of tradition.[58] MacIntyre has pointed to the difference between tradition and taboo. The latter is a totally irrational adherence to practices, customs, and ways of life—practices that when challenged or questioned collapse instantly. Such was the situation of the Hawaiians under Kamehameha II.[59] Europeans wondered why it was deemed so indecent for men and women to eat in each other's presence, in a society that was so casual about sexual intercourse. When asked to give an account of their customs, the Hawaiians were stumped. Their geographic isolation made them unfamiliar with this sort of challenge; they were not accustomed to giving an account of their beliefs and practices. And once challenged, their beliefs crumbled, since they had no vitality and were not part of the inner life of the people.

What is disconcerting in the current debate between the right and the left is that it is a debate between postmoderns who share the same view of the West. Allan Bloom does not deny that culture imposes its dominion through art, myth, illusion, and subterfuge. His point is that it is the function of the humanities to sustain the myths, to inculcate the illusions, and to maintain the dominance of the West. It seems to me that a culture is in trouble when its critics and its defenders describe it in the same terms—as domination camouflaged by sugar-coated lies.

## AFFIRMATIVE ACTION

Bloom's criticism of affirmative action is wildly hypocritical. His argument relies heavily on liberal ideals and sentiments. He objects to affirmative action on the ground that it undermines the primacy of merit and considerations of excellence that ought to govern university admissions. Preferential treatment for disadvantaged groups accomplishes nothing more than humiliating the very groups whose social position it is intended to improve. The reason is that everyone suspects that they have been admitted without having the credentials to make the grade, even when this is not the case.

The trouble with Bloom's argument is that it is disingenuous. No sooner does he finish extolling merit and excellence as the supreme criteria of admissions, he begins to wax nostalgic over the good old days when "aristocratic sentiments" prevailed, and when differentiations based on family and wealth were the rule. Unfortunately, Harvard, Yale and Princeton have

> abandoned preference for the children of their alumni and the exclusion of outsiders, especially Jews. Academic records and tests became the criteria for selection. New kinds of preference— particularly for blacks—replaced the old ones, which were class preserving, whereas these are class destroying. Now the student bodies of all the major universities are pretty much alike, drawing from the best applicants, with "good" meaning good at the academic disciplines. There is hardly a Harvard man or a Yale man anymore.[60]

Even Harvard and Yale, the "last resorts of aristocratic sentiments," have "lost their focus" and succumbed to democratizing pressures.

Clearly, Bloom approves of special treatment for the sons and daughters of Harvard and Yale graduates, but not for the sons and daughters of former slaves. He insists on academic excellence when it comes to admitting the latter but not the former. Because his devotion to excellence is suspect, his argument against affirmative action is hypocritical and manipulative in the extreme—it appeals to our liberal and meritocratic values but only to protect privileges based on birth, not merit or excellence.


## LOVE, SEX, AND FEMINISM

His objections to Freud notwithstanding, Bloom's discussions of love and sex, as well as his indictment of feminism are premised on Freudian assumptions about sexuality that he partly inherits from Leo Strauss.

Simply stated, these assumptions are as follows: Men are primarily interested in sex, and women are primarily keen on offspring. Women are therefore mothers by nature, but men are fathers only by convention. It is the function of civilization to transform natural men into fathers and husbands. Women are necessary accomplices in this process. By withholding their sexuality, women are the key to the existence of the family and to the process of sublimation.[61] Sublimation is the process by which frustrated sexual energy is redirected to other interests and pursuits. Like Freud, Bloom regards culture and the arts as the products of sublimation.

Although Freud welcomed the success that civilization has achieved in taming mankind and redirecting sexual energy into art and science, he warned civilization against being so encouraged by its success as to embark on even greater conquests over the instincts. He believed that the triumphs of civilization were won at the expense of the instincts and that there were limits to the oppression that the instincts can withstand without either becoming neurotic or rebelling against their intolerable burden.[62] Either case would be disastrous for the future of civilization. In light of his assessment of the situation, Freud would have welcomed outlets for the beleaguered instinct—birth control, rock and roll, free love, and feminism, for example. But Bloom's attitude is the very reverse. Bloom is a champion of civilization and its repressions.

Despite his reliance on Freud, Bloom departs from him in a significant way. Bloom is a romantic at heart. And he is most endearing when he speaks of the beguilements of love and the illusion of perfection it creates. He laments that the relations between the sexes have been demystified, and that the world has been robbed of love, romance, and enchantment. The rot began with the unerotic Freud. Bloom does not reject Freud's account of sublimation; he objects to the fact that the Freudian account implies that the pleasures of art and culture are second-best in comparison to the raw sexuality of nature. Bloom argues that Freud cannot answer the question: why sublimate instead of doing what comes naturally?[63] Of course, Freud devoted much energy to answering this question; but his answer usually took a social rather than an individualistic turn. Simply stated, he believed that the appetites when left to their own resources run afoul of reality, and make survival, peace and social order impossible. But Bloom is asking the question that Glaucon asked Socrates: Why should I (or any other individual) sublimate if I have the chance, in the context of the relative peace and order that society provides, to seek the greater satisfactions that nature affords? Freud's answer to that question is not all that clear. There is a hint of the Platonic answer that the appetites are self-destructive, and that they need to be restrained for their own good. If we eat all the time, then we will be unable to enjoy the pleasure of eating since that pleasure depends on being hungry.[64] What is true for food is true for drink and sex. But unfortunately, Freud does not state this explicitly, and is therefore vulnerable to Bloom's (and Glaucon's) objection.

In contrast to Freud, Bloom thinks that raw or natural sexuality is uninteresting and unerotic.[65] Repression is necessary to make natural sexuality erotic and sublime. What interests Bloom is what society does to sex. Eros is born out of the repressions and distortions of society. The latter account for what is sublime about sublimation. Failing to appreciate the wonders of repression, Freud supposedly failed to understand the sublime in sublimation. The result is a hopelessly unerotic account of sexuality. Freud's unerotic approach to sex is then carried to new heights by social scientists and their polling madness. Bloom rightly heaps abuse on the pseudoscience of the Kinsey report, with its clinical, unerotic, and totally banal approach to love.[66]

Bloom is convinced that the world has conspired to trivialize and demystify sexuality, and to sever it from its romantic moorings. Sexuality has therefore been reduced to its animal function.[67] Bloom considers his students living proof of the death of eros. He describes them as "prodigies of reason" who need not fear Othello's fate.[68] Gone is the "divine madness," gone is love and longing, gone is the "steamy sexuality" of Madame Bovary and Anna Karenina, gone are the "illusions of perfection" that love devises.[69] Bloom makes a gallant effort to revive romanticism, but to no avail. As one of his students asked incredulously, "Do you expect me to play the guitar under some girl's window?"

Bloom is repelled by the casual approach to sexuality that his students display—it goes along with sharing the rent and the dishes, and at the end of their university years, the couple parts company with a handshake. As one of Bloom's female students remarked, "It's no big deal."[70] For Bloom, this remark depicts the magnitude of the problem. If women are no longer willing to be accomplices of culture, in the transfiguration of natural man into father and citizen, then all is lost. If women give their sexual favors freely to men, then what incentive is left for marriage and family? Why should men pay dearly for what is now offered with no strings attached?

Although not freedom-loving in its inspiration, Bloom regards feminism to be parasitic on the de-eroticization of sexuality that was accomplished by Freud, the sexual revolution, and the social scientists. Bloom links this de-eroticization of sex with the dissolution of the family, which he believes to be at the heart of the feminist project. And insofar as the family is a microcosm of civilization, the fate of the latter is linked to the fate of the former.

According to Bloom, the decline of the family began with Locke's democratization of that institution, and ended with the feminist emasculation of men. Locke obliterated the authority of the father as the symbol of the divine on earth. And, in the absence of this fiction to nourish men's pride, male machismo seems to have evaporated.[71] Machismo is a sublimation of the aggressive and warlike instincts of men; it is the way that women and culture harness the ambitious and assertive nature of men and transfigure them into passionate attachment, loyalty, and protectiveness of "their own"—their own wives, children, and country. Of course, the feminists have not vanquished machismo singlehandedly; they simply completed a project that is at least as old as Hobbes.[72] In Bloom's view, the new order softens, emasculates, and feminizes men—its goal is to make them sensitive, caring, and nurturing. Whereas the old order worked *with* nature, the new order *subverts* it. Bloom therefore declares feminism highly unnatural.[73] It does not occur to Bloom to consider whether the feminist disenchantment with machismo is connected to the latter's decay in our time. In our world, machismo has become little more than false pride, egotistical self-absorption, and an excuse for violence and aggression.

Bloom compares the sexual revolution to the French Revolution, and feminism to the reign of terror that followed.[74] His point is that the sexual revolution was grounded in the demand for freedom, which is natural, whereas feminism is grounded in the demand for equality, which is artificial or socially contrived. The feminist world order demands the equality of the sexes; it demands that men and women have the same opportunities and employment prospects; it hopes for a world in which men and women are pilots, doctors, and bus drivers first, and men and women second. Bloom thinks that this sort of equality presupposes the subversion of eros.

Some objections are in order. First, Bloom assumes that women are mothers by nature, and that men have no natural desire for offspring—they must be swindled. Bloom's opinion reinforces the message of the beer commercials: real men are irresponsible sexual vagabonds. If Bloom is right about men, and if women are tired of playing tricks, then the family is a relic of history. But if Bloom is wrong, and both sexes have a keen interest in having and rearing their offspring, then the family is bound to have a rebirth. Seen in this light, the family is an arrangement for mutual advantage, intended to satisfy powerful natural instincts. The nature of these arrangements will inevitably depend on the historical and geographical conditions in which men and women live and rear their young. This is not to say, as feminists often imply, that only sameness of condition and function would qualify as justice between the sexes. It is also not to say, as feminists do, that the old divisions of labor between the sexes were relations of domination, or exploitation of women by men. The old arrangements were fair and practicable under the circumstances in which men and women lived. But modern conditions have created new circumstances that make the old arrangements inadequate. It is up to those who are critical of the traditional division of labor between the sexes to suggest a new order. But it is important not to assume at the outset that justice between the sexes requires sameness of condition or function, but merely an equitable distribution of benefits and burdens.[75]

Second, Bloom objects to the feminist project on the grounds that it is both oppressive and unnatural. But by his own account, culture is not an extension of nature; it involves some imposition, control, or sublimation. Somehow, the unnaturalness of feminism gets on Bloom's nerves. But in fairness, it must be admitted that if it is possible to transform sexual vagabonds into fathers and husbands, as Bloom maintains, then other transformations of men are also within reach. And in that light, the feminist project is not all that far-fetched. Its goal is to change the division of labor between the sexes, so that women need not be confined to their biological roles. This is certainly not unreasonable in an overpopulated planet. It means that occupations that were previously a male preserve must be made open to women, and that men must get used to the idea of working side by side with women in the office, at the factory, and on the assembly line. This will not be easy for men or women who are used to a greater segregation of the sexes, but it does not seem to be unnatural. As with every social change, there will be benefits as well as costs. Bloom is blind to the benefits, and painfully aware of the costs.

Third, there is no doubt that feminism comes into conflict with Bloom's romantic sensibilities, and *that* is the source of his antipathy to it. But however alluring Bloom's romantic sensibilities may be, they cannot withstand rational scrutiny. The decline of the family is certainly not the result of the death of eros and the demise of romanticism. On the contrary, the prevalence of romantic notions and expectations is closely linked to the rise in divorce rates. Marriage has its source in a view of love that is diametrically opposed to that of romanticism. The romantic cannot not pledge to love in sickness and in health, because love is something he falls into; it is not something he has any control over, and it is not subject to his will. Romantic love is a state of ecstasy, brought on by frustrated longings; it is a condition that cannot survive the pleasure of consummation, because it is a desire for the unattainable. Only in its bastardized twentieth-century incarnations, such as Harlequin Romances, does romantic love end in marriage. In its classic expression, romantic love ends in death. Johann Wolfgang von Goethe's *The Sorrows of Young Werther* (1774) and Emily Brontë's *Wuthering Heights* (1847) are examples.

Bloom's nostalgia for the glories of an enchanted past are as dangerous and as misguided as the dreams of Gustave Flaubert's Emma Bovary. Bloom reads the novel from Emma's point of view.[76] He regards her husband Charles and his friend M. Homais, as the personifications of the bourgeoisie—contemptible, self-satisfied imbeciles. But Bloom is full of empathy for Emma who cannot bear her bourgeois existence; she despises her husband, her neighbors, and her surroundings. She dreams of an enchanted world of great and glorious men who do not exist. And in comparison to her fantasy world, she finds her life so unbearable that she commits suicide. Bloom regards Emma's suicide as her "triumph" and her "only free act." He implies that sensitive women who are forced to live in this hideous modern world, a world bereft of glorious men, will naturally feel suicidal.

Bloom's reading of the novel is highly questionable. There is a higher and more objective perspective in the novel that Bloom rejects. Far from presenting Emma's perspective as the final insight into the nature of reality, Flaubert portrays Emma as a middle-class coquette whose world is constructed by myths, illusions, and romantic novels. When invited to an upper-class party, she is dazzled by the marquis and the marquise because she confuses "sensual luxury with true joy, elegance of manners with delicacy of sentiments."[77] She is equally enchanted with the old man sitting in the corner with gravy dribbling from his sagging lips because she discovers that he was the old Duc de Laverdière who was believed to have been the lover of Marie Antoinette.[78] Imagine living at court and sleeping in the bed of a queen! Far from endorsing Emma's view of the world, Flaubert unravels it. He allows us to understand that those who expect life to mirror romantic fairy tales will not have the courage to face reality. Emma is self-centered, self-absorbed, capricious, and cruel; she is incapable of loving the husband who adores her, or the father who cherishes her. Flaubert tells us that Emma "was not in the least kind-hearted, nor readily aware of the feelings of others."[79] She reads her romantic novels at the dinner table while her husband eats and talks to her. And she repays his devotion and continence with adultery. Her quest for romantic excitement fills her with torment, lust, rage, and hatred.[80] Emma is a selfish, frivolous, incontinent coward. But Bloom portrays her as a sensitive soul who preferred death to the banalities of bourgeois existence.

Bloom is sympathetic to Emma because he shares her romantic sensibilities. But this romantic longing is a dangerous and deadly fantasy. Emma is the paradigm of the romantic because her expectations of love are so extravagant. The romantic expects love to be her salvation; she expects it to deliver her from feelings of isolation, to rescue her from the drabness and tedium of existence; she expects it to bestow life with significance, ecstasy, and intensity. Flaubert describes the romantic sensibility brilliantly when he says of Emma that she believed love "had to come suddenly, with a great clap of thunder and a lightning flash, a tempest from heaven that falls upon your life, like a devastation, scatters your ideals like leaves and hurls your very soul into the abyss."[81] Such romantic expectations invite helplessness; they sever love from the will, and make one unable to face reality, affirm life, or love another. Emma's romantic fantasies make her incapable of loving her husband. Dull as he may have been, he was honest and continent; and there is no telling what transformations he might have undergone had he been truly loved. Emma was constantly in search of the man who will transfigure her existence; and as each lover proved disappointing, she became desperate. Far from making love glorious, romanticism blinds us to its sweetness. Consummation, satisfaction, and conjugal bliss are altogether foreign to the romantic.

What is charming about Bloom is that he is something of a sorcerer's apprentice: he falls prey to his own spell. Strauss is to Bloom what the master sorcerer is to the apprentice in the old Egyptian tale. According to Goethe's version of the story, the old master tells his disciple only what he thinks is safe for him to know.[82] But he does not teach him how he can dress a broom and turn it into a living servant. But the apprentice overhears the magic words, and when the master is out, he tries it. Sure enough, the broom comes to life, and obeys the command to fetch a pail of water. But the apprentice does not remember the magic words that would make the broom inanimate again. So the broom keeps fetching more and more water until the place is flooded. In despair, the apprentice takes an ax and smashes the broom to pieces; but every piece becomes yet another servant fetching water. Happily, the master sorcerer returns in time to save his apprentice from a watery grave. But no such luck for Allan Bloom. He knew that romantic love was one of those spells that, with the help of philosophers, culture devises. But Bloom has fallen prey to his own tricks.

In conclusion, Bloom's critique of America is a rejection of liberal society tout court; he rejects American pluralism as much as the American melting pot. His disdain for distinctive American art forms, such as blues and jazz, is a failure to recognize the triumph involved in turning the pain of slavery into art. His conception of higher education is little more than indoctrination in the myths that camouflage dominance. His critique of affirmative action is hypocritical in the extreme. His conception of the family as a sugar-coated outlet for male aggression is ripe for feminist invective. And his scorn for feminism is rooted in his hopeless romanticism. In short, Bloom's Straussian education fills him with repugnance for everything American. It makes him nostalgic for a European past, its grandeur, its art, its passions, and even its repressions. Like Emma, he lives in a dreamworld, loathing the real world around him.

## WILLMOORE KENDALL: THE POPULIST CURE

The third appropriation of Leo Strauss's ideas in America can be described as pragmatic, practical, and political. It combines the positions of Jaffa and Bloom. It accepts Jaffa's claim that America's foundations have an ancient lineage and are therefore not altogether modern, as well as Bloom's assertion that America's troubles have their source in her liberal modernity. But in this view, what is critical is the recognition that America's troubles are not totally incurable. They can best be addressed by curbing the excesses of her modernity. The key to nursing America back to health is to undermine her liberal modernity and bring to the fore vestiges of ancient wisdom that are deeply hidden and long forgotten. Unwilling to wallow in the gloomy prognostications of Allan Bloom, practical-minded Straussians adopt an all-American approach and take the bull by the horns.

To control the damage that liberalism wreaks on social life, America must be brought to her senses; she must be convinced that her love affair with liberalism must come to an end; she must recognize liberalism as the enemy. She must understand that the only vestige of good sense left in America is her people. The people alone can be relied on to recognize liberalism as the enemy and to unseat the liberal elite that rules them.

Populism is the cure for America's liberal malaise. The idea is to use American democracy to subvert American liberalism. The strategy has its foundation in Carl Schmitt's important distinction between liberalism and democracy. This is not a secret or sinister plot. It is a strategy that is embraced in good faith out of love for America. The trouble is that the cure might turn out to be worse than the disease.

No matter how politically or practically inclined, Straussian conservatives realize that politics alone will not do. There is much academic work to be done. It is up to political philosophers and historians to provide a theoretical basis for the political strategy at hand. Their role is to show that the populist project is not a betrayal of America's roots or her heritage, and that antiliberal, anti-individualist, and antisecularist ideas have always been a part of America's heritage, even if they have never been part of her official documents. The conservative spirit may not have inspired many American leaders, and as a result it has been politically overshadowed by the more flamboyant spirit of liberalism.

Straussian conservatives have provided several versions of this argument. The most radical version belongs to Willmoore Kendall. Kendall articulates Strauss and Bloom's objections to American liberalism in the clearest terms. In a famous essay on John Stuart Mill, "The

Open Society and Its Fallacies," Kendall argues that Mill's proposals are of unprecedented novelty.[83] Mill was the first philosopher in history to recommend a society without a public orthodoxy. If liberal society has any orthodoxy at all, it is skepticism. However, Kendall recognizes that liberal skepticism does not have its roots in nihilism, but in the love of truth and devotion to its pursuit. Liberalism is the organization of society on the model of a debating club, where freedom of speech and the pursuit of truth are the highest goods.[84] Nevertheless, liberalism rests on a total misunderstanding of the nature of society.

For Kendall as for Strauss and Bloom, society is by its nature closed. The liberal worship of truth, while not uncommendable in itself, is antipolitical. The love of truth requires a posture of "openness." The latter is a virtue suitable to philosophy, but it is contrary to the nature, health, and survival of political societies. Political societies must necessarily be closed in the sense of being unwilling to entertain opinions or values that differ from their own. What is important for society is not truth, but the unity of feeling and sentiment that only a public orthodoxy can create.[85]

Kendall is not an enemy of the pursuit of truth. Like Strauss and Bloom, he thinks that the pursuit of truth is for the few; and that it would be a very good thing for society to provide that select minority with the funds, leisure, and resources it needs for the pursuit of truth. It would also be a real boon if that select minority were to influence the society at large.[86] But no society can survive in the face of freedom of thought and speech.

Kendall scorns Mill's liberal sympathies for Socrates. Liberals regard Socrates as a sage who was ruthlessly persecuted by a mob of small-minded Athenians. In contrast, Kendall shares Strauss's view that Socrates got the punishment he deserved; for he should have known that the marketplace is no place for philosophy. All his talk had the effect of undermining the regime; and the Athenians were quite justified in condemning him in self-defense.[87] Society has every right to exercise its power to silence.[88] Anyone who challenges the public orthodoxy should find barriers. Socrates must have recognized the error of his ways when he submitted to the law, even though he had a chance to escape. Plato learned the lesson well, and retreated from the public arena and into the academy.

The Straussian assault on liberalism has its source in the assumption that freedom of thought and discussion may indeed allow the truth to emerge; but the truth is destructive of society because the latter cannot sustain itself in the face of the realization that there is no God, no rational foundation for morality, and no natural good other than pleasure. In the face of atheism, nihilism, and hedonism, social life is impossible. The Straussian objection to liberalism is rooted in a Nietzschean conviction that the true, the good, and the beautiful are at odds. But instead of following Nietzsche and disregarding the true in favor of the beautiful and noble, Straussians continue to hanker after the sordid truth. So understood, philosophy is a self-indulgent vice on the part of those who delude themselves into thinking that they are superior to the ordinary run of humanity. And this explains why philosophy must remain secret—not just to preserve the city, but to protect the philosophers.

Like Strauss and Bloom, Kendall complains that a liberal society is weak and vulnerable to dissolution because it courts the truth. But unlike them, he denies that America is liberal. A liberal society would be one in which neither Communists, anarchists, nor defenders of polygamy can be silenced. But this is not true in America. A liberal society would not be savvy enough to use the doctrine of the clear and present danger as Americans have done in their effort to defend themselves against the Communist threat. Nor would a liberal society display America's grassroots support for Senator Joseph McCarthy, whom Kendall naturally defends.[89]

Kendall is convinced that in her heart of hearts, America is not and has never been a liberal society, and that American history has been a grand swindle perpetrated by a liberal elite that has hoodwinked the people.[90] Abraham Lincoln's liberation of the slaves was a classic blunder. Lincoln was the first in a long line of liberal leaders who have created institutions and laws that reflect their own liberal modernity, and not the true sentiments of the people. The only reasonable political strategy is to unseat this pernicious and misguided liberal elite and to replace it with a conservative elite that understands what the people really need and want.

Kendall relies on the classic friend/enemy dichotomy. The enemies are "barbarians" or Communists who threaten America from without, and "heretics" or Communist sympathizers and liberals who undermine America from within.[91] The internal enemy is by far the most dangerous. Kendall is convinced that the liberal enemy may have won many battles, but it has not won the war. Liberals have succeeded in emancipating the slaves, expanding the suffrage, and adding the post–Civil War equality amendments. But there is a great deal more that they have not succeeded in accomplishing. Kendall thinks that the liberal agenda includes equalizing incomes through the reform of income-tax laws; closing the loopholes in the income tax act to prevent the rich from getting richer; and equalizing education through bussing. Kendall is convinced that liberals want every American child picked up in a yellow bus, whisked to a remote school, fed a free lunch, doctored, hospitalized, and educated for liberal democracy. Kendall interprets this as teaching people to eke out a living by soaking the rich and playing the angles. He fears that the end result will be a society of delinquent Socialists.[92] Kendall rejoices that all these plans have not succeeded, and tax loopholes have not disappeared so that it is still possible in the United States, as it is not in Britain, to get "smacking rich" and to will it all to your grandchildren.[93]

In contrast to Bloom, Kendall is neither gloomy nor depressed; he has a practical cure for America's liberal malaise. The solution rests in the people who are alone the repository of America's ancient lineage. The key is to turn the people against liberalism. For Kendall, a new populism in the service of conservative principles is of the essence. However, Kendall is not totally blind to the vagaries of the people. Despite his populist sympathies, Kendall is ambivalent toward the people. Although they are the repository of tradition, they may be manipulated by demagogues (a word reserved for liberals). The key to keeping the people honest is the elites. The latter must shape the will of the people. Kendall's populism is a Straussian populism that is peppered with a strong elitist element.

Democracy has traditionally rested on a strong faith in the common people, their decency, their rationality, and their common sense. But in American politics, the behavioral movement brought in a new and unprecedented democratic theory. Instead of putting its faith in the rationality of the people, it declared their irrationality. In fact, it repudiated the whole idea of the will of the people on the grounds that it was unintelligible—there is no such thing as the will of the people, since the people are a diverse collection of conflicting irrational interests and desires.[94] But this did not lead behaviorists to despair of democracy. Instead, they offered a new definition of democracy that was less utopian and more compatible with American political reality. They defined a democracy as a society in which elites compete for power.

Despite his castigation of the behavioral movement in political science, Strauss welcomes its emphasis on the "irrationality of the masses and the necessity of elites."[95] But he rightly criticizes the behaviorists for continuing to cling to democracy even though they are convinced of the irrationality of the people.

The behaviorists assume that since all values are equally irrational, there are no grounds on which to choose among them. Their solution to this meta-ethical dilemma is democracy. Democracy resolves the problem by allowing the will of the most numerous, or the most adept at the struggle for power, to triumph. Strauss repudiates this equality of all wills in favor of the superior will of the wise, who should rule over the unwise. The inequality of opinions leads Strauss to the antidemocratic conclusion that freedom of speech as well as elections based on universal suffrage are equally unwarranted.

Despite his antidemocratic elitism, Strauss chooses democracy as the lesser evil when compared to liberalism. The worst of all possible worlds is the coupling of liberalism and democracy—hence the "crisis of liberal democracy."[96] The problem is that liberalism is permissive and democracy is egalitarian. The coupling of the two allows a society to extend to all its citizens privileges that are only appropriate for the very few. The result is rampant and uncontrollable vice that undermines the discipline, self-sacrifice, and self-abnegation on which social life depends.

If the crisis of liberal democracy is to be averted, democracy must be used to defeat liberalism. The elite must turn the people against their own liberal institutions. This may not be as difficult as it may seem. For as Kendall has pointed out, the people are by no means as liberal as the regime. Joseph Cropsey makes a similar point when he distinguishes between the "parchment regime" and the "ungovernable" part of the American polity.[97] The parchment regime is articulated in America's official documents—the Declaration of Independence, the Constitution, Lincoln's Second Inaugural Address, judicial decisions, and others. But the unspoken, unofficial, and ungovernable part of the American heritage, the part of the tradition that is in the hearts or hips of the people, is at odds with the parchment regime. The idea is that Americans are not as liberal or as modern as the official documents that define their regime would lead one to believe.

There is something to be said for this view. There is a sense in which Americans have always been reluctant liberals. America's earliest settlers were Puritans who were escaping religious persecution in Europe. Their puritan heritage led them to accept liberalism as a necessity for securing their religious freedom. But there is a permissive quality in liberalism that ill-suits the puritan mentality. It would therefore not be difficult to convince a puritan-minded people that liberalism has outlived its usefulness and must be discarded because it is responsible for the death of God, the nihilistic indifference of the youth, and the moral decay of America. This is indeed what the leaders of the religious right in America have succeeded in convincing their devout followers. And while it is the case that liberal permissiveness must bear its share of the blame for America's vices, it must also get the credit for America's freedom. In my view, the tragic reality of life is that it is as impossible to have a free society without vice as it is to have a virtuous society without coercion and oppression. If the religious right has its way, and America makes virtue its supreme value, then it must be ready to lose most, if not all, of its hard-won freedoms.

In conclusion, Kendall does not confine himself to lamenting the triumph of modernity and the loss of the great tradition. He resolves to do something about it. He believes that it is possible to save America from herself. The idea is to drive a wedge between liberalism and democracy, and to use the popular will to defeat American liberalism. This is not to say that either Strauss or his American followers are democrats. The only democracy they could endure is a representative democracy in which the few rule over the many. Strauss's students generally praise republicanism, not democracy.[98] They appeal to the Founding Fathers: they appeal to Madison's fear of the tyranny of the majority, and to Jefferson's talk of the rule of the natural aristocracy.[99] What they like about republicanism is that it is aristocracy in a democratic guise.

For the Straussians, the practical political problem is to get the people to choose the natural aristocracy who should govern. Like Kendall, they believe that the task at hand is to unseat the liberal elite and replace it with a conservative elite that is more favorably disposed to the advice of the wise. In this way, America can recapture her ancient lineage and in so doing escape the deadly effects of her modernity.

The populist approach to the crisis of liberal democracy has its risks. Strauss himself warned of the vagaries of the people. But the elite must be wily. And because Strauss has such contempt for the masses, he encourages tactics that are antithetical to those of rational persuasion and mutual respect. In my view, manipulation and deceit are likely to result in political failure. These Machiavellian tactics are bound to be found out, and then the people's trust and faith in the elites will be severely damaged. In this way, the populist cure for America's liberal modernity may backfire. But for now, the populist cure to America's troubles has become a dominant motif of the American right.

As we shall see in the next chapter, Straussian ideas provide American neoconservatism with all its dominant themes: the internal enemy, the weakness of liberalism, the iniquity of liberal elites, the need for a public orthodoxy, and the populist cure for America's liberal modernity.

## CHAPTER FIVE

# NEOCONSERVATISM: A STRAUSSIAN LEGACY

THE TERM *NEOCONSERVATISM* WAS FIRST USED by a critic to refer to a new breed of conservatives who began to exert a certain influence on American politics after 1945.[1] The label was later adopted by Irving Kristol as a term of approbation to describe his own point of view and that of other American conservatives who shared his political outlook. Generally included among the neoconservatives are Daniel Bell, Jeane Kirkpatrick, Nathan Glazer, Norman Podhoretz, Seymour Martin Lipset, Samuel Huntington, James Q. Wilson, and others.[2]

In this chapter, I will focus on Kristol's work because his work is as delightful as it is candid, because the themes that preoccupy him are the dominant themes of the American right, because his neoconservatism has become the dominant ideology of the Republican party in the 1980s and 1990s, and because it constitutes a most serious challenge to American liberalism. When he started writing in the late 1940s and early 1950s, he never imagined that his ideas would make such inroads into the psyche of the nation, or that they would become the central ideology of the Republican party. Some of the credit for the political success of neoconservatism must go to his son, William Kristol, who is editor of *The Weekly Standard* and the leading political strategist of the Republican party. Jack Kemp, the Republican vice-presidential running mate with Bob Dole in the election of 1996, pays tribute to Irving Kristol as the most important source of his intellectual inspiration.[3]

Irving Kristol maintains that the two greatest intellectual influences on his thought are Leo Strauss and Lionel Trilling.[4] His only reservation about Strauss is that he may have been somewhat "too wary of modernity."[5] But as I will show, Kristol is just as wary of modernity as Strauss.

Unlike Strauss, Trilling was a fashionable, leftist liberal intellectual and literary critic whose work was as labyrinthine as it was stylish and elegant. One would think that Trilling would have influenced Kristol in a more liberal direction, but this is not so. On the contrary, Trilling's commentaries on modern literature are consistent with Strauss's rejection of modernity. Trilling was a secularist and a Freudian, but he found modern literature—Dostoevsky, Kafka, Joyce, Proust—disconcerting. He thought that the overriding theme of modern literature was the liberation of the unconscious. And like a good Freudian, he shrank from the dangerous prospect of a world without a superego. He was more at home in the self-contained worlds of Jane Austen and Charles Dickens. He rejected the existential quest for an authentic self in favor of a resigned attitude to "one's station and its duties." He found it difficult to reconcile his leftist politics with his literary studies. And he worried that a classless society might mean the death of literature, because he was convinced that literature was the study of character, and that character was shaped by class and station.[6] So, his politics notwithstanding, Trilling's writings point in the same direction as Strauss's—a decidedly antimodernist direction.

The connection between Leo Strauss and American neoconservatism is not that well known, and has never been fully explored or understood. In this chapter, I hope to show that almost all of the dominant motifs of neoconservatism are the bedrock of Straussian political thought: the preoccupation with religion, the conviction that nihilism is the source of the crisis of American liberalism, the deprecation of Enlightenment rationalism, the antipathy to liberalism, the emphasis on nationalism, the concern with the role of intellectuals in politics, and the preference for democracy over liberalism.

## WHAT'S "NEO" ABOUT NEOCONSERVATISM?

Conservatism is first and foremost a political temper characterized by moderation, caution, and fear of change. But conservatism is more than just a political disposition; it contains a concrete political ideal characterized by hierarchy, harmony, unity, order, virtue, reciprocity, shared values, and mutual concern. The feudal society of the Middle Ages came closest to actualizing this ideal. Each order in this hierarchical society had its place and its corresponding duties within the whole. The conservative ideal is based on mutual service and fidelity between the higher and the lower orders. The knights and nobles were responsible for the military protection of the lower classes, while the latter were duty-bound to plough and grow the crops necessary to feed the knights and nobles and to provide them with the leisure and privileges necessary for the fulfillment of their arduous duties. When the shared values of Christendom were shaken, and changing conditions made the privileges of the aristocracy seem unwarranted and even exploitative, liberal ideas inspired the revolutions of the seventeenth and eighteenth centuries. The liberal celebration of religious and economic freedom, competition, social mobility, and individualism soon replaced the stability and security of the medieval order. It was in the wake of the triumph of liberalism that classical conservatism was born. Classic conservatives such as Edmund Burke, Joseph de Maistre, and Louis de Bonald lamented the waning of the Middle Ages.[7]

The classic conservative ideal did not fit the American experience because the new world had no feudal aristocracy whose passing it could lament. In America such conservatism was rootless, except as a fiction and an "illusion."[8] Nevertheless, it was a fiction to which some agrarian Southerners clung. It is no wonder that Leo Strauss is popular south of the Mason-Dixon line where he is regarded as a classic conservative endorsing an agrarian society ruled by a landed gentry (that is, gentlemen who defer to the advice of philosophers). Lamenting the destruction of their society and their Confederacy, some agrarian Southerners harbored the illusion that their social order was a model of aristocratic harmony, virtue, and reciprocity. But if it was difficult to believe this idealized picture of social harmony where serfdom was involved, it was simply impossible to take it seriously when applied to a social order dependent on slavery. As a result, traditional conservatism was always suspect in America. But Kristol resolved to change all this by introducing a new and improved version of conservatism.

"Neo" has its origin in the Greek *neos,* which means new. As Kristol explains, neoconservatism is a new conservatism that is free from the nostalgia for the past that characterized the old conservatism. Far from looking back fondly at aristocratic society, the new conservatism accepts the present, the bourgeois present, and even celebrates the bourgeois ethos.

Kristol appears to make a total break with the old right in America and its nostalgia for the old South, as well as with the ideas of Strauss that harken back to the premodern past. After reading Leo Strauss and Allan Bloom, and wallowing in all the gloom of modernity, one is likely to conclude that the world in which we live does not contain a single redeeming attribute, that life in the modern world is not worth living, that it is as miserable as it is mundane, and had we been anything other than pitiful cowards, we would have committed suicide, like Emma Bovary. In light of this, there is something totally refreshing about a writer who is willing to celebrate the present—the *bourgeois* present!

In what follows, I will argue that all his efforts notwithstanding, Kristol is just as wary of modernity and just as nostalgic for the premodern world as was Strauss. And as a result, I am hard-pressed to find much that is "neo" about neoconservatism. And what little there is that is new, does not make neoconservatism a new and improved version of conservatism. On the contrary, I will show that neoconservatism is bereft of the moderation and modesty of its traditional counterpart.

## CELEBRATING THE BOURGEOIS ETHOS

If there is anything "neo" about neoconservatism, if there is anything that sets it apart from the nostalgia for the past characteristic of traditional conservatives and reactionaries, it is the celebration of the bourgeois ethos and modern bourgeois economics. As I will show, Kristol's account of the bourgeois ethos (though not without its attractions) is at odds with the reality of bourgeois society and oblivious to its appeal.

Contrary to Strauss's claim that the Jews are not at home in the modern world, Kristol thinks that the Jews are more at home in the capitalist bourgeois world than in any other.[9] The reason is that bourgeois commercial civilization is Jewish, even biblical, because it accepts this mundane world as the god-given world, and does not expect its transfiguration or its transcendence, except in the beyond. Here on earth we live, work, and multiply. And no matter what hardships, what trials and tribulations we encounter, we must stoically accept "our station and its duties."[10] No matter how humble our station, and no matter how onerous our duties, we must resign ourselves to the world as it is, because having been created by God, it must be good. And far from being demeaning, work, including commerce, is elevating. There is absolutely nothing wrong with bettering one's material condition, or getting rich. Unlike Christianity, Judaism has never had any objections to commerce or wealth. As a result, the bourgeois ethos is "perfectly congruent with the world view of postexilic Judaism."[11] Like Judaism, bourgeois society has a "domestic conception of the universe and of man's place therein."[12] The bourgeois ideal of human fulfillment is being a "good citizen, good husband, and good provider."[13]

Bourgeois civilization is literally prosaic. Like the novel, it does not revolve around aristocratic heroes who triumph over monstrous obstacles with boldness and bravado; it is about the ordinary adventures of ordinary people. Bourgeois society is "organized for the convenience and comfort of ordinary men and women, not for the production of heroic, memorable figures."[14] Bourgeois civilization understands the common good as security and liberty under law. It promises a steady increase in material prosperity "for those who apply themselves to that end."[15] The virtues of bourgeois society—honesty, sobriety, diligence, and thrift—are directly connected to worldly success.[16]

Kristol laments that the bourgeois ethos is in crisis because the connection between the bourgeois virtues and worldly success has been severed by a secular set of ideas that has replaced the Puritan and religious ones. Kristol attributes this corruptive and corrosive doctrine to David Hume and Bernard Mandeville. According to this view, distributive justice is not connected with virtue or merit. On the contrary, the capitalist market is driven by greed, selfishness, and avarice. In the very exercise of these private vices, individuals unwittingly contribute to the public good. Because this perspective rejects the connection between the bourgeois virtues and success, it fails to distinguish between the speculator and the entrepreneur. It maintains that any distributions that result from the free market are just. But Kristol objects that this account of inequality will not do. People need a "metaphysical" justification of economic inequalities, and will not be satisfied with a haphazard and arbitrary account that is based on luck and not merit.[17] In Kristol's view, this is where Adam Smith and the early moderns went astray.[18]

Kristol believes that American bourgeois society is as egalitarian as any society has ever been. So much so, that there is a direct correspondence between the natural distribution of human talents in the population and the bell curve of income distribution in America.[19] This leads him to conclude that all is well with bourgeois economics, since its inequalities are a reflection of nature. Indeed, the economics of capitalism are the "saving grace" of bourgeois society; it is the ethos of bourgeois society that needs revitalizing. Only a theologian or a philosopher can do this, not an economist.[20]

Two criticisms of Kristol's conception of the bourgeois ethos are in order. First, Kristol speaks as if the ethos of bourgeois society can be severed from the realities of capitalist economics. Even though capitalism may reward talent, diligence, and hard work, it is still the case that its greatest rewards are linked to daring, risk, and luck, not diligence. The bourgeois ethos cannot be separated from this reality, without becoming merely a pious fiction in the Straussian sense.

Kristol's account of the bourgeois ethos may lead one to surmise that he is a champion of petit bourgeois economics, but this is not so. Unlike other champions of the prosaic and puritanical bourgeois virtues,[21] Kristol does not harken back to the infancy of capitalism; he is a champion of corporate capitalism—of growth and unlimited production (and consumption). And because he thinks that bourgeois economics, unlike the bourgeois ethos, is healthy, he is opposed to efforts on the part of liberal governments to interfere in the economic affairs of corporations or to limit their power. He does not object to antitrust laws, but he is hostile to other governmental regulations, including environmental ones, because they cost corporations millions of dollars. Kristol laments the unhappy fate of corporate men in America. He thinks that it is unhealthy for a society to despise its most important people. He deplores the fact that businessmen and chief executive officers are portrayed as villains in movies, novels, and television; he complains that they are despised by the media, the intellectuals, the educators, and even their own children. Kristol is nostalgic for the days when Horatio Alger's novels were read and taken seriously, because he is the only novelist to portray businessmen as heroes.[22] Alger was not romanticizing the naked pursuit of wealth, but admirable qualities of character—veracity, probity, diligence, self-reliance, and self-respect.[23]

The trouble with Kristol's celebration of corporate capitalism is that it cannot be sustained in the face of reality. Horatio Alger is fiction;

the modest and prosaic qualities that Kristol extols are in conflict with the realities of corporate capitalism—its limitless pursuit of profit, its tendency to endless exploitation of the earth without any heed to future generations, its strategy of planned obsolescence, its greed, love of luxury, and commitment to endless consumption. All these things undermine Kristol's prosaic bourgeois ethos. Nor can Kristol rely on corporate executives to serve as models of bourgeois virtue. Kristol realizes that the ethical practices of corporate capitalism's chief executive officers are often less than exemplary. He gives examples of highly unethical practices where stock options and bank loans are involved—practices that reveal the unwillingness of executives to take the risks or bear the losses that other stockholders are expected to bear.[24] But even if we set aside their questionable financial practices, corporate men are despised not just because they wield so much wealth and power, but because they are faceless, and hence unaccountable. Kristol realizes this, but he defends them anyway because he thinks that the power they wield is beneficial to society as a whole, because he thinks that limitless growth and the never-ending quest for prosperity is necessary for social health and well-being, and because he thinks that the paternalism of the corporation protects people from the cut-throat competition of capitalist economics.[25] These are questionable assumptions. Even if it is true that the activities of corporate men benefit society, it remains the case that those who have so much power to benefit, also have the power to harm, unless that power is checked. Besides, the corporate policy of limitless growth often comes into conflict with a prosaic ethos that is modest and mindful of future generations. Corporate paternalism was a rare phenomenon in the 70s, and is almost unheard of in the corporate culture of the 90s where downsizing is the order of the day.

Second, Kristol's conception of the bourgeois ethos is puzzling because it seems somewhat at odds with the attractions of bourgeois society. There is no doubt that Kristol is right in thinking that the success of capitalist society is closely linked with the Protestant ethic of sobriety, diligence, and thrift. But the submissive attitude to one's station and its duties is not what the appeal of bourgeois society was all about. If bourgeois society was really as prosaic as Kristol maintains, it would never have succeeded as well as it did. The attraction of the bourgeois world had to do with the fact that it was a *liberal* capitalist world, not just a capitalist one. Kristol's account of the bourgeois ethos omits the liberal dimension. Bourgeois society is not as prosaic, rabbinic, or unromantic as Kristol makes it out. It did indeed have a work ethic, but the latter was connected to its individualism and competitiveness. The appeal of the bourgeois ethos had nothing to do with resigning oneself to God's will, or submitting to one's station and its duties. Its appeal was connected to the idea of pulling oneself up by one's bootstraps, being self-reliant, and self-made. The bourgeois ethos was individualistic, vigorous, and dynamic, as opposed to being submissive to fate, class, or station. What is distinctive about neoconservatism is not so much its celebration of bourgeois economics but of corporate capitalism.[26] The latter is compatible with a hierarchical vision of life in which one prosaically submits to one's station and its duties.

## DUALISTIC THINKING: ORTHODOXY AND ITS ENEMIES

Irving Kristol is a profoundly dualistic thinker. This is probably a legacy from his youth when he was an ardent Marxist and Trotskyist. These early political convictions got him in the habit of thinking about life and history in terms of a cosmic struggle. But having abandoned his Marxist hopes, he came to regard history as a never-ending struggle between the forces of orthodoxy and its enemies, which he refers to as "countercultures." Orthodoxy is practical and prosaic, rather than poetic or romantic. Orthodoxy is not fancy, but it is real, attainable, wholesome, and good. Its classic representative is rabbinic rather than prophetic Judaism. Religion, law, and the family are the three pillars of orthodoxy.

Religion satisfies the "theotropic" nature of man by providing a transcendent dimension to life.[27] Religion provides "comforting rituals" that help human beings withstand the drudgery and mundanity of existence. Religion also provides a belief in an afterlife, which is essential to the well-being of orthodoxy. The decline in the belief in an afterlife is particularly deleterious to the stability of orthodoxy; when this life on earth is all there is, people are inclined to demand more of politics than orthodoxy can offer.[28]

Because orthodoxy takes the doctrine of original sin for granted, it relies on law backed by religious sanctions to restrain the natural evil of humanity. Law also inculcates virtuous habits that sanctify daily life.

Orthodoxy is totally committed to "family values" and takes seriously the biblical injunction to be fruitful and multiply. Since the family is the "citadel of orthodoxy," orthodoxies are characterized by their opposition to homosexuality, abortion, sexual abstinence, and sexual licentiousness.[29]

Orthodoxy does not pretend to diminish or explain the evils of the world. It realizes that "this world we live in is, in fact, a hell."[30] But it tells us honestly and plainly that it does not know why these evils exist, and that all we can do is to "have faith that, in some larger sense, they contribute to the glory of the world."[31] Orthodoxy therefore tries to cultivate a "stoical temper" toward evil.[32]

In contrast to orthodoxy, countercultures are neither practical nor prosaic; they are idealistic, and their expectations of life are extravagant and totally unattainable. Unable to withstand the burden of existence, and wishing to be liberated from all the evils of the world, countercultures mobilize natural human discontent. Kristol regards Christianity as the "granddaddy of all countercultures."[33] Like Christianity, all countercultures "engender a millenarian temper" that leads to the belief that the evils of the world can be escaped, corrected, or redeemed.[34] What gives countercultures an advantage over orthodoxy is that they are animated by a "spiritual energy" that is totally unlike anything that orthodoxy can muster.[35]

Countercultures undermine everything that orthodoxy relies on to make human life tolerable: established religion, law, and family values. Their "prophetic fervor" makes them hostile to the rabbinic qualities of established religion, which they regard as "stale and decadent."[36] Like Christianity, they are antinomian, which is to say that they are opposed to established laws and institutions. They regard the coercive nature of law to be antithetical to the spiritual nature of love and worship. Moreover, countercultures are enemies of family values because they are invariably interested in the liberation of women and sex.[37] Their sexual preoccupations lead to either total sexual abstinence (Christianity) or total licentiousness (the counterculture of the 1960s)—both extremes are incompatible with family life.

In the conflict between orthodoxy and counterculture, Kristol sides totally with orthodoxy. He assumes that all evils have their source in countercultures, but never in orthodoxies. He counsels the latter not to yield, appease, placate, or compromise with the counterculture under any circumstances.[38] He chides the church for compromising with modernity. He counsels it to insist that its young people "wear sackcloth and ashes" and that they "walk on nails to Rome."[39] He counsels American society to resist its enemies, especially radical feminists, and gay rights activists, because in typical countercultural fashion, their complaints are fictitious and they are bent on undermining family values.[40] Kristol is not only intolerant of criticism, but of diversity; he has no use for liberal pluralism, and thinks that it leads only to "moral anarchy."[41] His advice amounts to counseling liberal society to become illiberal and intolerant.

By the same token, Kristol is certain that the demands for greater equality in our own time have absolutely nothing to do with the inequalities of capitalist bourgeois civilization. On the contrary, he believes that the more egalitarian a civilization becomes, the more enraged are its critics. He insists that "there are no reforms that are going to placate the egalitarian impulse."[42] He considers the real problem of bourgeois society to be nihilism, not inequality.[43]

Kristol's position is harsh, uncompromising, autocratic, and down-right repressive. But for him to behave otherwise is unorthodox. His rationale seems to be twofold. First, the discontent of the counterculture is totally groundless. It has nothing to do with the shortcomings of orthodoxy. Discontent is a function of the shortcomings of life itself; therefore, reforming the established order is unnecessary. Second, what countercultures desire is to redeem existence and to escape the harsh realities of life. But there is nothing whatsoever that can be done that would accomplish this, and this is another reason for not trying to appease them. Orthodoxies that try to placate their countercultures succeed only in destroying themselves.

Kristol thinks that a tough and uncompromising posture is the key to the success and survival of orthodoxy, but he is wrong. This arrogant, uncompromising spirit on the part of the established order succeeds in fueling the discontent of its critics. The advice that Kristol gives to orthodoxies in general is as bad as the advice that Louis XVI got from his ministers and close associates. The advice is to dig in your heels, insist that all is well with the established order, and that all the trouble rests with the critics whose demands are too idealistic, unrealistic, and unattainable. I believe that Hegel was quite justified in connecting the ferocity of the French Revolution to the intransigence of the ancien regime in general and the Catholic Church in particular.

Even if it is the case that countercultures are often motivated by the unavoidable wretchedness of life, and even if it is the case that their own visions are utopian and unattainable (as Marx's Communist ideal was), it does not follow that their criticisms of orthodoxy are unfounded, and that orthodoxy cannot be strengthened by reforms that address these criticisms. An admirer of bourgeois capitalism should not fail to recognize the extent to which the success and survival of capitalism is linked to the fact that it has reformed itself in ways that have made it less vulnerable to Marxist criticism.

Kristol shares Strauss's assumption that the established order is like a house of cards that cannot withstand examination, let alone criticism. But this is not true of great traditions. Far from being destroyed by listening to their detractors, or by responding to criticism and bettering themselves accordingly, traditions are strengthened. If they play deaf and dumb, if they shroud themselves in mystery, if they refuse to give an account of themselves, then they will be reduced to stale and lifeless dogma. There is no reason for a great tradition to shun the life of the mind. A tradition that cannot respond to criticism or give an account of itself is a tradition built on quicksand, a tradition filled with senseless repressions and taboos, a tradition rooted in the arbitrary lies of ambitious priests and arrogant philosophers, a tradition whose customs are as dull as they are decadent.

Moreover, a religion that insists on the rabbinic to the detriment of the prophetic and the spiritual will sap the life from its congregation. Like Strauss, Kristol cannot side wholeheartedly with the rabbinic elements of religion without destroying religion itself, because religion thrives on the life of the spirit. Without the latter, everything is just ritual and rote. And far from sanctifying the mundane and monotonous, such meaningless rituals can intensify alienation and despair. Kristol's orthodoxy is not just mundane and prosaic, it is a loveless affair that is dogged and dutiful but devoid of spirit or heart.

## THE AMERICAN UN-FOUNDING?

In Kristol's view, the most regrettable error of the American Founding Fathers was the disestablishment of religion. The Founders were misled by the secular humanist counterculture into thinking that an established religion was unnecessary, and that religion can be made into a private affair and still survive. And even in the absence of religion, they thought that reason was sufficient to lend support to the Judeo-Christian morality. For Kristol as for Strauss, reason is impotent in lending support to morality, and this is the root of the "crisis" of modern society.[44]

Kristol believes that religion is "far more important *politically*" than the Founders and other liberal humanists realized.[45] To reverse the error of the Founders, and to rescue America from the countercultural experiment that gave it birth, it is necessary to breath "new life into the older, now largely comatose religious orthodoxies."[46]

In view of his Straussian assumptions, Kristol's conclusion is logical but puzzling. It is the sort of solution that takes no heed of either the present or the past realities of American life. It ignores the existence of a plurality of religions in American society; it ignores the fact that America was settled by Puritans and other religious sects who were escaping the religious persecutions of Europe; it ignores the fact that freedom of religion was and continues to be one of the main attractions for all those who leave their native lands to seek a new home.

Besides, even if it were possible for America to have an established religion, which one would it be? Like Strauss, Kristol does not care; almost any will do. But whatever it is, it is likely to be one sect of Christianity or another. It is not likely to be Judaism. Kristol realizes this, and despite his own Jewish heritage, is not deterred. He encourages the Republican party to court the religious right in America, and insists that the party cannot succeed unless it does. He points to the religious character of neoconservatism as one of the most important things that sets it apart from British and European conservatism with their secular and detached dispositions.[47] It seems that Kristol prefers to risk the horrors of religious persecution than to risk nihilism.

Like Strauss and Marx, Kristol tends to overestimate the extent to which religion is the opium of the people. But the history of Europe, especially in the sixteenth and seventeenth centuries, testifies to the contrary, as does the politics of the Middle East in our time. The political prominence of the religious right within the Republican party is likely to make American politics resemble the politics of the Middle East—a politics of extremism fueled by religious hatred. Insofar as the disestablishment of religion is the bedrock of the American founding, the neoconservative rejection of this principle sows the seeds of the American un-founding.

## NATIONALISM OR PATRIOTISM?

In 1973, Kristol was suspicious of nationalism, saying that this "secular myth," while more successful than enlightened self-interest in providing a rationale for loyalty and self-sacrifice to the nation, has proven to be "utterly subversive of the bourgeois order."[48] But in 1983 he declared that neoconservatism was "nationalist," and that its foreign policy must reflect its nationalist proclivities. And again in an essay of 1993, he declared that "the three pillars of modern conservatism are religion, nationalism and economic growth."[49] Capitalist economics is important for providing incentives for human beings who are not naturally inclined to work. Religion and nationalism are important for providing motivations for people who are not by nature moral or political animals.

The reason behind the insistence on the political importance of nationalism, as well as religion, is an erroneous Straussian assumption about the nature of human beings and the nature of reason. Following Strauss, Kristol argues that the error of Enlightenment rationalism is to assume that enlightened self-interest would suffice to provide a rationale for moral and political obligation. But Strauss and Kristol deny that all the benefits of communal life can possibly outweigh the sacrifice involved in dying for one's country. They conclude that such a sacrifice cannot make sense.[50] Their objection to enlightened self-interest is compelling, but only if self-interest is defined as narrowly as it was defined by Thomas Hobbes. Like Hobbes, those who define self-interest narrowly find it difficult to account for altruistic behavior. Hobbes surmised that when we give alms to a beggar, we do it only to make ourselves feel good. But this observation does not necessarily prove that human beings are hopelessly selfish and self-absorbed. It suggests that people are not only capable of being altruistic, but that they even take pleasure in it. Far from undermining the altruism involved, the "selfish" enjoyment enhances the goodness of the act. It is not necessary to suffer in order to do good. On the contrary, those who act rightly only after a titanic struggle with the forces of evil in their breast cannot be counted among the most virtuous.

Even the ultimate sacrifice of one's life is not necessarily incompatible with a certain "selfish" enjoyment, because it is reasonable to prefer death to alternatives that are sordid, demeaning, or degrading, like betraying one's friend or one's country. There is nothing illogical about wanting to live only if one can continue to be the sort of person one takes pleasure in being. There is nothing irrational in preferring death to foul deeds. But to say all this is not to say that all, most, or even many people will be motivated by this sort of reasoning.

There is a difference between saying that most people are not motivated by rational considerations, and saying that there are no rational foundations for moral or political obligation. Strauss's position confuses the claim that most people need myths to motivate them to be moral with the claim that there are no rational reasons for behaving decently, even heroically. Kristol makes the same error. This leads them to believe that religion and nationalism are necessary, not only because people need powerful incentives to motivate them to behave well, but because there are no rational foundations for moral or political obligation. Just because Plato provides a myth about the rewards of the just and the punishments of the wicked in the afterlife, does not mean that the rational arguments about the alliance of justice with inner peace and happiness that he develops throughout the *Republic* are invalid.[51] It only means that not everyone will be motivated by rational considerations about the real nature of human happiness and well-being. Strauss erroneously assumes that the myth of Er at the end of the *Republic* is Plato's subtle way of suggesting that there are no rational foundations for morality, and that the whole *Republic* is nothing more than a display of Plato's sophistic virtuosity—his ability to make the weaker argument appear the stronger, and his capacity for splendid lies. This interpretive subterfuge allows Strauss to rely on the convergence of the great philosophers from Plato to Nietzsche as a source of authority without arguing his case.

Even if the Straussian and Hobbesian view of man and of reason is false, there would still be a problem finding enough people willing to die for their country. Hobbes thought that the solution is to make it mandatory for people to go to war when the sovereign declares one, and that those who refuse would be shot. In this case, the choice is between certain death (being shot) and uncertain death (going to war). Since human beings are rational as well as selfish, they can be depended on to choose the prospect of uncertain death. But even though Strauss and Kristol share Hobbes's view of human nature, they are not satisfied with Hobbes's solution. Coercion is not enough for those whose goal is to make selfish people rush willingly into battle and headlong to their death. Religion and nationalism are more sublime solutions to the problem of human selfishness.

In his book entitled *Nationalism,* Kenneth Minogue distinguishes between nationalism and patriotism. He argues that patriotism is compatible with a conservative temper, but that nationalism is not. Patriotism is loving one's country as it is, and being willing to defend it against foreign aggression in order to keep it as it is. Before her ships set out to defend England against the invasion of the Spanish Armada, Queen Elizabeth I climbed onto the decks and delivered a passionate speech about her love of England and her willingness to make the sacrifices necessary to preserve her country. Minogue regards the speech as the epitome of patriotism. In contrast, nationalism is a devotion to a certain ideal conception of one's country that is yet to be realized. German nationalism is the paradigm in this case. The nation becomes a sort of Sleeping Beauty that is yet to be awakened. But before this awakening is possible, it is necessary to ask who put her to sleep in the first place. The answer is usually in the form of wicked aristocrats, greedy capitalists, or, as in the Quebec referendum of 1995, "the ethnic vote." Nationalist politics is then characterized by a struggle against the "enemies" of the nation. Once the enemies of the nation are eliminated, then Sleeping Beauty will awaken; then harmony and concord will reign, and all will be well with the world. The trouble is that in the nearly endless struggle against her enemies, Sleeping Beauty starts to look more like Frankenstein.[52]

Kristol also distinguishes between patriotism and nationalism, but unlike Minogue, he rejects patriotism in favor of nationalism. He explains his preference as follows: "Patriotism springs from love of the nation's past; nationalism arises out of hope for the nation's future, distinctive greatness. . . . Neoconservatives believe . . . that the goals of American foreign policy must go well beyond a narrow, too literal definition of 'national security.' It is the national interest of a world power, as this is defined by a sense of national destiny, . . . not a myopic national security."[53] Written in 1983, these words clearly reveal that his nationalism is not backward-looking or conservative of America as it is, but radical and forward-looking.

American foreign policy must be guided, not by the concerns of national security, but by a yet unrealized vision of America's destiny as the Zion that will light up all the world, to use the words of Harry Jaffa. This perspective is not conservative or defensive, but radical and aggressive. It is not about resisting aggression, but about encouraging belligerence. This aggressive foreign policy was expressed by Kristol and other neoconservatives such as Norman Podhoretz in the pages of *Commentary* and *The National Interest*. The neoconservatives left the Democratic party in favor of the Republican party largely because President Jimmy Carter was too soft on the Soviets and too "even-handed" in disputes between Israel and its Arab neighbors.[54] Even Republican President Ronald Reagan was not always hawkish enough for them. Their foreign policy was characterized by a deep and uncompromising hostility to the Soviet Union as the representative of cosmic diabolical forces that must be defeated in every corner of the globe. Accordingly, Kristol and his fellow neoconservatives were ardent supporters of the war in Vietnam—a war that was not inspired by a narrow or myopic conception of national security. Kristol's complaint is that the war was not conducted with the force necessary to insure victory.[55]

Kristol is delighted by the popularity of the movie *Rambo* because it proves that people love war.[56] This is a good thing supposedly because only the menace of a common enemy and the threat of annihilation can unite a people. This is an important political assumption for Kristol as for Strauss, and it explains why they admire Machiavelli's political wisdom, despite calling him a "teacher of evil."[57] But this view neglects the extent to which people can be united by a shared love, such as the love of freedom, rather than a shared hatred of a common enemy.

Kristol's nationalism not only encourages a belligerent foreign policy, it assumes that American values are the only true values. This highly presumptuous attitude ignores the plurality of human groups and civilizations. It rejects plurality as a slippery slope to relativism and nihilism. But this is not so. There is a plurality of human groups and civilizations because there is a genuine plurality of human goods that are not always mutually compatible. This is not to deny that there is good and evil, right and wrong. It is merely a recognition that political disputes are not always conflicts between good and evil. Political disputes are often disputes between incommensurable goods. This is not to say that such disputes are not lethal. Unfortunately, much of the evil that men do has its source in an overzealous pursuit of a single good and a stubborn blindness to other competing goods. Nevertheless, failing to recognize the good that the other stands for is the sign of ignorance and fanaticism.

Kristol's nationalism not only invites an aggressive foreign policy, it also destabilizes domestic politics by depicting it in terms of the distinction between friend and foe—the enemies of the nation and the friends of Sleeping Beauty. This dualistic mentality has the effect of turning the political contest for power into an all-out war. The Watergate scandal that ended the presidency of Richard Nixon was a manifestation of this mentality on the domestic scene. When political opponents are demonized, simple ambition is reinforced and politicians are tempted to overstep the bounds of law. When domestic politics is turned into a contest between the forces of good and the forces of evil, when political opponents are regarded as the enemies of civilization, the results are dishonest political tactics, corruption and conflict.

Kristol begins with Hobbesian assumptions about human nature but ends by thinking that religion and nationalism are the magical cures for the human predicament. He is blind to the fact that these cures may be more lethal than the disease.

## THE TREASON OF THE INTELLECTUALS

Even though Kristol has written many a diatribe against the intellectuals of his day, reviewers of his work who assume that he is an "anti-intellectual intellectual" are mistaken.[58] On the contrary, Kristol takes intellectuals seriously. He thinks that they are crucial to the vitality of any culture, and that their proper function is to lend support to the civilization that nourishes them. Kristol is appalled that the liberal intellectuals of our time not only criticize their society for failing to live up to its own ideals, they criticize the ideals themselves. He therefore holds them responsible for the crisis of bourgeois civilization.

Those who attribute to intellectuals a special importance tend to think, as Kristol does, that ideas make history.[59] He thinks that what we need to revitalize bourgeois society is the inculcation of the right ideas. But the trouble is that the intellectuals are recalcitrant. They have always been hostile to bourgeois society and have refused to lend it support. Instead, they have developed an adversary culture that has held bourgeois civilization in a state of siege, and robbed it of its soul.[60] Bourgeois civilization must struggle to exist while being perpetually sabotaged by its own intellectual elite. Kristol thinks that the existence of an "adversary culture" is an "unprecedented" social phenomenon. Culture is supposed to enrich, enhance, and support the civilization that nourishes it, rather than holding it hostage.

Far from being anti-intellectual, Kristol shares the grandiose Straussian conception of the role of intellectuals in society. He echoes the Straussian view of the intellectuals as the propagandists of society. But this conception of the role of intellectuals, is not as salutary as Kristol thinks. Liberal intellectuals who think of themselves as the conscience of their society are likely to do it more good. Societies rarely welcome the truth about themselves, and if the intellectuals refuse to deliver the harsh realities, then who will? What is the point of furnishing society with noble fictions intended to deceive it about its true nature? Supposedly, these consummate lies will promote acceptance of the status quo and engender stability. But this claim overestimates the capacity of ideas to shape social reality. Ideas that are so transparently at odds with the lived reality cannot possibly accomplish this stabilizing task. On the contrary, they are more likely to fuel discontent. When the gulf between the reality and the ideals of a society is too great, cynicism sets in.

Is Kristol's conception of the bourgeois ethos a noble fiction perpetuated by neoconservative intellectuals? Are people gullible enough to believe that a capitalist economy is one in which those who are disciplined and diligent will be assured material success? Are they gullible enough to believe that the inequalities of their society are but the reflection of the inequalities of nature? Does Kristol himself believe that there is a correspondence between the bell curve of talent and that of income? Are such fictions likely to resign people to their fate? Will they foster social stability? I will argue that this neoconservative fiction is both damaging and disingenuous. And far from encouraging stability, it fuels discontent.

## THE POPULIST PLOY

Kristol blames most of the ills of our society on the liberal intellectuals. The latter are part of what Kristol calls the "new class" which is to say, a new ruling class that includes journalists, educators, city planners, government bureaucrats, as well as scientists, doctors, and lawyers who work in the public sector. As Christopher Lasch rightly points out, the preoccupation with the new class is a hangover from Marxist habits of thought that allows neoconservatives to attack the "elites" without attacking big business.[61] Kristol regards the intellectuals as the most poisonous component of this liberal elite. The intellectuals have turned against bourgeois culture because it is too prosaic, too domestic, too ordinary, and too boring for their liking. The virtues of honesty, hard work, and thrift do not interest them. The aspirations of ordinary people for a better living do not capture their fancy. The intellectuals are bent not only on the destruction of bourgeois civilization, but on the destruction of all morality, restraint, and decency. The nihilism of the elite is boundless, and it threatens not only bourgeois capitalist society, but all of Western civilization. Kristol prefers the days when the highbrow or the avant-garde culture was separate from popular culture. He laments the fact that the nihilistic culture of the intellectuals has infected the popular culture. Robbed of its "soul" by the nihilism of the adversary culture, the bourgeois order is "sick." This explains rampant crime, pornography, and promiscuity. Since the intellectuals are the source of the problem, they cannot be relied upon to breathe new life into the bourgeois order. Neoconservatism must therefore turn to the people.[62]

Kristol hangs all his hope on the people, the average middle-class people who are the "rock" of bourgeois capitalist society. He is certain that they will not allow cultural nihilism to triumph, because even though they are not "uncommonly wise," they are "uncommonly sensible."[63] They are certainly more reasonable and more dependable than the liberal intellectual elite. They alone can be relied on to "turn back the clock" on the liberal revolution. Kristol thinks that the popular referendum is unquestionably the most conservative piece of legislation passed by the state legislatures in the last century.[64] Popular referenda have succeeded in defeating the "most cherished liberal ideas"—school integration is one example, but there will be others—legal abortions, homosexual rights, women's equality, and so on.

Kristol asserts that since the 1960s the people have had to endure a liberal "revolution-from-above"—a revolution that the people did not want, and that their common sense rejected. It is time for them to retrieve the power that they have entrusted to the elite, and to "turn back the clock" on the liberal revolution.[65] Kristol's hope is that the people will defeat the liberal elite, rescue bourgeois capitalist society from its spiritual atrophy, and provide it with the religious solace it needs.

Kristol is aware of the fact that the Founding Fathers were not populists. They went to great lengths to protect the American polity from the tyranny of the majority. The bicameral Congress, the separation of powers, and the Constitution itself, are all intended to avoid the tyranny of the ruling elite as well as the tyranny of the people. But in his essay "The New Populism: Not to Worry," Kristol argues that populism is a necessary measure in view of the current circumstances. The Founders assumed that the people will choose the best among them to govern. But this has not happened; in the current "crisis of our disoriented elites" we must rely on the common sense of the people, not the "un-wisdom of its governing elites"—in politics, the judiciary, the universities, and the media.

Kristol's confidence in the people, his repudiation of the liberal elite, and his radical politics are echoed by Newt Gingrich in *The Contract With America*: "There's at least a better than even chance that it is the people and not the elite who are right."[66] Gingrich also echoes Kristol's conviction that the newly emerging neoconservative elite represents "the vast majority of Americans."[67] Armed with such confidence in the true will of the people, Gingrich announces his readiness to move America in a "dramatically different direction" that takes no cognizance of history because the latter is merely the failed experiment of countercultural elites.[68] Needless to say, this heady mandate has tempted this populist politician to proceed with such reckless abandon that it nearly cost him his political career.[69]

The populist ploy has become a dominant motif of the American right. The basic strategy of populist leaders is to exploit the inarticulate discontent of the people, and their resentment toward the elite. Every populist leader tells the people that they have been betrayed by the elites whose corrupt habits and newfangled ideas cannot be trusted. Supposedly, the leader in question is someone who can be trusted because he is not a leader at all, but one of the people, and therefore shares their interests, their pains, and their concerns. Ross Perot, who ran for the presidency in 1992, is a multimillionaire, but he still managed to convince a sizable proportion of the American population that he represented the common people. The Republican candidates who swept Congress in the congressional elections of 1994 brought the populist resentment of Washington elites to a feverish pitch.[70] Patrick Buchanan's campaign for the Republican presidential nomination in 1996 was particularly rich in populist demagoguery. Buchanan appealed not just to the middle class, but to the working people, and unlike Kristol and the neoconservatives, he did not exclude businessmen and corporate executives from the "elite." His populist appeal was more coherent and thoroughgoing, and as a result it was a threat to the neoconservative philosophy that dominates the Republican party.

Oliver North was one Republican hopeful who overplayed his hand. Far from avoiding his reputation as the U.S. marine lieutenant who coordinated the Iran-Contra affair, then lying about it to Congress, he used his record to advantage, and narrowly won the Republican party's nomination to run for the Senate. During his campaign, he used the usual populist tactics and complained about the pernicious elite in Washington that must be unseated. But he went a step further. He spoke of his covert activities during the Iran-Contra affair as a guerrilla war of liberation. He compared Washington with Europe and his own campaign with the liberation of Europe that began on D-day. Clearly, this was more than the credulity of the American people could withstand, and North lost the election.

Despite the inclination to eulogize the populace and their common sense, the neoconservative commitment to populism is questionable. Kristol makes this clear in discussing the importance of preventing the market from determining the values of society. Kristol recognizes the need for public authority to set limits on the excess and debauchery to which the market economy is inclined. But this sort of posture is incompatible with one who pays tribute to the common sense and decency of the people in comparison to the elites. For what are market preferences if not a reflection of the tastes and preferences of the populace? Is it not the same people who love *Rambo* that determine the values of the market? And are not these the very people that Kristol is depending on to make the neoconservative revolution?

Far from being a democratic trust in the common sense and decency of the people, neoconservative populism is a desperate ploy by which neoconservatives hope to unseat the liberal elite that presides over America's "parchment regime." It is a technique that pits American liberalism against American democracy. The idea is to use democracy to defeat liberalism, which is identified as the greatest threat to America and the source of the crisis of the West. But this populist ploy displays a profound contempt for the people, and hence for democracy itself.

There is nothing democratic about populism. To be a democrat is to trust in the goodwill and good judgment of the people; it means treating the people with respect as rational persons and not as an irrational bundle of appetites; it means insuring that the people are well informed enough to make an intelligent decision; it means respecting the people enough to tell them the truth, even when the truth is harsh or unpleasant; it means refraining from demagoguery, systematic lying, flattery, deception, and manipulation; it means having leaders who are willing to give an account of themselves and their policies, and not leaders who will rely simply on their charisma. The reliance on charisma and image manipulation is a betrayal of the democratic spirit because it appeals to people on a subliminal and nonrational level. Charismatic leadership cannot give an account of itself; its authority depends on the personality and not the policies of the leader; it expects people to follow the leader because of *who* he is and not *what* he says. A leader who believes in democracy must be willing to tell the truth; he must be willing to give a rational account of his policies; and he must be willing to have these policies rejected by the electorate, a risk that democrats must take if they believe in democracy, or if democracy is to have a fighting chance. Insofar as our leaders are refusing to take this risk, insofar as they are relying on the professional panderers, the image-makers, the manufacturers of charisma, and a plethora of other masters of manipulation, democracy has become the rule of craft, guile, and cunning. It is in this context that neoconservatism can successfully resort to populism as a weapon against American liberalism.

## WHAT'S CONSERVATIVE
## ABOUT NEOCONSERVATISM?

Conservatism is at its best a certain political disposition. In Michael Oakeshott's words, being conservative means being disposed to "prefer the familiar to the unknown, to prefer the tried to the untried, fact to mystery, the actual to the possible, the limited to the unbounded, the near to the distant . . . the convenient to the perfect, present laughter to utopian bliss."[71] For conservatives, politics is the art of the possible; and in view of their unflattering conception of human nature, their estimation of what is possible is quite low. Conservatives not only shun utopianism and idealism of every sort, they have no illusions that politics can conform to any of the rules of abstract justice. There is a sense in which conservatives are cynical about life and politics. Ironically, this cynical posture is what recommends conservatism in a century that has suffered so many horrors at the hands of idealists. The appeal of conservatism derives precisely from its modest expectations of politics. Politics cannot hope to transfigure life or give it meaning. And there is no doubt that the romantic quest for the unattainable in politics, as in love, is the source of the greatest human misery.

Conservative resignation to things as they are, assuming that things are not intolerable, is a source of stability and security in politics. By the same token, the conservative disposition can result in a detrimental attachment to decrepit traditions, unnecessary evils, and irrational customs. The trouble with the conservative temper is that it is bound to engender an aversion to every new spirit, and every fresh breeze; it is bound to cultivate a general repugnance to innovation, adventure, and even youth itself.

Conservatism is suspicious not only of innovation, risk, and adventure, but of reason. It prefers incomprehensible traditions to reasonable innovations. Conservatives tend to deprecate the rationalist spirit, and are particularly distrustful of philosophy. They reject reason in favor of "the wisdom of the ages," which is how they designate traditions whose rationale is all but totally lost, or customs that they cannot explain. It is no wonder that John Stuart Mill dubbed conservatism as "the stupid party."

Even though Irving Kristol pays tribute to stupidity, he is not satisfied with the stupid party.[72] He longs to transform conservatism into an intellectually and culturally attractive proposition. He wishes to define it as something more than just accommodation to present realities. He wants to turn it into a political philosophy that stands for something. He feels that the trouble with the Republican party in the United States has been its stupidity. For the last half century, it has played second fiddle to the Democratic party, which has become the naturally governing party, the party of the people. In contrast, the Republican party is the party of vested interests, the party of the minority, the few, the rich, the capitalists. Republicans have won elections, but only by default, only as a result of Democratic foibles. And when in office, they have done little more than restrain the fiscal excesses of the Democrats. The Republican party cannot hope to revitalize itself unless it changes its mind about what George Bush dismissed as "the vision thing." Kristol surmises that politics today has become too enmeshed with the "life of the mind," and a stupid party that does not stand for anything will be lost. Kristol was saying this in 1976, and it seems as if the Republicans have been listening. The Republican Contract with America is an articulation of just what the Republican party stands for. Newt Gingrich even brags that he belongs to "the most explicitly ideologically committed House Republican party in modern history."[73] Kristol assumes that the ideological intensity of the Republican party will make it more intellectually interesting as well as more politically successful. I can testify to the truth of the former, but only history can determine the truth of the latter.

Kristol is no admirer of political radicalism; but he is a radical in spite of himself. He is compelled to shun the conservative disposition because of what he considers to be the pitiful conditions of modernity. He echoes the Straussian alarm about the crisis of liberal democracy.[74] And he understands that crisis as Strauss did: as a spiritual malaise caused by the death of God and the triumph of nihilism. Kristol wants politics to rescue liberal society from its current crisis. In light of the dire conditions imposed by modernity, Kristol rejects Oakeshott's account of conservatism as "thin gruel."[75] Neoconservatism is much more ambitious. A neoconservative regime must do much more than maintain order and secure liberty under law. It must address the spiritual disorder of modernity; it must defeat the reigning nihilism, and reinvest life with meaning.

When I say that Kristol pays tribute to stupidity, I mean that he regards himself as one of the ardent champions of the conservative disposition. However, he denies that it is the right disposition for our times. According to Kristol, we need to bring back the past, or "turn back the clock" as he puts it, before we can start being conservative.[76] This is not a conservative posture; on the contrary, it is the sort of posture that is shared by radicals, revolutionaries, and reformers of every stripe. Once things are radically different from what they are, once things are just the way they should be, then all revolutionaries are content to turn conservative. But that defeats the whole point of being conservative.

Kristol rejects Oakeshott's account of what it means to be a conservative simply because the conservative disposition does not fit neoconservatism.[77] The truth of the matter is that neoconservatism is not conservative, but radical and reactionary. Its radical nature is manifest in Kristol's refusal to accept the basic tenets of the American founding and in Newt Gingrich's declaration that it is time "to erase the slate and start over."[78] Neoconservatism is also reactionary in the technical sense of the term. Reactionaries are not interested in conserving the present as it is. On the contrary, it is the present that they find intolerable. As Kristol explains, "there is so much to deplore in this American present that Oakeshott's paean to present-mindedness is singularly inapt."[79] Neoconservatives are repelled by the liberal present, and they hunger for radical change intended to restore a lost golden age.

Bob Dole, the Republican presidential candidate in the election of 1996 reflected the neoconservative nostalgia for the past. Dole promised the electorate that he would turn back the clock, that he would build a bridge to the past, and that he would restore the America that was lost.

To say that neoconservatism is radical and reactionary is not to condemn it. Failing to keep abreast of the times, resisting the dominant tide, or obstructing the progressive trajectory of history, are admirable qualities. There is no reason to go along with the tide, and every tide deserves a little resisting. But neoconservatism is an expression of modernity, and of the radical and immoderate spirit of our times. It fits the model of politics that Michael Oakeshott referred to as "the politics of faith"—not for its religiosity, which is suspect, but for its conception of politics as a mode of conduct that seeks to bring all human activity within its domain of control.[80] The neoconservative vision relies on the huge expansion of the power and sphere of government that is characteristic of modern times, and to which writers as diverse as Michel Foucault (in his dramatic Kafkaesque style) and Michael Oakeshott (in his diffident and understated style) have pointed.

Neoconservatism has a peculiarly modern conception of politics as a sphere of action that shapes the religious, moral, psychic, sexual, and economic lives of its citizens. It is very far from being a champion of limited government. Even its supply-side economics is not strictly speaking laissez-faire. It requires government to act on the economy in a manner that is intended to stimulate growth; it involves a giant gamble—huge tax cuts for the rich in the hope that they will reinvest the money into the economy and stimulate growth. If they do not, then the government will be left with huge deficits. It is the sort of gamble that is fiscally irresponsible and lacks moderation and diffidence. Nor is the devotion to perpetual growth, and the attendant exploitation of natural resources, a conservative posture because it takes no heed of our responsibilities to future generations.

I am a skeptical liberal, a liberal without illusions, a liberal who is painfully aware of the shortcomings of liberalism, its pretensions, its myths, its radical spirit, and its suicidal tendencies. I am a liberal who believes that the liberal spirit needs to be moderated by a conservative temper that would undermine the inflated expectations that modern men and women have of political life. A conservative temper has the effect of resigning us to the present, and even to its injustices. A conservative temper promotes an atmosphere of sobriety and stability that every society badly needs. But unfortunately, that sobriety is precisely what is missing in America's Strauss-inspired neoconservatism.

## THE WORST OF BOTH WORLDS

What is new about neoconservatism is not the absence of nostalgia for the past, but the exchange of an aristocracy of birth for an aristocracy of talents. In other words, neoconservatism rejects the classic conservative account of inequality in favor of the liberal account. But it endows the liberal view with its own unique pretensions.

The difference between the traditional conservative view of inequality and the liberal view can be explained simply as follows. On the conservative view, social inequality is the result of good birth, which is a matter of good fortune. Being born to a privileged household means having all sorts of opportunities for the cultivation of one's god-given potentialities—moral, intellectual, artistic, musical, or athletic. In a traditional society, social inequality is the result of the accident of birth, and the unequal privileges and opportunities that go along with it. The idea that the social hierarchy is a reflection of the natural inequalities or the natural aristocracy is laughable precisely because all the talents and potentialities furnished by nature are worthless and come to naught without social privileges that provide the opportunity for their develop-ment. Without such opportunity, all the intellectual, athletic, artistic, and musical talents come to nothing. What nature provides is mere potentialities and not full-blown capacities. This is not to say that the natural lottery distributes talents equally, it is merely to say that the talents nature provides are worthless in the absence of the socially acquired opportunity to cultivate them. Nor is it to say that all those who are born privileged will necessarily take full advantage of the opportunity to cultivate their god-given potentialities. However, it means that those who succeed in doing so, and who lead more complete and more fulfilled lives, owe a debt to society for making such a blessed life possible. This is the meaning of noblesse oblige. It refers to the obligations and duties that the nobility or the more fortunate owe to the less fortunate. It is not a question of charity; it is a debt. The labors, the drudgery, and the attention to the biological details of life that are the lot of the unfortunate make the leisure necessary for self-cultivation of the privileged possible. For conservatives, aristocracy is a highly artificial phenomenon—a result of arbitrarily bestowed social privileges and opportunities. Even when he used the term *natural aristocracy,* Edmund Burke meant by it something "bred" by a combination of privilege and education: never seeing anything sordid, learning to respect oneself, getting used to living in the glare of the public eye, learning to despise danger in the pursuit of honor and duty, having the leisure to reflect and converse, recognizing that the slightest fault can have ruinous conse-quences, setting an example, becoming a benefactor of mankind, learning vigilance, foresight, and circumspection. Clearly, the cultiva-tion of this sort of aristocracy is natural only in the sense that "art is man's nature."[81]

In contrast to the conservative view, liberals regard social life as a competition in which the more talented, more able, more determined, and more diligent succeed. Liberalism replaces a hierarchy based on birth (that is, an aristocracy) with a hierarchy based on merit (that is, a meritocracy). Liberalism accepts inequality on the condition that every-one enjoys equality of opportunity. If everyone has the same starting point, then the inequalities that emerge are justified on the basis of differentials in effort and ability. In the liberal vision, inequalities are never the result of chance or the accident of birth. Our status in society, our success and failure, is entirely our own doing. Social inequalities are, or are supposed to be, the result of natural inequalities; the socially privileged are those whom nature has blessed; society is therefore a reflection of the natural aristocracy.

Inequality is much harder to bear in a liberal society because one has only oneself and one's inadequacies to blame for one's poor social standing. But in more traditional or aristocratic societies, where chance and the accident of birth determine ones prospects and opportunities, one can always curse one's luck. The more we believe that liberalism has been actualized, the more we believe that our society provides us with equality of opportunity, the more we believe that there is a fair starting gate for all, the more difficult it is to deal with the fact of inequality. Of course, it could be argued that liberalism is bogus, and that the ideal of equality of opportunity has not or cannot be attained, or that it can only be partially realized. For the most part, liberal society is painfully aware of this, and therefore invents schemes by which the conditions that justify inequality can be actualized. The current preoccupation with affirmative action is one such scheme; and when it is abandoned, new schemes will no doubt take its place.

Far from endorsing the sobriety of the conservative view of social inequality, neoconservatism is a passionate exponent of liberal mythology. It rejects noblesse oblige in favor of the myth of natural aristocracy. But it pretends that liberal ideals have been actualized and that social inequalities are indeed a reflection of natural inequalities. This view flatters the fortunate by allowing them to believe that they are self-made men and women who emerged from the womb with their talents and abilities full-blown, and that they owe their fulfillment and self-cultivation to no one but themselves. Bluntly put, they assume that everyone who is rich must be clever and industrious, while everyone who is poor must be lazy and stupid. The unfortunate have only themselves to blame, and the fortunate, having acquired their fortunes by their own efforts, owe nothing to the society that made their achievements possible. Needless to say, these pretensions aggravate the discontent at the heart of liberal society.

Neoconservatism becomes uglier when it adopts a strident biological and racial account of inequality. It is easy to see why neoconservatism falls prey to the pseudoscientific theories that try to find the source of inequality in nature alone, or try to prove the superiority of white Anglo-Saxon males—the very group that is anxious about the effects of affirmative action on its prospects.[82] But this deadly fascination with biology can only silence the moral conscience of society by pretending that social hierarchy is a reflection of nature.

A more resigned and more conservative posture is to admit that bourgeois society, like every other society, has its foundation in convention not nature. Far from being the embodiment of natural justice, its inequalities are often arbitrary and capricious. But in its defense, one can argue that all its shortcomings notwithstanding, liberal society affords a degree of mobility that is unknown in traditional societies. Besides, every order has its price, and the relative prosperity and freedom that bourgeois society affords may be worth the price in arbitrary inequalities and injustices. This would certainly be a conservative posture, but it is not the posture adopted by neoconservatism. Instead of acknowledging the historical, conventional, and haphazard nature of inequality, neoconservatism echoes Leo Strauss's enthusiasm for nature and for a natural aristocracy. The wedding of liberal mythology and neoconservative pretensions fuels the discontent at the heart of liberal society, and makes its inequalities even harder to bear. Neoconservatism rejects all liberal efforts to make equality of opportunity a reality, because it is convinced that it already is. Kristol's conviction that the bell curve of income corresponds to the bell curve of talent is a case in point. In this way, neoconservatism deludes those who are better off into thinking that they are entitled to their privileges and that they owe nothing to the rest of society; if they help the poor, it is only out of charity. In short, the neoconservative melange of liberal and conservative ideas can provide us only with the worst of both worlds.

## FAMILY VALUES:
## THE UNDECLARED WAR ON WOMEN

The neoconservative enthusiasm for meritocracy does not extend to women. Since neoconservatism regards the equality of women to be incompatible with family values, women must be excluded from the meritocratic society. Neoconservatism confines women to the household at a time when the status of the home, of childbearing, and child rearing is at an all-time low. In a world where the bell curve of incomes parallels the bell curve of talents, one can only conclude that those who have no incomes also have no talents, and are therefore worthless members of society. If the market is the measure of success, then women who stay home and raise their children are failures. "Family values" is little more than a hypocritical slogan that conceals the disparagement and hostility toward women at the heart of the neoconservative political agenda; it is a code for making women into second-class citizens. This may explain the antipathy of women to the Republican party in the presidential election of 1996.

Tanya Melich is one Republican who has recognized the fact that her party is no longer the party of Lincoln—that is, the party of equality and freedom. In *The Republican War Against Women,* she documents the takeover of the Republican party by the radical right.[83] She uncovers the hypocrisy at the heart of "family values," and reveals the hostility of the party toward women, and its determination to exclude them from opportunities for self-cultivation and self-actualization.

Journalist Barbara Ehrenreich has been the most incisive analyst of the political gap between the sexes that was reflected in the presidential election of 1996. She suggests that the gender gap has its origin in the fact that the neoconservative agenda of the Republican party appeals to the sort of perverse masculinity that is represented in magazines such as *GQ* for whom fatherhood is a totally foreign ideal. Instead of being fathers and husbands, men are the inhabitants of "guy land" where life is one large sports network, supplemented with fast cars, guns, and an endless parade of "gal pals"—lovely women who are programmed to satisfy male sexual fantasies and then magically disappear without a trace, let alone a child. It does not surprise her that men are easily "seduced by the social Darwinism of the political right, with its vision of the world as a vast playing field for superstar linebackers and heroic entrepreneurs."[84] In the absence of the Nanny State (the anathema of right-wing politics), men live out their days in fantasyland, using public funds only for bombs and spaceships, while women spend their lives caring for children and the elderly. In this way the political gender gap grows, not because women are different, but because men have turned their backs on the human race. Ehrenreich's cynical vision is a testimony to the failure of the neoconservative appeal to family values—a failure that stems from its hypocrisy, its double standard, and its insipid conception of masculinity.

It would be unfair to find the origin of the neoconservative hostility toward women in the writings or character of Irving Kristol. His marriage to Gertrude Himmelfarb has been described as the best marriage of the century—an assessment that he has never denied. And it is clear that his own devotion to family life is based on his understanding of marriage as a long-term friendship, which is impossible in the absence of equality and mutual respect. Nevertheless, Kristol is terrified by liberated women. He tells of an incident at a dinner party where he no sooner settled down with his plate of food in the middle of the couch, when Hannah Arendt sat to his left, Mary McCarthy to his right, and Diana Trilling directly opposite. He recalls sinking into a "terrified paralysis of body and mind."[85] For nearly an hour, he could not swallow a bite nor could he follow the conversation about Freud, the libido, and other scandalous subjects. He could only pray that his wife Bea (Gertrude Himmelfarb) would come to his rescue. But she was busy eating and laughing at the other end of the room, totally oblivious to his plight.

There is no doubt that Kristol is committed to a prosaic domesticity. He tells us that the enemies of family values always begin with the liberation of women and sex. This explains his fear and trembling in the company of liberated women. But there is no reason to think that the sexual liberation of men is any less of a threat to the family. If it goes unexamined, this double standard invites the sort of gender gap that has been rightly attributed to the ascendancy of the right.

Kristol's good intentions notwithstanding, the gender gap as analyzed by Ehrenreich is inherent in the neoconservative affirmation of bourgeois economics on one hand, and family values on the other. Bourgeois economics is for men, and family values is for women. This would not be a bad arrangement were it not for the fact that we live in a society where all worthwhile achievement is deemed to be outside the home. Besides, the neoconservative effort to endow the private realm with dignity is invariably betrayed by the misogyny at the heart of its intellectual lineage.

The phalocratic character of Leo Strauss's philosophy is undeniable. In an article on Aristophanes's *Assembly of Women,* Strauss criticizes Aristophanes for allowing the women to triumph at the end of the play. The play is a comedy in which the women of Athens manage to swindle the men into surrendering their political power. The women take over the assembly and proceed to re-organize the world. They abolish private property as well as the family, and they liberate sex. Moved by an egalitarian spirit appropriate to their Athenian heritage, they insist on an equal distribution of sexual pleasure. Praxagora, the leader of the women, decides that young men cannot bed with young women unless they first bed with old ones. Her husband asks her what will happen to old men who no longer have the money to buy the favors of young women as they used to in the old days. Praxagora decides that young women too must bed with old men before they can bed with young ones. In interpreting this hilarious comedy, Strauss is particularly repelled by the scenes in which the "old hags" pursue young men in the streets; he finds these scenes hideous and unnatural. What makes the play repulsive for Strauss is that it is the inversion of what he regards as the natural order of things—the rule of men over women.[86] Strauss cannot understand why Aristophanes did not condemn the triumph of the women at the end of the play.[87] The reason that Aristophanes does not denounce the triumph of the "old hags" is that he does not assume, as does Strauss, that the old order is natural. Why is the control of the assembly by the women and the total exclusion of men any more absurd than the reverse? Why is it unnatural for the "old hags" to bed with young men, but not unnatural for erotically challenged old men to bed with young women routinely as they did in Athens, and as they do in our own society?

Strauss insists on the rule of men over women because he believes that women are inferior to men—not just in strength or intelligence, but in moral goodness. He tells us that the Bible and Greek philosophy agree on the "superiority of the male sex" and the inferiority of the female sex, especially where justice is concerned.[88] Plainly stated this means that women are more evil than men. Strauss supports his views by using the authority of Greek philosophy as well as the Bible. Apparently, the wise Euripides held this view, and Strauss assures us that "there is no question as to the truth of what Euripides said about the female sex."[89] Nor was Euripides alone; Strauss insists Aristophanes "expressed the same view throughout the plays."[90] What's more, the Bible blames the fall of man on Eve, and Plato blames the demise of the ideal state on the covetousness of a woman.[91] With so much wisdom and authority piled high against the female sex, we cannot but conclude that women are evil, and a "force to be reckoned with."[92] This is a classic case of how Strauss uses the old books to impart his dubious wisdom.[93]

As I have shown earlier, Allan Bloom is staunchly unsympathetic to feminism because it de-eroticizes the world, destroys the family, and subverts the natural hierarchy in which men must rule over women. Setting aside the self-congratulatory conviction that men are superior to women and should rule over them, as well as the equally questionable conviction that the patriarchal family is a form of male domination softened by romantic mystifications, Bloom's support for the family is a failure because it is based merely on social utility. Bloom defends the family because it provides men with a supposedly harmless outlet for their aggression, while supplying women with a provider for themselves and their children. In a radio interview on the Canadian Broadcasting Corporation, Bloom ridiculed the whole idea of marriage, saying that it was ridiculous to think that the person you marry today will still be physically attractive ten years hence; and as to conversation, that is likely to be exhausted in much less than five years. It is no wonder that he recommends the institution only for others and not for himself. Strauss expresses the same view by using the term *gentlemen* pejoratively to mean dupes who genuinely relish the prospects of being husbands and fathers.[94]

Thomas Pangle repeats Strauss and Bloom's views of women and the family. Like Bloom, he poses as a defender of family values. He denounces Locke as the destroyer of the family. He maintains that Locke was subversive of the biblical tradition, which supposedly insists not just on the inferiority of women, but on the necessity of their subjugation. But the allegedly outrageous Locke would educate women like men and would give mothers as much authority over their progeny as fathers. Locke, the father of liberalism, is therefore condemned as the enemy of the Bible and the wisdom of the ages. Locke is painted as the mad and dangerous liberator of women and the destroyer of family values.[95] Pangle asserts the superiority of the tradition against Locke's scandalous innovations. The book leaves one wondering what became of Christianity's glad tidings? What happened to the gospel of love and freedom? Pangle's efforts to blacken the name of the father of liberalism are a colossal failure. Instead of making the reader despise Locke, Pangle's book breeds contempt for the Bible according to Strauss. If the Bible is really as black as Pangle maintains, then Locke's rebellion against this gospel of domination and injustice is heroic. All of Pangle's efforts notwithstanding, Locke emerges as a prince of light in the midst of darkness.

The Straussian roots of neoconservatism, coupled with its celebration of a bourgeois ethos in which the natural distribution of talent corresponds to the bell curve of income, betrays its hostility to women.

It is difficult not to conclude that talent, excellence, individuality, and accomplishment are for men, and family values are for women. It is no wonder that more and more women have discovered that family values is a code word for their subjugation and humiliation.

## THE POLITICAL SUCCESS
## OF NEOCONSERVATISM

Neoconservatism is bent on undoing the liberal heritage of America—it rejects the Constitution's disestablishment of religion, it begrudgingly accepts desegregation, it has no intention of taking any measures to improve equality of opportunity, it is opposed to the equality of the sexes, it is filled with nostalgia for the past, and it hypocritically champions religion for political reasons. How has such an ideology managed to garner any support in America? How can its political success be explained?

It seems to me that there are several possible explanations. First, neoconservatism has an uncanny ability to ally itself with almost all of the current critics of liberalism while disseminating liberal myths in their most artless form. The political weakness of liberalism in American politics is the second factor. The natural and perennial weakness of liberalism is the third. And fourthly, neoconservatism has successfully capitalized on the puritanical spirit of America that is at odds with the permissive character of liberalism. I will discuss each of these in turn.

The first key to the success of neoconservatism is its ability to ally itself with all of the critics of liberalism, with the exception of the postmodern left. These critics include the Libertarians, Communitarians, Republicans, and feminists.

Libertarians harken back to the heyday of capitalism when it was embraced enthusiastically by liberals. Capitalism was historically a natural ally of liberalism because it replaced the oligarchic and monopolistic practices of the mercantile system and allowed individual initiative, innovation, and competition to thrive. This new economic order was congenial to the individualistic spirit of liberal politics. But unfortunately, the rugged individuality of early capitalism gave way to the large exploitative and dehumanizing factories of the nineteenth century and the corporate capitalism of the twentieth century. To allay the evils of capitalism, liberalism resorted to ideas borrowed from the socialist tradition. In this way, the liberal state gave way to the social welfare state and its bureaucratic machinery. Libertarians are nostalgic for capitalism in its infancy. Robert Nozick is the most radical of the Libertarians, with a decidedly anarchic spirit.

Neoconservatism capitalizes on the libertarian discontent with the social welfare state. The association of liberalism with fiscal bankruptcy and economic disarray has allowed neoconservatism to ally itself with all those who are interested in fiscal restraint and responsibility. Its rhetoric is filled with contempt and hostility for big government. And it has managed to redefine liberalism as the political philosophy of big government. But while neoconservatism is indeed eager to limit the size of government, *it has no intention of limiting its scope.* It has every intention of using the power of the state to uphold religion, lend legal support to the social values it deems worthy, and interfere in the norms that govern private life. It is not only profoundly anti-individualist, but it has abandoned itself to corporate capitalism. It saves us from the clutches of big government only to leave us at the mercy of big business.

Communitarianism does not have a liberal inspiration. It is not disenchanted with liberalism because of what it has become, but because of what it has always been—namely an antisocial philosophy. Communitarianism blames liberalism for the alienation, isolation, and anomie of individuals in modern postindustrial society. Communitarians such as Alasdair MacIntyre, Michael Sandel, and Amitai Etzioni contend that liberalism is corrosive of community and that efforts on the part of the state may be necessary to save, protect, and promote the fragile flower of social life.[96] Communitarianism promises warmth, oneness, togetherness, a sense of belonging, having a place or station, knowing what you are, who you are, and what is expected.

Neoconservatism shares the Communitarian emphasis on the primacy of the community over the individual, and it is eager to use the arm of the law to enforce and protect the values of the community. Its legal moralism harkens back to the days when homosexuality, sodomy, prostitution, and other "victimless crimes" were enshrined in the law.

In the presidential election of 1996, community was the catchphrase. In line with their neoconservative inspiration, the Republicans emphasized the primacy of the community and promised to be tough on crime, without specifying what would count as crime. The Democrats followed suit; President Clinton presented a vision of America as a single community working together to achieve its collective goals. Meanwhile, First Lady Hillary Rodham Clinton wrote a book entitled *It Takes a Village*. The American spirit of individualism was altogether absent from the campaign, and community was touted on all sides.

Republicanism is as old as Aristotle, Polybius, and Machiavelli, and as new as Hannah Arendt. Although it is a complex and multifaceted tradition, its critique of liberalism can be stated simply as follows. Liberalism has an antipathy to politics; it regards the latter as a necessary evil and does its best to limit the scope of government. Liberalism sets a premium on private life and private associations and pursuits, while subtly neglecting or undermining public life. In so doing, liberalism fails to understand politics in general, and democratic politics in particular. It fails to recognize that politics is first and foremost an opportunity. It is an opportunity to exercise our rational as well as our moral capacities. It allows us to deliberate on matters of public concern. Instead of pursuing our private interests, instead of concerning ourselves with our private needs and desires, politics forces us to consider our collective good. Through this process, it lifts us out of our selfishness and transforms us into social beings. Because it provides an opportunity for speech and mutual exchange, politics satisfies and completes our gregarious inclinations. In short, it is a delightful part of life, and an integral element in the completion and fulfillment of humanity.[97]

The practical policy implications of republicanism is to have more politics. This can be accomplished by a process of decentralizing and democratizing American society. The decentralization and democratization of society will allow more people to participate in the deliberative process. And while this is an end in itself, it also has beneficial consequences—it will give people control over their lives; it will strengthen the ties of community; and it will undermine the feelings of alienation and isolation that individuals supposedly experience in liberal society.

Neoconservatism capitalizes on the republican love affair with the people, its hostility toward elites, its antipathy to the federal government, its resolve to give power back to the people, to the state legislatures, and to local governments. But the neoconservative esteem for the people and for local governments does not have its source in a special fondness for deliberative reasoning, or an appreciation of the delights of politics, or a commitment to democracy; it has its source in its confidence that the sentiments of the people are far less liberal than those of the Washington elite, and can therefore be relied on to reverse the liberal tradition.

Feminism is a multifaceted philosophy. There are liberal feminists, socialist feminists, Marxist feminists, and postmodern feminists. Not all feminists are opposed to liberalism. However, feminists who are disenchanted with the "pornographic state" blame the situation on liberalism.[98] They rightly believe that the liberal devotion to freedom of speech has wittingly or unwittingly engendered a huge industry that appeals to the basest instincts of men and demeans women by turning them into sexual commodities.

Feminists are hostile to neoconservatism, and as I have argued, rightly so. Nevertheless, neoconservatives manage to ally themselves with feminists on the question of pornography. Kristol's essay on pornography and obscenity is likely to win the hearts of many a liberal feminist.[99] But this is not because neoconservatism is committed to the equality of the sexes. Neoconservatives are committed to the family and believe that it cannot survive the equality, let alone the liberation, of women.

The political success of neoconservatism is largely due to its ability to capitalize on these diverse sources of discontent, coupled with its uncanny ability to feed off liberal assumptions while disseminating liberal myths in their most artless form.

The *second* explanation for the political success of neoconservatism has its source in the condition of political disarray that characterizes American liberalism. American liberalism is besieged from all sides, and there are no American politicians who are willing to defend it. In fact, the very word *liberal* has become a term of abuse and opprobrium in American politics. Republicans accuse Democrats of being liberals, and instead of proudly accepting the label, Democrats deny and shun it. When George Bush accused Michael Dukakis of being a liberal in the presidential election of 1988, Dukakis denied it as if it were a terrible accusation. In the elections of 1996, Bob Dole accused Bill Clinton of being a "closet liberal," and Clinton vigorously denied the accusation. It was clear by then that anyone who was going to be a liberal had better keep it a secret. Liberalism has indeed become the L-word, as Terence Ball put it.[100]

The word *liberal* was first used in its political sense in England in the nineteenth century when the Tories referred to their Whig opponents as *liberales*. This was intended pejoratively, and indicated that the ideals espoused by these politicians were somehow un-English. But in Spain, the word *liberale* was used to refer to ideas that were politically advanced, and very English—Lockean principles of constitutional monarchy, limited government, and respect for human rights. The point is that the English politicians who were called *liberales* rejoiced in the name, and this accounts for the transformation of the word in the English language. It went from its Shakespearean sense of gross or licentious to its modern sense of generous, bountiful, openhearted, and open-minded. But in the context of late twentieth-century American politics, the word liberal is once again taking a turn for the worse. Liberal has become once again a word denoting extravagance and licentiousness, but this time with the public purse.

Bob Dole delivered the neoconservative message clearly in the election of 1996; he described himself as the candidate who trusted the people to decide for themselves and govern their own lives, while painting his Democratic opponent as the candidate who trusts the central government and expects it to dictate and control many aspect of life. Bill Clinton could have replied that he does indeed trust the federal government because it is the handiwork of the wisdom of the Founding Fathers. After all, it has a constitution in which the rights of individuals are enshrined, it insists on the liberal principle of the separation of powers, which is a precaution against tyranny, including the tyranny of the majority. Clinton could have said that he has no intention of sweeping away America's liberal traditions in favor of the whims of the people. But Clinton was on the run—just as he denied being a liberal, so he denied being anything other than a populist who put his trust in the people. The reluctance and cowardice of liberal politicians in the face of their opponents is a sure sign of the current *political* weakness of liberalism in America. This is the sort of weakness that will allow neoconservatism to succeed by default.

The *third* explanation for the political success of neoconservatism is the *natural* weakness of liberalism and the inevitable resurgence of a fierce gregariousness that makes men shrink from freedom. The neoconservatives champion an America made up of a single, homogeneous identity shaped by shared religious and nationalistic sentiments, while the postmoderns on the left insist on a multicultural mosaic in which individual identities are shaped by their respective groups. In my view, the difference between neoconservatism and the postmodern left is not as great as is generally believed. Both affirm the primacy of the group over the individual; in other words, they both manifest the human proclivity that accounts for the natural weakness of liberalism.

The fashionable postmodern heirs of Heidegger will have no trek with either liberal rationalism or liberal individualism. They insist that a cold and calculating rationality has smothered us with its barrage of electronic information, its technological wizardry, and its purposeless efficiency. Painfully aware of the reductive scientism and inhumanity that reason has propagated, postmodernism denounces reason altogether as inherently flawed. Reason is condemmed as nothing more than "white mythology" that has been a powerful tool in the colonization of women and the non-Western world. The appeal of postmodernism is its liberating impulse, which is unmistakably attractive in a world where the efforts to manipulate, control, and homogenize human beings have reached new heights of sophistication and audacity. The object of postmodernism is to "deconstruct" the rationalist regime of power, uncover the lie, and liberate us from its clutches. But unfortunately, postmodernism has no faith either in truth or in the possibility of liberation. The only truth that emerges is that there is never any truth independent of power, of groups and their visions, interests, and identities. The individual turns out to be a figment of reason's imagination. The result is a "politics of identity" that leaves individuals entrapped in a cultural, historical, and linguistic web from which they cannot escape. In this way, groups proliferate, and claim the status of the marginalized and silenced. America's liberal heritage notwithstanding, it has become a society in which being on the margins—being excluded, ignored, or left out—is the worst evil.

There is no doubt that liberalism has overstated its inclusiveness. But in truth, liberalism cannot possibly protect individuals from being marginalized, excluded, or ostracized. The liberal ethos encourages individuals to resist the pressures of social conformity; it encourages them to have the courage of their convictions; it hopes that they will be true to themselves even when it is difficult or painful. Liberalism has made great strides in the legal domain; but it cannot protect nonconformists from the effects of social disapprobation and contempt; it cannot shield individuals from social ostracism; nor is it reasonable to expect it to do so. Nonconformists cannot expect approval, acceptance, and approbation. People have to realize that there is a price to pay for standing apart, and if they are strong-minded, they would find it a price worth paying.

Society will always demand conformity. Liberalism cannot change that. What is positively sheepish is the eagerness to belong and to be a nonconformist at the same time. The nonconformists of our time lack the liberal spirit of individuality. They long for acceptance, approval, and recognition. Homosexuals wish to be considered normal; they would like the larger society to think of their brand of sexuality as equally worthy and on a par with heterosexuality; they would like to participate in holy matrimony. They are no longer willing to look upon their lifestyle as unusual and eccentric. They are no longer willing to accept their position on the margins of society, remain defiant, and take pride in their eccentricities.

On the right, the neoconservatives and their Communitarian allies champion a homogeneous America held together by the cement of religion and nationalism—an America that mirrors the homogeneous communitarianism of the old world, a melting pot without individuals, without immigrants, and without plurality. The more the neoconservatives defend the melting pot against multiculturalism and diversity, the more it looks like a straightjacket, and the more it looks like the hypocritical and racially monolithic America that haunts leftist nightmares. This is the America in which only white males need apply. This is the America that has reinvented the golden rule: Those who have the gold make the rules. The clash between left and right polarizes American politics while eclipsing the liberal center.

Their differences notwithstanding, the right and the left contribute to the ascendancy of the lemming spirit. Both reject liberalism because it is supposedly destitute of community. But being destitute of community is a most unlikely affair. Human beings are intensely gregarious, even lemminglike. Liberalism is a remedy for our pathological gregariousness. It is a heroic achievement against nearly insurmountable odds. It appeals to us as individuals, and not as members of groups. It implores us to stand alone, to be autonomous, to think for ourselves, and to resist conformity. In a sense, liberalism defies what comes naturally, what is easy and pleasant—the desire to belong, to be accepted, and to be recognized. As a result, its triumph is necessarily precarious.

The *fourth* explanation for the political success of neoconservatism is connected to the political strategy that I have called the populist ploy.

There is a sense in which America is more puritan than liberal at heart. Her puritan instincts inspire her with a desire for modesty, sobriety, and restraint. In contrast, her official documents, or her "parchment regime" as Joseph Cropsey calls it, push her in the direction of immodesty, permissiveness, and licentiousness. The result is that she has become repellent to herself. She has been dubbed the "pornographic state," but this is not altogether accurate. A pornographic state is hedonistic and carefree, but America is tortured by her own moral failing. She is like a prostitute with the heart of an ayatollah. Her puritanism is at war with the permissive character of her liberalism. In this state of self-loathing it is not difficult for wily politicians to convince her that her liberal regime is the albatross around her neck and that if she is to save herself and regain her honor, she must realize that liberalism has outlived its purpose and has now become a liability. Its original purpose was to secure religious freedom; it was but a means to an end. As it turned out, so the story goes, this freedom was secured at the expense of her soul. Liberalism provided religious liberty, but the cost was the atrophy of religion itself. Having driven it into the private sphere, liberalism has robbed religion of its public life, its vitality and its power. Relying on the conflict between America's puritanical spirit and her liberal regime, the neoconservative strategy consists in driving a wedge between American democracy and American liberalism. Convinced that America's liberalism will prove to be her undoing, the Strauss-inspired neoconservatives are bent on rescuing America from her liberal heritage. The strategy relies on America's puritanical longing for virtue—a longing that is ultimately incompatible with the love of freedom. The political success of neoconservatism depends on the capacity for the desire for virtue to triumph over the love of freedom.

Instead of cautiously guarding against the ills of democracy, neoconservatism has embraced a populist strategy that leaves America vulnerable to the tyranny of the not-so-silent majority. Like Strauss, the neoconservatives are convinced that democracy is preferable to liberalism, especially if the right elite is in power; and they fancy themselves the aristocrats that will lead the people back to political health and well-being. But unhappily, this Strauss-inspired elite combines democratic populism with a profound disdain for the populace. It is the sort of elite that is ready, willing, and able to use almost any means to achieve its end. It is not a question of a thirst for power; the neoconservatives believe that

the glory of their end is bound to excuse any means that may prove to be necessary or useful. For their mission is nothing short of the salvation of America—in fact, of Western civilization itself. The sense of impending catastrophe and crisis naturally leads people to assume that in these perilous circumstances, extraordinary measures are both necessary and justifiable. Not surprisingly, neoconservatives identify their political opponents as the enemy, and therefore introduce into domestic politics a friend/foe mentality that transforms the political contest into a life-and-death struggle against diabolical forces.

In short, neoconservatism is the legacy of Leo Strauss. It echoes all the dominant features of his philosophy—the political importance of religion, the necessity of nationalism, the language of nihilism, the sense of crisis, the friend/foe mentality, the hostility toward women, the rejection of modernity, the nostalgia for the past, and the abhorrence of liberalism. And having established itself as the dominant ideology of the Republican party, it threatens to remake America in its own image.

# NOTES

## PREFACE

1. Richard Lacayo, "But Who has the Power?" *Time* (June 17, 1996), p. 43.

## CHAPTER 1

1. Leo Strauss, *On Tyranny* (Ithaca, N. Y.: Cornell University Press, 1963), p. 26.
2. Gordon S. Wood, "The Fundamentalists and the Constitution," *New York Review of Books* (February 1988), pp. 33-40.
3. Hanna Rosin, "Memo Master," *The New Republic* (November 7, 1994), pp. 22-28. Documents the political style of William Kristol, son of Irving Kristol and Gertrude Himmelfarb. He went to a private school, then to Harvard where he studied with Straussian guru, Harvey C. Mansfield, Jr., who is well known for his study of Machiavelli and his interest in executive power. Kristol wrote a doctoral dissertation arguing that the judiciary should assume its role as the elite, and stop the popular desire for radical change. Rosin paints him as an unprincipled political opportunist and partisan politician whose timely memos are quick to set the agendas of Republican politicians on the issues of the day. See also Jacob Weisberg, "The Family Way: How Irving Kristol, Gertrude Himmelfarb, and their son William Kristol, became the family that liberals love to hate," *The New Yorker* (October 21 and 28, 1996), pp. 180-89. Describes the think-tank founded by William Kristol and called Project for Republican Future, as consisting merely of William Kristol and a fax machine. But the memos he generated became important strategies for the GOP during President Bill Clinton's first two years in office. William Kristol is credited with the defeat of health-care reform; apparently, he sent a memo arguing that Republicans must reject *whatever* Clinton proposes because any health-care reform would be a credit to the Democrats. William Kristol also founded a magazine, *The Weekly Standard,* where he predicted the defeat of Bob Dole in the presidential elections of 1996, and supported Colin Powell for president and leader of the Republican party, even though he admitted that he did not agree with Powell on anything—but

no matter, Powell looked like a winner, and that's the necessary first step. Once the election is won, the candidate can always be reconstructed. These attitudes to politics and power are not surprising for someone nourished on the ideas of Leo Strauss and Machiavelli.

4. For an account of Straussian intellectuals in Washington, see Jacob Weisberg, "The Cult of Leo Strauss: An Obscure Philosopher's Washington Disciples," *Newsweek* (August 3, 1987), p. 61; James Atlas, "Look Who's the Opinion Elite Now" *New York Times Magazine* (February 12, 1995), sec. 6; Robert Devigne, *Recasting Conservatism: Oakeshott, Strauss, and the Response to Postmodernism* (New Haven, Conn.: Yale University Press, 1994), pp. 58-59, esp. note 76. Devigne provides a long list of less well-known Straussians who left the academy in favor of politics. In my view, the Straussian move out of the academy and into the political arena makes perfect sense. William Kristol said he could not imagine himself being a scholar for the rest of his life. The reason is that a scholar is someone who feels that the search for truth is incomplete, but Straussians emerge from the academy knowing the truths of political life. The only logical thing left to do is to change the world accordingly, or whisper in the ears of those who are powerful enough to do so.

5. Richard Bernstein, "A Very Unlikely Villain (or Hero)," *New York Times* (January 29, 1995), p. E4.

6. See for example, Brent Staples, "Undemocratic Vistas: The Sinister Vogue of Leo Strauss," *New York Times,* November 28, 1994, p. 14.

7. The best account of the history and the spirit of Weimar is Peter Gay's *Weimar Culture* (New York: Harper Torchbooks, 1968).

8. Plato, *Republic,* translated by G. M. A. Grube, (Indianapolis, Ind.: Hackett Publishing Co. Inc., 1974), Book VIII.

9. "Preface," *Spinoza's Critique of Religion* (1930), E. M. Sinclair, trans. (New York: Schocken Books, 1965), p. 1.

10. Hiram Caton, "Explaining the Nazis: Leo Strauss Today," *Quadrant* (October 1986), pp. 61-65.

11. Allan Bloom, *The Closing of the American Mind* (New York: Simon & Schuster, 1987), p. 151.

12. Ibid., p. 152.

13. Leo Strauss, "Why We Remain Jews: Can Jewish Faith and History Still Speak to Us?" *Leo Strauss: Political Philosopher and Jewish Thinker,* Kenneth L. Deutsch and Walter Nicgorski, eds. (Lanham Md,: Rowman & Littlefield, 1994), p. 11.

14. Leo Strauss, *Liberalism Ancient and Modern* (New York: Basic Books, 1968), pp. 260 ff.

15. Ibid.

16. Harry Neumann points out that Rudolph Hess invented the idea of the politically infallible führer and turned it into a reality. A man could become infallible if everyone around him treated him and his commands

as such, and under no circumstance criticized him or appealed to independent standards to evaluate him. In this way, the nihilist void would be filled. See his *Liberalism* (Durham, N.C.: Carolina Academic Press, 1991).

17. John Stuart Mill, *On Liberty* (1859) (New York: W. W. Norton & Co., 1975).

18. For a fuller elaboration on this and other aspects of Leo Strauss's political philosophy, see Shadia B. Drury, *The Political Ideas of Leo Strauss* (New York: St. Martin's Press, 1988), p. 84.

19. Joseph Cropsey, "The United States as Regime and the Sources of the American Way of Life," in Robert H. Horowitz, ed., *The Moral Foundations of the American Republic* (Charlottesville, Va.: University Press of Virginia, 1986), pp. 177, 171.

20. Leo Strauss, *City and Man* (Chicago, Ill.: University of Chicago Press, 1964), introduction.

21. Ibid.

22. Charles R. Kesler, "Is Conservatism Un-American?" *National Review,* vol. 38, no. 5 (March 22, 1985), pp. 28-37; Clinton Rossiter, *Conservatism in America: The Thankless Persuasion,* 2nd ed. (New York: Knopf, 1962).

23. This is the subtle message of Thomas Pangle's book, *The Ennobling of Democracy* (Baltimore, Md.: The Johns Hopkins University Press, 1992).

24. Leo Strauss, *What is Political Philosophy?* (New York: Free Press, 1959); Leo Strauss, *Persecution and the Art of Writing* (Westport, Conn.: Greenwood Press, 1952).

25. Reported in *Time* (May 15, 1995), p. 22.

26. See "The Gospel According to Ralph," *Time* (May 15, 1995), pp. 18-27.

27. Ibid., p. 21.

28. Michael Lind, "Rev. Robertson's Grand International Conspiracy Theory," a review of Pat Robertson, *The New World Order* in *New York Review of Books* (February 2, 1995), pp. 21-25.

29. Reed is quoted by Michael Lind, ibid., p. 21.

30. *Contract With America* (New York: Random House, 1994), p. 182.

31. Ibid.

32. Listed in "Enemies of the State," *Time* (May 8, 1995), pp. 16-27.

33. Quoted in *Time* (May 1, 1995), p. 27.

34. Leo Strauss, *City and Man* (Chicago, Ill.: University of Chicago Press, 1964), pp. 87, 97, 111; Leo Strauss, *On Tyranny* (Ithaca, N.Y.: Cornell University Press, 1968), p. 94; Leo Strauss, *Xenophon's Socrates* (Ithaca, N.Y.: Cornell University Press, 1972), p. 50; Leo Strauss, *Xenophon's Socratic Discourse* (Ithaca, N.Y.: Cornell University Press, 1970), p. 85; Leo Strauss, *Natural Right and History* (Chicago, Ill.: University of Chicago Press, 1953), p. 150 n.

35. For a brief but excellent account of the history of liberalism, see Terence Ball and Richard Dagger, *Political Ideologies and the Democratic Ideal* (New York: HarperCollins Publishers Inc., 1991).

36. John Stuart Mill, *On Liberty.*

37. Ibid., ch. III.

38. T. H. Green, *Political Theory,* John R. Rodman, ed. (New York: Meredith Corporation, 1964); John Rawls, *A Theory of Justice* (Cambridge, Mass.: Harvard University Press, 1971).

39. Isaiah Berlin, *Four Essays on Liberty* (Oxford, England: Oxford University Press, 1969). There is a wealth of literature on this topic. See, for example, Charles Taylor, "What's Wrong with Negative Liberty," in A. Ryan, ed., *The Idea of Freeedom* (Oxford, England: Oxford University Press, 1979), pp. 175-93; John Gray, "On Negative and Positive Liberty," *Political Studies,* vol. 28 (1980), pp. 507-26; Quentin Skinner, "The Idea of Negative Liberty: Philosophical and Historical Perspectives," *Philosophy in History: Essays on the Historiography of Philosophy,* R. Rorty, J.B. Schneewind, and Q. Skinner, eds. (Cambridge, England: Cambridge University Press, 1984), pp. 193-221; Gerard MacCallum, "Negative and Positive Freedom," *The Philosophical Review,* vol. 76 (July 1967), pp. 312-34.

40. Paul Gottfried and Thomas Fleming, *The Conservative Movement* (Boston, Mass.: Twayne Publishers, 1988). A critical account of the rise of American conservatism written from the point of view of a traditional or classical conservative as opposed to a neoconservative.

41. The most recent representative of libertarianism is Robert Nozick, *Anarchy, State, and Utopia* (New York: Basic Books, 1974).

42. The information is from Seymour Martin Lipset, "American Intellectuals—Mostly on the Left, Some Politically Incorrect," in his *American Exceptionalism* (New York: W.W. Norton & Co., 1996). Lipset explains how the neoconservatives were wooed by Ronald Reagan and the Republicans.

## CHAPTER 2

1. Leo Strauss, "Why We Remain Jews: Can Jewish Faith and History Still Speak to Us?" A lecture delivered on February 4, 1962, at the Hillel Foundation, published posthumously in *Leo Strauss: Political Philosopher and Jewish Thinker,* Kenneth L. Deutsch and Walter Nicgorski, eds. (Lanham, Md.: Rowman & Littlefield, 1994), p. 73.

2. Ibid., pp. 49, 60.

3. Ibid., p. 44.

4. Ibid., p. 49.

5. Ibid., p. 55.

6. Ibid., p. 44.

7. Leo Strauss, "Progress or Return?" in *Rebirth of Classical Political Rationalism*, T. L. Pangle, ed. (Chicago, Ill.: University of Chicago Press, 1989), p. 241.

8. Leo Strauss, "Preface," *Spinoza's Critique of Religion* (1930), translated by E. M. Sinclair (New York: Schocken Books, 1965), pp. 2-3.

9. Ibid., p. 15.

10. Ibid., pp. 9, 13, 15. It is significant to note that the book is dedicated to the memory of Franz Rosenzweig. It is not unfair to describe Rosenzweig as a Jewish existentialist because he eschewed the philosophical search for essences as an abstract and meaningless way of reaching the truth. Instead, he suggested starting with human experience, particularly the human fear in the face of death. He thought that this experience is the root of the experience of God. And even though Rosenzweig was tempted to convert to Christianity, he decided against it because he thought that being a Christian meant searching for God, but that being Jewish meant being already with God, or chosen to be with God.

11. Strauss, "Why We Remain Jews, " p. 45.

12. Ibid., p. 46.

13. Strauss, "Preface," *Spinoza's Critique of Religion*, p. 5; Theodor Herzl is a leading Zionist and author of *The Jewish State*.

14. Strauss, "Why We Remain Jews," p. 75.

15. Strauss, "Preface," *Spinoza's Critique of Religion*, p. 6; Strauss, "Progress or Return?," pp. 227-70; Strauss, "Why We Remain Jews," p. 49.

16. Strauss, "Why We Remain Jews," p. 49.

17. Ibid.

18. Karl Marx, "On the Jewish Question," in *Early Writings*, T. B. Bottomore, ed. and trans. (New York: McGraw Hill, 1963), pp. 3-31.

19. Erich Fromm, in *Escape From Freedom* (New York: Holt, Rinehart and Winston, 1941) applies this idea to the understanding of the holocaust. He argues that the dissolution of feudalism and the triumph of capitalism was the source of profound human alienation and homelessness that accounts for the appeal of the Fascist demand for oneness and unity in the state. The freedom of capitalist individualism was intolerable; people needed an escape from freedom. His argument relies heavily on Marx's essay in the next note.

20. Marx, "On the Jewish Question," p. 29.

21. Ibid., p. 30, Marx's emphasis; Rousseau, *Social Contract*, bk. II, ch. 7.

22. Strauss, "Preface," *Spinoza's Critique of Religion*, p. 7.

23. Ibid.

24. Strauss, "An Introduction to Heideggerian Existentialism," in *The Rebirth of Classical Political Rationalism*, p. 42.

25. Ibid., see also Strauss, "Why We Remain Jews," p. 67.

26. For a full account of Strauss's view of religion, see Shadia B. Drury, *The Political Ideas of Leo Strauss* (New York: St. Martin's Press, 1988), esp. ch. 3.

27. Strauss, "Why We Remain Jews," p. 69; Strauss, "Preface," *Spinoza's Critique of Religion,* p. 21.

28. This is one of the themes of Emil L. Fackenheim's work. See for example his *God's Presence in History: Jewish Affirmations and Philosophical Reflections* (New York: New York University Press, 1970), and *What Is Judaism?* (New York: Collier Books, 1987). Fackenheim's view is that God was present at Auschwitz, even though we don't understand what he was doing there. But out of the cataclysm has emerged a new commandment: Jews, do not give Hitler a posthumous victory, survive and do not despair of the God of Israel, lest Judaism perish. Fackenheim is caught in an impossible dilemma: After the holocaust, it is difficult to be Jewish in the old sense of accepting Jewish martyrdom as God's will, but at the same time, it is difficult to assimilate. For Fackenheim, the state of Israel is the solution.

29. Isaiah Berlin, "Jewish Slavery and Emancipation," *Hebrew University Garland,* Norman Bentwich, ed. (London, England: Constellation Books, 1952).

30. There is a remarkable resemblance between Berlin's position and that of Justice Clarence Thomas regarding the assimilation of black people in America. See Juan Williams, "A Question of Fairness," *The Atlantic Monthly* (February, 1987), pp. 71-82. For an account of this essay and essays by Thomas see Annotated Bibliography.

31. Strauss, "Preface," *Spinoza's Critique of Religion,* p. 5; Strauss, "Why We Remain Jews," p. 60.

32. Strauss, "Why We Remain Jews," p. 51. According to Strauss, Spinoza was the first to propose political Zionism as a solution to the Jewish problem. But Spinoza also thought that their religion made the Jews so effeminate that they were unlikely to restore the state by their own efforts. Strauss, "Why We Remain Jews," p. 50; also Strauss, "Preface," *Spinoza's Critique of Religion,* pp. 5-6; Strauss, "Progress or Return?," in *The Rebirth of Classical Political Rationalism,* p. 231.

33. Strauss, "Why We Remain Jews," p. 51.

34. A more extreme version of this position is held by Rabbi Joel Teitelbaum according to whom the holocaust was God's punishment for Zionism because the latter is not content to wait for God's messianic redemption.

35. Strauss, "Why We Remain Jews," p. 60. For Strauss, political Zionism is arid and must be supplemented with something more. Cultural Zionism has attempted to fill the void, but a few folk dances will not do. Culture is not enough; divine revelation—the Bible, the Talmud, and the Midrash—is necessary.

36. Ibid., p. 56.

37. See the correspondence between Strauss and Karl Löwith, *Independent Journal of Philosophy,* vols. 5 and 6 (1988), p. 185, where Strauss ends one of his letters by saying, "By the way: I am *not* an orthodox Jew!" (his emphasis).

38. Strauss, "Why We Remain Jews," p. 61.

39. Strauss, "Preface," *Spinoza's Critique of Religion*, p. 2.

40. Joseph Mazzini, *The Duties of Man and Other Essays* (New York: E. P. Dutton & Co., 1907).

41. I am deeply indebted to Elie Kedourie's brilliant and lucid work, *Nationalism*, fourth expanded edition (Oxford, England: Blackwell, 1993).

42. Leo Strauss, "The State of Israel, " *National Review*, vol. 3, no. 1 (5 January, 1957), p. 23.

43. Ibid.

44. Gotthold Ephraim Lessing, *Nathan the Wise* (1779), Bayard Quincy Morgan, trans. (New York: Frederick Ungar Publishing Co., 1955).

45. See Drury, *The Political Ideas of Leo Strauss,* esp. chs. 4, 5, and 11.

46. Strauss, "Exoteric Teaching," originally in *Interpretation: A Journal of Political Philosophy,* vol. 14 (1986), pp. 51-59, reprinted in Leo Strauss, *The Rebirth of Classical Political Rationalism*, pp. 63-71. I will refer to the latter.

47. Gotthold Ephraim Lessing, "Ernst and Falk: Conversations for the Freemasons," William L. Zwiebel, trans., in Lessing, *Nathan the Wise, Minna Von Barnhelm, and Other Plays and Writings,* Peter Demetz, ed., with a foreword by Hannah Arendt (New York: Continuum Publishing Co., 1991). "Lessing's Dialogues for Freemansons," was also translated by Chaninah Maschler for *Interpretation,* vol. 14, no. 1 (January 1986), pp. 1-49. I will refer to the translations by Zwiebel. To further support his theory, Strauss relies on Jacobi's claim that Lessing came to prefer ecclesiastical despots to secular ones: Strauss, "Exoteric Teaching," p. 70. This is a highly dubious claim because it is both irrational and contrary to the spirit of Lessing. It is irrational to think that ecclesiastical despots are better than secular ones because despots are despots regardless of how they justify their treachery. But it is plausible to argue that ecclesiastical despots are far more odious than secular ones because their hypocrisy and their lies defile the beautiful and sacred core of the faith that they exploit. In a posthumously published fragment, Lessing describes monks and soldiers as comparable: the former are the defenders of the church, the later are the defenders of the state. And he adds that neither is to be preferred to the other any more than mice are to be preferred to slugs. Quoted in James Sime, *Lessing,* vol.II (London, England: Kegan Paul, 1896), p. 288.

48. Stanley Rosen, *Hermeneutics as Politics* (Oxford, England: Oxford University Press, 1987), esp. ch. 3. Rosen suggests that Strauss's secret teaching was but an empty vessel, a ploy to acquire disciples. But when asked why bother acquiring disciplines, Rosen's is that ideas make the world, and if you have enough people in influential positions thinking in a particular way, then you have the power to shape the world. But if that is the case,

then there must be some teaching or doctrine according to which the world is to be changed. Rosen's view is flawed.

49. Lessing, "Ernst and Falk," p. 299.

50. Gotthold Ephraim Lessing, "The Religion of Christ" (1780) Henry Chadwick, trans., in *Nathan The Wise, Minna Von Barnhelm, and Other Plays and Writings,* pp. 334-35.

51. Lessing, *Nathan the Wise,* p. 7.

52. Strauss, "A Note on Lucretius," *Liberalism Ancient and Modern,* (Ithaca, N.Y.: Cornell University Press, 1968), pp. 76-139. See also Drury's discussion of Strauss on Lucretius in *The Political Ideas of Leo Strauss,* pp. 62-71.

53. Jacobi was the subject of Strauss's doctoral dissertation at the University of Hamburg in 1921. Jacobi was a Christian who believed that reason leads to atheism, skepticism, nihilism, and maybe even to megalomaniacal delusions about being the center of the universe. Jacobi knew Lessing, and after the latter's death, Jacobi published an account of a conversation in which he claimed that prior to his death, Lessing confided in him that he was a follower of Spinoza, which in those days meant that he was an atheist. This was important in corroborating Jacobi's own belief that rationalism leads to atheism. But Lessing's friend, Moses Mendelssohn, saw it as libel of his dear friend, and naturally came to his defense, sparking the famous controversy between Jacobi and Mendelssohn over Lessing's pantheism—a controversy that continues to this day. It seems to me that whether Lessing was an atheist, a deist, a devout Christian, or a pantheist like Spinoza, is not that important, because for Lessing, conduct was more important than belief. Nevertheless, Jacobi's story is probably quite reliable since Lessing was influenced by Spinoza, who was a liberal-minded rationalist like himself. Strauss takes Jacobi's side in maintaining that reason is destructive of faith and that faith cannot be based on reason. But unlike Jacobi, Strauss does not opt for a leap of faith. See Gérard Vallée, ed., *The Spinoza Conversations Between Lessing and Jacobi,* G. Valée, J. B. Lawson, and C. G. Chapple, trans. (Lanham, Md.: University Press of America, 1988).

54. See, for example, Kenneth Hart Green, *Jew and Philosopher: The Return of Maimonides in the Jewish Thought of Leo Strauss* (Albany, N.Y.: State University of New York Press, 1993); see also Shadia Drury's review essay of Hart's book, "The Jewish Thought of Leo Strauss?" *Shofar: An Interdisciplinary Journal of Jewish Studies,* vol. 13, no. 2 (Winter 1995), pp. 81-85.

55. Leo Strauss, "The Literary Character of the *Guide for the Perplexed,*" in Strauss's *Persecution and the Art of Writing* (Chicago, Ill.: University of Chicago Press, 1952); Strauss, "How to Begin to Study the Guide of the

Perplexed," in Moses Maimonides, *The Guide of the Perplexed*, Shlomo Pines, trans. (Chicago, Ill.: University of Chicago Press, 1963), pp. xi-lvi.

56. Leon Roth, *The Guide For the Perplexed* (New York: Hutchinson's University Library, 1948), p. 10.

57. For an account of the debates about Maimonides within the Jewish tradition, see Marvin Fox's excellent work, *Interpreting Maimonides* (Chicago, Ill.: The University of Chicago Press, 1990).

58. Leo Strauss, *Philosophy and Law: Essays Toward the Understanding of Maimonides and his Predecessors* (1935), Fred Baumann, trans., with a foreword by Ralph Lerner (New York: The Jewish Publication Society, 1987), p. 13.

59. Ibid., p. 15.

60. Ibid., pp. 15, 17.

61. Ibid., pp. 13-18.

62. Ibid., p. 18.

63. Ibid.

64. Ibid., p. 46.

65. Ibid., p. 47.

66. Leo Strauss, "On Abravanel's Philosophical Tendency and Political Teaching," *Isaac Abravanel: Six Lectures,* J.B. Trend and H. Loewe, eds. (Cambridge, England: Cambridge University Press, 1937), p. 97.

67. Strauss, *Philosophy and Law,* pp. 62, 69.

68. Ibid., p. 63.

69. Ibid., pp. 64, 65.

70. Ibid., pp. 64, 69, 74, 82.

71. Ibid., p. 66.

72. Ibid., 67, 69.

73. Ibid., pp. 67, 68. Strauss acknowledges that there are many passages in which Averroës speaks of the superiority of revelation over reason, but Strauss doubts their authenticity. When Averroës says that the truths of law are beyond reason, Strauss denies that this is an indication of the superiority of law, but merely the claim that the truths contained in the law are not rationally knowable or supportable.

74. Ibid., p. 72.

75. Ibid., p. 74.

76. Ibid.

77. Ibid., p. 82.

78. Ibid.

79. Ibid., pp. 47-48.

80. Ibid., p. 84.

81. Ibid., p. 84.

82. Ibid., pp. 90-91, 51.

83. Ibid., pp. 50, 97-98, 103.

84. Ibid., pp. 103, 50, 97, 98.

85. Ibid., p. 99.

86. Ibid.

87. See Drury, *The Political Ideas of Leo Strauss,* ch. 4.

88. Strauss, *Philosophy and Law,* p. 99.

89. Ibid., p. 89. Strauss reports that Maimonides expects the prophet to be morally excellent, but Strauss refuses to put too much emphasis on that requirement.

90. Ibid., pp. 56, 103, 110. Strauss thinks that despite appearances to the contrary, Maimonides and the Falasifa are more Platonist than Aristotelian. But Strauss undermines the difference between Plato and Aristotle. Both agree that philosophy is the highest life and the philosopher is the most perfect man. But whereas Aristotle leaves philosophy in its natural freedom, Plato "compels" it to play a political role.

91. Maimonides, *Guide of the Perplexed,* pp. 6, 10, 15, 20.

92. Ibid., p. 20.

93. Ibid., p. 18.

94. Gershom G. Scholem, *Major Trends in Jewish Mysticism* (New York: Schocken Books, 1946); Gershom Scholem, *On the Kabbalah and Its Symbolism,* Ralph Manheim, trans. (New York: Schocken Books, 1977). I have also learned a great deal from David Bakan, *Sigmund Freud and the Jewish Mystical Tradition* (Toronto, Ontario: D. Van Nostrand Co., Inc., 1958).

95. Scholem, *On the Kabbalah and Its Symbolism,* p. 57.

96. Maimonides, *Guide of the Perplexed,* p. 6.

97. Franz Rosenzweig, *The Star of Redemption,* William W. Hallo, trans. (New York: Holt, Rinehart and Winston, 1970).

98. Strauss does not use those terms, but he argues explicitly against the soft version in his "Exoteric Teaching," pp. 67-69.

99. Strauss, *Philosophy and Law,* p. 89.

100. Plato, *Republic,* G. M. A. Grube, trans. (Indianapolis, Ind.: Hackett Publishing Co., 1974), 382A–382D.

101. Strauss was respectful of Cohen, but for the most part he thought of him as someone who provided "comfort" not truth, and hence not a philosopher in Strauss's sense of the word. See Strauss's comments on Cohen in his "Preface," *Spinoza's Critique of Religion;* also his introduction to the English translation of Cohen's *Religion of Reason Out of the Sources of Judaism* (New York: Frederick Ungar, 1972), also reprinted in Strauss, *Studies in Platonic Political Philosophy,* T. L. Pangle, ed. (Chicago, Ill.: University of Chicago Press, 1983), pp. 233-47.

102. Hermann Cohen, *Reason and Hope: Selections from the Jewish Writings of Hermann Cohen,* Eva Jospe, trans. (New York: W. W. Norton & Co., Inc., 1971); see also Ernst Cassirer, "Herman Cohen, 1842-1918," *Social Research,* vol. 10 (1943), pp. 233-47. Cassirer was a student of Cohen's.

103. "A Giving of Accounts: Jacob Klein and Leo Strauss," an exchange between Klein and Strauss at St. John's College, Annapolis, Maryland, January 30, 1970, published in *The College,* vol. 22 (April 1970), pp. 1-5, see especially p. 4 where Strauss admits that in his scheme of things, morality does not enjoy a particularly high status.

104. Bakan, *Sigmund Freud and the Jewish Mystical Tradition,* p. 264.

105. Strauss thought that Maimonidies was the first Kabbalist, and that he was the first to transmit the secret teaching in writing, and hence his need for caution; see Strauss, *Persecution and the Art of Writing,* p. 51.

106. Bakan, *Sigmund Freud and the Jewish Mystical Tradition,* p. 41. These lines were echoed by Mephistopheles in Goethe's *Faust,* Part I, scene 4.

107. Strauss, *Persecution and the Art of Writing,* pp. 35-36. For a more detailed discussion of this work see Drury, *The Political Ideas of Leo Strauss,* ch. 2.

108. Strauss, "Jerusalem and Athens," *Studies in Platonic Political Philosophy,* pp. 147-73; also Strauss, "On the Interpretation of Genesis," *L'Homme: revue française d'anthropologie,* vol. xxi, no. 1 (Janvier-Mars 1981), pp. 5-20.

109. I am very indebted to Bakan's discussion of sexuality in Jewish mysticism. See his *Sigmund Freud and the Jewish Mystical Tradition,* pp. 272 ff. See also Scholem, *Major Trends in Jewish Mysticism,* p. 235 ff.

110. Leo Strauss, *City and Man* (Chicago, Ill.: University of Chicago Press, 1964), p. 111. This is also Freud's view.

111. Bakan, *Sigmund Freud and the Jewish Mystical Tradition,* p. 277.

112. Leo Strauss, *Rebirth of Classical Political Rationalism,* pp. 116-17.

113. Strauss, "Jerusalem and Athens," in *Studies in Platonic Political Philosophy,* p. 164; Strauss, *Natural Right and History* (Chicago, Ill.: University of Chicago Press, 1953), pp. 93-94; Drury, *The Political Ideas of Leo Strauss,* ch. 3.

114. Scholem, *Major Trends in Jewish Mysticism,* pp. 290, 293.

115. When Zevi went to Turkey declaring that, as part of his messianic mission, he was going to dethrone the sultan who ruled over the holy land, he was arrested. The Turkish authorities gave him a choice; either death or conversion to Islam. He converted in a public ceremony. Yet strangely, his apostasy did not disillusion all his followers. Many continued to believe that he was the Messiah, and that his apostasy was part of the necessary descent into the realm of darkness that was represented by Islam.

116. Scholem, *Major Trends in Jewish Mysticism,* p. 318.

117. Strauss accepts the Machiavellian doctrine according to which moral considerations have no place in politics and power. This explains why he felt compelled to undermine Maimonides's insistence on the moral perfection of the philosopher-prophet. See his *Thoughts of Machiavelli* (Chicago, Ill.: University of Chicago Press, 1958). See also Drury, *The Political Ideas of Leo Strauss,* ch. 6.

CHAPTER 3

1. The best available account of Strauss's early intellectual life in Germany is by John G. Gunnell, "Strauss Before Straussianism: The Weimar Conversation," *Vital Nexus,* vol. 1, no. 1 (May 1990), pp. 73-104. Other versions of the same paper can be found in *The Review of Politics,* vol. 53, no. 1 (Winter 1991), pp. 53-74, and Kenneth L. Deutsch and Walter Nicgorski, eds., *Leo Strauss: Political Philosopher and Jewish Thinker* (Lanham, Md.: Rowman & Littlefield Publishers Inc., 1994). See also John G. Gunnell, *The Descent of Political Theory* (Chicago, Ill.: University of Chicago Press, 1993). See the annotated bibliography.

2. Victor Farias, *Heidegger and Nazism,* Paul Burrell and Gabriel Ricci, trans. (Philadelphia, Penn.: Temple University Press, 1989). The strength of Farias's book does not rest with the lucidity of its prose or the sharpness of its philosophical analysis. But there is no denying that the book reveals, through never before published letters and documents, a new Heidegger. Heidegger can no longer be regarded as the naive philosopher overtaken by shrewd worldly political men and the events of the 1930s. No longer can his defenders regard his escapade with nazism as the childish enthusiasm of a philosopher whose head was in the clouds and who could not be expected to understand politics (as Hannah Arendt would like us to believe). Farias's book reveals a man who has always been keenly interested in politics, and not just a fumbling theoretician who did not know what he was doing. See also Thomas Sheehan, "Heidegger and the Nazis" and "A Normal Nazi," *New York Review of Books* (June 16, 1988 and January 14, 1993, respectively), pp. 38-47 and 30-50.

3. Martin Heidegger, *Being and Time,* John Macquarrie and Edward Robinson, trans. (New York: Harper & Row, 1962); see also Richard Wolin, ed., *The Heidegger Controversy: A Critical Reader* (New York: Columbia University Press, 1991), a collection of essays on Heidegger's involvement with the Nazis that includes Heidegger's political speeches as well as his famous interview with *Der Spiegel* of 1966, which was published only after his death.

4. Leo Tolstoy, *The Death of Ivan Ilych* (1886) (New York: Penguin Books, 1960). This story is often regarded as a superior version of Heidegger's account of human angst in the face of death. But Tolstoy's ending is not Heideggerian. Ivan experiences a conversion on his deathbed. He realizes that he has not lived rightly and that this is why he has so much angst in the face of death.

5. Jean-Paul Sartre, *Saint Genet* (Paris, France: Gallimard, 1952).

6. Ralph Waldo Emerson, *Essays and Lectures* (New York: The Library of America, 1983), p. 262.

7. Heidegger's political speeches can be found in Richard Wolin, ed., *The Heidegger Controversy: A Critical Reader* .

8. Karl Löwith, "My Last Meeting with Heidegger in Rome, 1936," and "The Political Implications of Heidegger's Existentialism," both in *New German Critique,* no. 45 (Fall 1988), pp. 115-34. The latter essay was originally published in *Les Temps Modernes,* vol. 14 (1946-47), pp. 343-60. The view that Heidegger's philosophy is logically connected to his support for the Nazi party is widely supported by scholars today. See Richard Wolin, *The Politics of Being: The Political Thought of Martin Heidegger* (New York: Columbia University Press, 1990). See also Richard Wolin, ed., *The Heidegger Controversy: A Critical Reader,* which includes critical essays by Löwith, Marcuse, Habermas, Jaspers, and others.

9. Leo Strauss, "An Introduction to Heideggerian Existentialism," in *The Rebirth of Classical Political Rationalism,* T. L. Pangle, ed. (Chicago, Ill.: University of Chicago Press, 1989).

10. Leo Strauss, "Preface," *Spinoza's Critique of Religion,* E. M. Sinclair, trans. (New York: Schocken Books, 1965), p. 4.

11. See the excellent discussion of Nazi ideas in James M. Rhodes, *The Hitler Movement: A Modern Millenarian Revolution* (Stanford, Calif.: Hoover Institution Press, 1980). The book contains the Nazi campaign poster that I am describing.

12. Strauss, "Preface," *Spinoza's Critique of Religion,* p. 12.

13. Ibid.

14. Strauss, "Heideggerian Existentialism," *The Rebirth of Classical Political Rationalism,* p. 40.

15. Ibid.

16. Strauss, "Preface," *Spinoza's Critique of Religion,* p. 12; see also "Philosophy as Rigorous Science and Political Philosophy," reprinted in *Studies in Platonic Political Philosophy,* T. L. Pangle, ed. (Chicago, Ill.: University of Chicago Press, 1983), p. 32.

17. Strauss, "Heideggerian Existentialism," *The Rebirth of Classical Political Rationalism,* p. 40.

18. Ibid., p. 41.

19. Ibid., see also Strauss, "Preface," *Spinoza's Critique of Religion,* p. 12.

20. Ibid.

21. Strauss, "Heideggerian Existentialism," *The Rebirth of Classical Political Rationalism,* p. 41; see also Leo Strauss, *Natural Right and History* (Chicago, Ill.: University of Chicago Press, 1950), p. 26, where Strauss draws a close parallel between Nietzsche and Plato.

22. Strauss, "Heideggerian Existentialism," *The Rebirth of Classical Political Rationalism,* p. 42.

23. Ibid., p. 14.

24. Ibid., p. 42.

25. Ibid.

26. Ibid., p. 41.

27. Ibid., pp. 30, 36; Strauss, "Philosophy as Rigorous Science," *Studies in Platonic Political Philosophy,* p. 30.

28. Strauss, *Natural Right and History,* p. 26.

29. Strauss, *The Rebirth of Classical Political Rationalism,* p. 206.

30. Leo Strauss, *On Tyranny* (Ithaca, N. Y.: Cornell University Press, 1968), p. 210.

31. Victor Gourevitch, "Philosophy and Politics: II," *Review of Metaphysics,* vol. 22, no. 2 (December 1968), p. 325; James F. Ward, "Experience and Political Philosophy: Notes on Reading Leo Strauss," *Polity,* vol. 13, no. 4 (Summer 1981), p. 681.

32. Terence Penelhum, *God and Skepticism: A Study in Skepticism and Fideism* (Boston: D. Reidel Publishing Company, 1983). I am indebted to Terence Penelhum for the discussion of skepticism that follows. See also Philip P. Hallie, ed., *Scepticism, Man, & God: Selections from The Major Writings of Sextus Empiricus,* Sanford G. Etheridge, trans. (Middletown, Conn.: Wesleyan University Press, 1964).

33. Terence Penelhum, "Does Philosophy have a central Place?" delivered at a conference on the Justification of the Humanities, March 1995, organized by Dr. Hugo Meynell and sponsored by the Calgary Institute for the Humanities. Penelhum reveals the similarities between ancient skeptics and modern ones.

34. Strauss associates this view with Rousseau, and it was part of the reason that he admires him. See Strauss, *Natural Right and History* (Chicago, Ill.: University of Chicago Press, 1953), ch. 6.

35. Strauss, *City and Man* (Chicago, Ill.: University of Chicago Press, 1964), pp. 59-60.

36. The exchange with Kojève, in Strauss, *On Tyranny,* is an example; for a discussion of this exchange, see Shadia Drury, *Alexandre Kojève: The Roots of Postmodern Politics* (New York: St. Martin's Press, 1994), ch. 10.

37. On Strauss's view of the philosopher-king as a Nietzschean superman, see Shadia Drury, *The Political Ideas of Leo Strauss.* On Heidegger's view of how special "creators" must become the definitive interpreters of Being as a way to save the West from its decadence, see Gregory Fried, "Heidegger's *Polemos,*" *Journal of Philosophical Research,* vol. 16 (1990-1991), pp. 159-95. Fried argues that this was Heidegger's view during the period of his Nazi involvement. Richard Wolin also refers to this as one stage of Heidegger's development; later he despaired and thought that only a god could save us. See Richard Wolin, *The Politics of Being.*

38. See Jacob Weisberg, "The Cult of Leo Strauss: An Obscure Philosopher's Washington Disciples," *Newsweek* (August 3, 1987), p. 61.

39. Martin Heidegger, *Parmenides,* André Schuwer and Richard Rojcewicz, trans. (Indianapolis, Ind.: Indiana University Press, 1992).

40. Leo Strauss, *City and Man,* pp. 77, 83-85.

41. Allan Bloom has made much of this in the interpretive essay that follows his translation of Plato's *Republic* (New York: Basic Books, 1968), pp. 380 ff.

42. Jacob Klein and Leo Strauss, "A Giving of Accounts," *The College,* vol. 25 (1970), p. 3.

43. George Steiner, *Martin Heidegger* (Chicago, Ill.: University of Chicago Press, 1989), p. 12.

44. Karl Jaspers, "Letter to the Freiburg University Denazification Commission," December, 1945, in Richard Wolin, ed., *The Heidegger Controversy,* pp. 144-51.

45. For Strauss, truth is not equally harmless to all, see Strauss, *On Tyranny,* p. 26.

46. Plato, *Republic,* G. M. A. Grube, trans. (Indianapolis, Ind.: Hackett Publishing Co. Inc., 1974), 382A ff.

47. *Republic,* 391E.

48. *Republic,* 414C.

49. Plato, *Republic,* 359D ff.

50. Nietzsche, *The Uses and Abuses of History,* Adrian Collins, trans. (New York: Library of the Liberal Arts, 1949), sec. vi, pp. 35 ff.

51. Ibid., sec. ii, pp. 12-15.

52. Nietzsche, *Beyond Good and Evil,* Walter Kaufmann, trans. (New York: Vintage Books, 1966), part II, "The Free Spirits."

53. Hannah Arendt, "Truth and Politics," in *Between Past and Future* (New York: Viking Press, 1954).

54. Carl Schmitt, *Political Theology: Four Chapters on the Concept of Sovereignty,* George Schwab, trans. (Cambridge, Mass.: MIT Press, 1988), p. 36.

55. Ibid.

56. Carl Schmitt, *The Crisis of Parliamentary Democracy,* Ellen Kennedy, trans. (Cambridge, Mass.: MIT Press, 1985), p. 52; Schmitt, *Political Theology,* p. 38.

57. See Shadia Drury, *Alexandre Kojève: The Roots of Postmodern Politics* (New York: St. Martin's Press, 1994). The thesis of the book is that postmodernism is a revolt against the arid mechanism of reason and a celebration of madness, arbitrariness, and ultimately violence.

58. Schmitt, *The Crisis of Parliamentary Democracy,* pp. 22.

59. Ibid., p. 27.

60. Ibid., p. 26.

61. Ibid., p. 11.

62. Ibid.

63. Schmitt, *Political Theology,* p. 65.

64. Carl Schmitt, *The Concept of the Political,* with an introduction and notes by George Schwab, trans., with a reply to Schmitt by Leo Strauss (New Brunswick, N.J.: Rutgers University Press, 1976), pp. 71-78.

65. Michel Foucault, *Discipline and Punish,* Alan Sheridan, trans. (New York: Vintage Books, 1979).

66. Ibid., p. 74.

67. Carl Schmitt, *Political Romanticism* (1919), Guy Oakes, trans. (Cambridge, Mass.: MIT Press, 1986). Schmitt rails against the romantics saying that they are morally, intellectually, and politically bankrupt. Romanticism is vacuous because anything at all can become the object of romantic sympathy. The romantics have romanticized the Middle Ages—castles, knights, and chivalry; but they have also romanticized Napoleon and the French Revolution. They have romanticized history, the people, the state, and the church. Politically speaking, romanticism is a rejection of the present in favor of a romanticized past or future. It attaches to whatever it pleases a certain set of attributes that it regards as positive: animate, organic, genuine, and legitimate—attributes that are opposed to the mechanical, mathematical, rigid, inorganic, surrogate, and deceptive (p. 101). Schmitt is eager to distinguish the romantics from conservative and reactionary writers such as Edmund Burke, Louis de Bonald, and Joseph de Maistre, whom he admires. He associates romanticism with Adam Müller, Friedrich Schlegel, and Novalis. If romanticism has a single core idea, Schmitt thinks that it is a secularization of the occasionalism of Nicolas Malebranche. Instead of thinking of every event as the occasion for God's activity or interference, the romantic replaces God and makes everything in the world the occasion of his own creativity. Schmitt is contemptuous of romantic creativity as nothing more than the creation of a mood. Politically speaking, romanticism is uncommitted; but if there is a political regime that is affirmed by romanticism, it is the liberal bourgeois state, because liberalism makes the "detached, isolated, and emancipated individual" the absolute point of reference (p. 99). Schmitt is right in pointing to the romantic fascination with unique individuality as an important dimension of liberalism; by the same token it must be admitted that the romantics betray individuality in longing for a communitarian oneness in which the individual is fulfilled and recognized. The tension is particularly evident in Rousseau's work, and Schmitt is quite justified in considering him an important precursor to the romantics. Schmitt is also justified in thinking that romanticism does not lend itself to decisiveness. The romantics loved paradox and irony. Romantic irony has its source in the recognition that the world is paradoxical and that every situation can be looked at from more than one side. In contrast to the romantics, Schmitt regards himself as a decisive, hardheaded political realist, and a critic of the liberal bourgeois state.

Despite his indictment of the romantics, it must be admitted that many of the qualities that Schmitt attributes to the romantics are characteristic of his own thought. He rejects the present in favor of an idealized past. He rejects the modern mechanization of the state in favor of something more alluring and mystical. He romanticizes politics, the state, and war. His preoccupation with the exceptional and unusual is a familiar romantic motif. He also shares the romantic hostility to the Enlightenment and its rationalism.

It is worth noting that romantics such as Adam Müller, on whom Schmitt heaps the greatest abuse, did not have the same aversion as Schmitt to everything universal, including the moral law. Müller romanticized the state and insisted that man is nothing without the state; but he also advocated a "league of nations" where different states recognize that they are equals under God, diverse manifestations of divine will—a beautiful tapestry of a world not unlike the vision shared by Mazzini. In contrast to this moderate nationalism, Schmitt was violently opposed to the idea of natural moral law as an anarchical assault on the political. However, Schmitt was extremely admiring of the Catholic Church, and somehow did not find her universalism objectionable. He paints her as the eternal mother who transcends all opposition and divisions among her children. See Carl Schmitt, *The Idea of Representation*, E. M. Codd, trans. (Washington, D.C.: Plutarch Press, 1988). See also H. S. Reiss, ed., *The Political Thought of the German Romantics 1793-1815* (Oxford, England: Basil Blackwell, 1955); Joseph Mazzini, *The Duties of Man and Other Essays* (New York: E. P. Dutton & Co., 1907).

68. Schmitt, *Political Theology*, pp. 62-63.
69. It is worth noting that Strauss's analysis of the "crisis of the West" follows the exact same lines of argument: the West has lost faith in itself.
70. Schmitt, *The Crisis of Parliamentary Democracy*, p. 7.
71. Schmitt, *The Concept of the Political*, p. 26.
72. Ibid., p. 27.
73. Ibid.
74. Ibid., p. 46.
75. Ibid., pp. 46, 47.
76. Joseph W. Bendersky, *Carl Schmitt: Theorist for the Reich* (Princeton, N.J.: Princeton University Press, 1983) is a detailed account of his political career and involvements, including his interpretation of article 48 of the Weimar constitution dealing with the emergency powers of the president. Schmitt interpreted that article as giving the president the right to suspend civil liberties and do whatever is necessary, regardless of the law, to save the regime. See also George Schwab's introduction to Schmitt, *The Concept of the Political*; Ellen Kennedy's introduction to Schmitt's *The Crisis of Parliamentary Democracy*; and Guy Oakes's introduction to Schmitt's *Political Romanticism*.
77. See Joseph W. Bendersky, "Carl Schmitt at Nuremberg," the transcripts of the "Interrogation of Carl Schmitt by Robert Kempner (I-III)," and Carl Schmitt's "Answers to the Allegations," in a special issue on Carl Schmitt in *Telos*, no. 72 (Summer 1987), pp. 91-129. A fascinating interview,

where Schmitt relies heavily on his political realism. When the interrogator asks him what he thought of his alliance with the Nazis, he says that
*now,* from his vantage point in 1945, he thinks that it was foolish. Which
is to say that had he known in 1933 that the Hitler regime would not
succeed, he would not have joined the party. In other words, his decision
was based on a bad prophecy. Having banished moral considerations from
politics, Schmitt's only guide to action was his ability to forecast the
future. He must have known the terrible risks this involved, since he tells
his interrogator that he is an intellectual adventurer, and that he does not
consider himself an innocent victim. Like a good existentialist, he takes
responsibility for groundless choices that are made in a moral vacuum.

In his *Political Romanticism,* Schmitt defines a "legitimate usurpa-
tion" as one that is historically durable (p. 63). But what could "legitimate" mean in this context? Nothing at all other than successful. Had the
Hitler regime endured, Schmitt would not have had to appear before the
interrogator at Nuremberg, or suffer solitary confinement. This is a fact
that tells us nothing about the legitimacy of the regime.

78. George Schwab, "Enemy or Foe: Conflict of Modern Politics," *Telos,* no.
72 (Summer 1987), pp. 194-201. This is a fascinating account in which
Schwab acknowledges that Schmitt romanticized the absolute state as the
peak of European civilization. Schwab thinks that this view of the absolute
state is quite justified because the latter had the effect of civilizing war.
The ancient Greeks saw their non-Greek opponents as barbarians who
were inferior to themselves, as a result, they felt it was legitimate to do
anything whatsoever to them—kill them, enslave them, or take their
property. The same is true for the Romans. The rise of Christian
civilization did nothing to make war any less barbaric, because the
Christians saw their opponents as infidels and agents of the devil, in
contrast to themselves, who were fighting for the one and only true God.
The result was the Crusades and the concept of a holy war. The decline of
the Catholic Church led to the rise of independent states that dared to
challenge the power of the popes. The emergence of the state was like a
fresh breeze, because the state was secular, its ends were material, and it
was devoted only to its own interests. The state had no illusions about
itself and it did not claim to represent transcendent interests or universal
ends. Supposedly, the pragmatism and cynicism of the sovereign state was
the key to its redemptive powers. Because it knew that its cause was not
sacred, it saw other states as equals, rather than as racially inferior, or as
agents of the devil. This equality among absolute states, each absolute in
its own sphere of influence led to the emergence of civilized rules of war.
In this way, a more controlled and more civilized type of warfare replaced
the total war that dominated previous eras. A clear demarcation was made
between combatants and noncombatants, combative areas and noncom-
bative areas. It became contemptible and illegitimate to destroy civilians,

or cultural and sacred monuments. It also became illegitimate to harm prisoners of war or combatants who had laid down their arms; they were to be treated humanely, and given proper medical treatment. All these rules of war were supposedly the achievements of the sovereign state. As a political realist, Schwab agrees with Schmitt that war cannot be eradicated from human life, and that the sovereign state is the highest achievement of European civilization. So understood, Schmitt is no friend of either the Communists who promise to destroy the final enemy of humanity (that is, the bourgeoisie) or the Fascists who promise to destroy the inferior races. Both demonize the enemy and reintroduce total war. So, why did Schmitt join the Nazis? Schwab's answer is that he was an opportunist. See his "Carl Schmitt: Political Opportunist?" *Intellect*, vol. 103 (February 1975), pp. 334-37. Schwab's view is that Schmitt's political philosophy is not Fascist, only antiliberal. He argues that his alliance with the Nazis was not so much a logical outcome of his political philosophy, but a break with the latter—a break that backfired.

As fascinating as Schwab's tale is, a few objections are in order. I share Schwab's view of the state as pragmatic, crass, and materialistic. But as we have seen, Schmitt abhors the crass, mechanical, and materialistic view of the state in favor of an existential, irrational, and mystical conception. And even though I would prefer a lowbrow conception of the state, there is no guarantee that materialistic concerns with self-interest and self-aggrandizement necessarily curb the violence of war or contain its chaos. Besides, for the sake of historical accuracy, it is worth mentioning that the rules of war antedate the emergence of sovereign states; they are connected to the moral prohibition against killing innocent people. But for Schmitt, there is no taming of the political, which represents the wildness, partiality, and evil of man.

Sympathetic interpreters accept this view of Schmitt as a political realist. These include Hans Morgenthau, *Scientific Man Vs. Power Politics* (Chicago, Ill.: University of Chicago Press, 1946); Joseph W. Bendersky, *Carl Schmitt: Theorist for the Reich* (Princeton, N.J.: Princeton University Press, 1983); and Paul Gottfried, *Carl Schmitt: Politics and Theory* (New York: Greenwood Press, 1990).

For less sympathetic interpreters, see Stephen Holmes, "The Scourge of Liberalism," *The New Republic* (August 22, 1988), pp. 31-36; Richard Wolin, "Carl Schmitt: The Conservative Revolutionary Habitus and the Aesthetics of Horror," *Political Theory*, vol. 20, no. 3 (August 1992), pp. 424-47; John P. McCormick, "Introduction to Schmitt's 'The Age of Neutralizations and Depoliticizations,'" *Telos*, no. 96 (Summer 1993), pp. 119-42.

79. Schmitt, *The Concept of the Political*, p. 29.
80. Ibid., p. 33, my emphasis.

81. Ibid., p. 49.

82. This is the reason that Marcuse counts Schmitt among the existentialists. See his *Negations: Essays in Critical Theory* (Boston, Mass.: Beacon Press, 1968), pp. 30-31.

83. Hannah Arendt, *Eichmann in Jerusalem* (New York: Viking Press, 1965), revised edition; see also Shiraz Dossa, *The Public Realm And The Public Self: The Political Theory of Hannah Arendt* (Waterloo, Ontario: Wilfrid Laurier University Press, 1989), especially ch. 5.

84. See Carl Schmitt, "The Age of Neutralizations and Depoliticizations," (1929) Matthias Konzett and John P. McCormick, trans., *Telos*, no. 96 (Summer 1993), pp. 130-42.

85. The admirable thing about Schmitt is that he does not succumb to Heidegger's pathetic romanticism in his treatment of technology. Schmitt eschews the romantic dualism according to which spirit, life, vitality, and dynamism are pitted against the rationalization, quantification, mechanization, and technification of life. This he says is to pit life against death, the organic against the inorganic, and soul against soullessness. But Schmitt points out that a life that knows only death as its enemy is near to death itself. In Schmitt's view, life struggles with life and spirit with spirit.

86. Leo Strauss, *City and Man*, p. 111.

87. Strauss, "Notes on Carl Schmitt," in Schmitt, *The Concept of the Political*, pp. 92-93. Strauss enlarges on these sentiments in his later work in the course of an exchange with Alexandre Kojève. See Leo Strauss, *On Tyranny* (Ithaca, N. Y.: Cornell University Press, 1963). On the exchange between Strauss and Kojève, see also Shadia B. Drury, *Alexandre Kojève: The Roots of Postmodern Politics,* ch. 10. Kojève also knew Schmitt, and his analysis of Hegel and the "end of history" are clearly indebted to Schmitt's work; see especially ch. 3 of Schmitt, *The Crisis of Parliamentary Democracy.*

88. Strauss, "Notes on Carl Schmitt," *The Concept of the Political,* pp. 88, 91.

89. Ibid., p. 89.

90. Ibid., pp. 87, 97; see also Shadia B. Drury, *The Political Ideas of Leo Strauss* (New York: St. Martin's Press, 1988), pp. 78 ff: Strauss thought that Plato secretly held such a view.

91. This fact has come to the attention of a German admirer of Strauss, but surprisingly, it has not led him to find fault with Strauss's view of politics. See Heinrich Meier, *Carl Schmitt and Leo Strauss* (Chicago, Ill.: University of Chicago Press, 1995).

92. Paul Edward Gottfried, *Carl Schmitt: Politics and Theory* (New York: Greenwood Press, 1990). A stimulating and philosophically incisive work. Gottfried is particularly persuasive when he joins Schmitt in arguing against the fraudulent neutrality of liberalism.

93. There is also what Jürgen Habermas calls the "aesthetics of violence" that explains the kinship of spirit between Schmitt and the Fascist intelligen-

tsia. Habermas is puzzled by the interest in Schmitt of Strauss's American followers. See Jürgen Habermas, "The Horrors of Autonomy," in his *The New Conservatism*, Shierry Weber Nicholsen, ed. and trans., with an introduction by Richard Wolin (Cambridge, Mass.: MIT Press, 1989). See also Schmitt, *The Crisis of Parliamentary Democracy*, ch. 4. The aesthetics of violence are particularly evident in his discussion of Georges Sorel and Benito Mussolini.

94. Carl Schmitt, *Political Romanticism* (1919), Guy Oakes, trans. (Cambridge, Mass.: MIT Press, 1986), p. 3.

95. See Shadia B. Drury, *The Political Ideas of Leo Strauss*, especially ch. 5.


## CHAPTER 4

1. Gordon S. Wood, "The Fundamentalists and the Constitution," *New York Review of Books* (February 1988), pp. 33-40. This is an excellent piece, and the most comprehensive account available of the Straussian writings on the American founding.

2. Charles Kesler, "Is Conservatism Un-American?" *National Review*, vol. 38, no. 5 (March 22, 1985), pp. 28-37.

3. Strauss's understanding of the ancients—Plato, Aristotle, Xenophon, and others—is radically at odds with the conventional view. This fact is not always understood by his students, and this is a reason for much confusion. See Shadia Drury, *The Political Ideas of Leo Strauss* (New York: St. Martin's Press, 1988), ch. 4.

4. Harry V. Jaffa, *Crisis of the House Divided: An Interpretation of the Issues in the Lincoln-Douglas Debates* (Chicago, Ill.: University of Chicago Press, 1959).

5. Leo Strauss, *City and Man* (Chicago, Ill.: University of Chicago Press, 1964), pp. 75 ff.

6. Ibid.

7. This is not the case for Straussians such as Allan Bloom, Walter Berns, and Thomas Pangle. Their own views of Strauss are hardly distinguishable from mine, only the criticism is lacking. Jaffa finds the views of these "eastern Straussians" appalling, and totally at odds with his own thirty-year association with Strauss. See Thomas L. Pangle, "Facing the Founders: Patriotism American Style," and Harry Jaffa's "Reply" in *National Review* (November 29, 1985). For an account of what is at issue between Jaffa and Pangle, see Shadia Drury, "Esotericism Betrayed" in *The Political Ideas of Leo Strauss*. Jaffa regards my book as an exposé of the eastern Straussians, but totally at odds with his own understanding of Strauss.

8. Jaffa is aware of the fact that Strauss regarded Locke as a modern whose philosophy was a disguised version of Hobbes's. Nor does Jaffa deny this

interpretation; Jaffa simply says that the Locke who influenced the Founders was the exoteric Locke whose views represent a practical compromise with the ideals of classical writers such as Aristotle. In what follows I will give reasons why the differences between the Lockean and the Aristotelian traditions are too great to be overlooked. See Jaffa, *The Conditions of Freedom* (Baltimore, Md.: The Johns Hopkins University Press, 1975), p.7.

9. For a more critical account of Jefferson, see Joyce O. Appleby, "Without Resolution: The Jeffersonian Tensions in American Nationalism." Oxford University Inaugural Lecture, April 25, 1991 (Oxford, England: Clarendon Press, 1992). Jefferson inherited, bought, and acquired from his wife more than 200 slaves; and "throughout his life, he sold slaves to offset his debts, thus participating in the cruelest aspect of slavery. When his slaves ran away, as they frequently did, he hired slave-catchers to bring them back," and he kept meticulous records in his own hand of the punishments meted out to the runaways (p. 19). Even though Jefferson was opposed to slavery, he was not an advocate of a biracial society because of the deep-rooted prejudices of whites, the black memory of the injuries they have sustained, and the "real distinctions which nature has made" (p. 20). He suggested that they be gradually emancipated and recolonized.

10. Jaffa, *Crisis of the House Divided.* Jaffa's debates with Willmoore Kendall focus on the fact that Kendall sees Lincoln as a villain whereas Jaffa sees him as the hero who saved the Declaration. See Willmoore Kendall and George Carey, *The Basic Symbols of the American Political Tradition* (Baton Rouge, La.: Louisiana State University Press, 1970) and Harry Jaffa's reply to Kendall, "Equality as a Conservative Principle," in Jaffa's *How to Think About the American Revolution* (Durham, N.C.: Carolina Academic Press, 1978).

11. Jaffa, *Crisis of the House Divided,* Harry V. Jaffa, "Equality as a Conservative Principle," *How To Think About the American Revolution* (Durham, N. C.: Carolina Academic Press, 1978); Harry V. Jaffa, "What is Equality? The Declaration of Independence Revisited," *The Conditions of Freedom* (Baltimore, Md.: The Johns Hopkins University Press, 1975); Harry V. Jaffa, *American Conservatism and the American Founding* (Durham, N. C.: Carolina Academic Press, 1984); Harry V. Jaffa, G. Anastaplo, R. L. Stone, et al., *Original Intent and the Framers of the Constitution* (Washington, D.C.: Regnery Publishing, 1994).

12. John C. Calhoun, *Union and Liberty,* Ross M. Lence, ed. (Indianapolis, Ind.: Liberty Fund, Inc., 1992), pp. 565-66.

13. Harry V. Jaffa, "Equality as a Conservative Principle," *How to Think About the American Revolution.*

14. Although historicism is no part of classic liberalism, it has become a fashionable aspect of its postmodern reincarnation, thanks mainly to Richard Rorty. The recent historicization of liberalism, coupled with the

fact that the L-word has become a political liability, accounts for the currency of the term *progressive* to refer to modern liberals. In contrast to liberalism, conservatism has always contained a certain historicist element, in the sense that it has always given credence to what is historically established as opposed to what is right and rational in the abstract.

15. In *How to Think About the American Revolution,* Jaffa registers a clear sense of crisis: America was nothing, then it became everything, and now it is on the brink of being nothing again. The reason is that Americans have wondered from the foundations of their republic, the foundations that made America great, the principles enshrined in the Declaration of Independence.

16. M. E. Bradford, *A Better Guide than Reason: Studies in the American Revolution* (La Salle, Ill.: Sherwood Sugden & Co., 1979). A Confederate who was very critical of Lincoln and his egalitarian ideas as millenarian, impossible, and unattainable.

17. Willmoore Kendall, *The Conservative Affirmation in America* (Chicago, Ill.: Gateway Editions, 1985); George Carey and Willmoore Kendall, *The Basic Symbols of the American Tradition* (Baton Rouge, La.: Louisiana State University Press, 1970).

18. William F. Buckley, Jr., *God and Man at Yale* (Chicago, Ill.: Regnery Gateway, 1951). Buckley displays his admiration for his teacher by telling the story of Kendall and the janitor, see annotated bibliography.

19. See Harry V. Jaffa, "Looking at Mr. Goodlyte," in Jaffa, *American Conservatism and the American Founding*.

20. On the intellectual pitfalls of original intent, see Terence Ball, "Constitutional Interpretation: What's Wrong With 'Original Intent'?" *Reappraising Political Theory* (Oxford, England: Clarendon Press, 1995). For a brief summary of Ball's argument see the annotated bibliography.

21. Lino A. Gralia, "Jaffa's Quarrel with Bork: Religious Belief Masquerading as Constitutional Argument." Unpublished manuscript by Gralia, Dalton Cross Professor of Law, University of Texas School of Law. A classic polemic against judicial activism; he is saddened by Jaffa's polemics against fellow conservatives, and is critical of Jaffa's natural law philosophy, which he regards as religious and mystical. Gralia's position clearly illustrates the connection between original intent and legal positivism. See also Lino A. Gralia, "Interpreting the Constitution: Posner on Bork," *Stanford Law Review,* vol. 44, no. 5 (May 1992), pp. 1020-43. See also Walter Berns, *Taking the Constitution Seriously* (New York: Simon and Schuster, 1987), which argues against judicial activism or government by the judiciary branch.

22. Clarence Thomas, "Toward a 'Plain Reading' of the Constitution—The Declaration of Independence in Constitutional Interpretation," *Howard Law Journal,* vol. 30 (1987), pp. 691-703; Clarence Thomas, "The Higher Law Background of the Privileges or Immunities Clause of the

Fourteenth Amendment," *Harvard Journal of Law and Public Policy,* vol. 12 (Winter 1989), pp. 63-70. See Annotated Bibliography for more information.

23. It may be argued that Justice Taney was in the unfortunate position of having to apply a law that was unjust. What is a judge to do if he finds himself in this situation? Should he stick to the law as it is written and intended? Or should he reinterpret it creatively? Advocates of a strict interpretation of original intent must hold the view that Justice Taney did the right thing; and that he was a good conservative judge who was not inclined to the "judicial activism" fashionable in our time. This is the position that those who insist on a strict interpretation of original intent must take. But it can be argued that in the Dred Scott case, the judge's situation was not that desperate. It is significant to remember that the Missouri Compromise (1820-1821) by which Congress outlawed slavery in the territories, had been repealed by the Kansas-Nebraska Act (1854), which allowed settlers in the territories of Kansas and Nebraska to decide the matter for themselves, according to what Stephen A. Douglas (chairman of the Senate Committee on Territories) called "popular sovereignty." Accordingly, Judge Taney denied the validity of the Missouri Compromise. But it must also be remembered that Scott left the slave state of Missouri for the free state of Illinois and later went to the Wisconsin Territory in 1834—a time when the Missouri Compromise was still in effect. It was after returning to Missouri and after the death of his master that Scott decided to sue his master's widow for his freedom, saying that having lived in a free state and in a territory where slavery was outlawed, he was an American citizen who was entitled to the constitutional rights of citizenship. It seems to me that a judge whose love of justice was as great as his respect for the law could have decided the case in favor of Scott without thwarting the letter of the law, especially in view of the fact that the Missouri Compromise was in effect during the time in dispute. This would be a way of avoiding both the dead hand of original intent, and the arbitrary creativeness of the living Constitution.

24. Harry V. Jaffa, "Dear Professor Drury," *Political Theory,* vol. 15, no. 3 (August 1987), pp. 316-25.

25. This is what is at issue between Jaffa and his fellow Straussian Walter Berns. See their exchange of letters in Jaffa's *American Conservatism and the American Founding.*

26. I have defended a pluralistic version of rationalism in the final chapter of my *Alexandre Kojève: The Roots of Postmodern Politics* (New York: St. Martin's Press, 1994).

27. Aristotle, *Politics,* T. A. Sinclair, trans. (London: Penguin Books, 1951), 1335 B19. See also Plato, *Republic,* G.M.A. Grube, trans. (Indianapolis, Ind.: Hackett Publishing Co., 1974), 460 C.

28. Jaffa is not alone in thinking that the American regime is the fulfillment of the classical ideal. See the annotated bibliography for an account of Hilail Gildin, "Leo Strauss and the Crisis of Liberal Democracy," in Kenneth L. Deutsch and Walter Soffer, eds., *The Crisis of Liberal Democracy: A Straussian Perspective* (Albany, N.Y.: State University of New York, 1987).

29. On the Christian dimensions of the American founding, see Ellis Sandoz, *A Government of Laws: Political Theory, Religion and the American Founding* (Baton Rouge, La.: Louisiana State University Press, 1990).

30. This point was eloquently made by my colleague Tom Hurka of the Philosophy Department at a conference at the University of Calgary on the American Constitution, where Harry V. Jaffa was a guest speaker.

31. Bernard de Mandeville, *Fable of the Bees*, F. B. Kaye, ed. (London, England: Oxford University Press, 1924), vol. 1, p. 4; see also discussion of Mandeville and Madison by Arthur Lovejoy, *Reflections on Human Nature* (Baltimore, Md.: Johns Hopkins University Press, 1961), p. 41. Lovejoy argues that Mandevillian rather than Lockean ideas were the source of the genius of the fathers of the American Constitution. He thinks that it was only natural that Mandevillian ideas were popular at a time when despairing of human nature was rampant.

32. Alexander Hamilton, James Madison, John Jay, *The Federalist Papers*, selected and edited by Roy P. Fairfield (New York: Doubleday & Company, Inc., 1966), no. 51.

33. The fact is that laws, no matter how wisely framed, need equitable persons to adjudicate them because justice has both a substantive and a procedural dimension. Substantive justice refers to the content of law, whereas procedural justice refers to the equitable administration of law. A law that requires everyone who parks illegally to be beheaded is not substantively just because the punishment does not match the crime, even if it were equitably administered, with everyone, rich or poor, black or white, treated the same. But historically speaking, injustice usually makes its appearance in the world by the demise of procedural justice, because people are not inclined to enshrine their iniquitous intentions in the law.

34. Americans often confuse the doctrine of the separation of powers with the idea of a mixed regime. There is good reason to think that the idea of a mixed regime, which has its source in Aristotle, Polybius, and the Roman Republic, played a role in the thought of the American Founders. For an excellent argument to that effect, see Carl J. Richard, *The Founders and the Classics* (Cambridge, Mass.: Harvard University Press, 1994).

35. Bloom provides the most colorful and radical example of this position, but he was by no means the first Straussian to take this view. It was defended much earlier by Martin Diamond, "Democracy and the Federalist: A Reconsideration of the Framers' Intent," *American Political Science Review*, vol. LIII (1959), pp. 52-68, and "Ethics and Politics: The American Way,"

Robert H. Horowitz, ed., *The Moral Foundations of the American Republic* (Charlottesville, Va.: University Press of Virginia, 1986). Summaries of both articles can be found in the annotated bibliography.

36. Allan Bloom, *The Closing of the American Mind* (New York: Simon and Schuster, 1987), p. 187.

37. Harry V. Jaffa, "Humanizing Certitudes and Impoverishing Doubts: A Critique of *The Closing of the American Mind,*" *Interpretation,* vol. 16, no. 1 (Fall 1988), pp. 111-38. Also reprinted in Robert L. Stone, ed., *Essays on The Closing of the American Mind* (Chicago, Ill.: Chicago Review Press, 1989). Jaffa is one of the few who recognizes that Bloom is no defender of the "old-time philosophy" and that he is thoroughly Nietzschean. See also Jean Bethke Elshtain, "Allan in Wonderland," *Cross Currents,* vol. 37 no. 4 (Winter 1987-88), pp. 476-79, this work documents beautifully Bloom's uses and abuses of nature.

38. On Bloom's understanding of the charms of culture, see Shadia B. Drury, "Allan Bloom's Last Men," in her *Alexandre Kojève: The Roots of Postmodern Politics* (New York: St. Martin's Press, 1994).

39. Bloom, *The Closing of the American Mind,* p. 147: Bloom's taxi driver from Atlanta is a case in point. He tells Bloom that he was once unhappy and dissatisfied with himself. But after some Gestalt therapy, he has been cured. Now he likes himself and is happy and contented. The story makes Bloom dyspeptic; what the taxi driver calls therapy serves only to cure him from the last vestiges of his humanity; the therapy made him contented with himself and smug in his brutishness. Bloom thinks that in a properly founded society, he would have learned to despise himself and worship God.

40. John Stuart Mill, *On Liberty* (1859) (London, England: W.W. Norton & Company, 1975), ch. II.

41. Mill uses Carlyle's expression, ibid., p. 22.

42. Ronald Dworkin, *A Matter of Principle* (Cambridge, Mass.: Harvard University Press, 1985).

43. Bloom regards Americans as "spiritually unclad, unconnected, isolated" (*The Closing of the American Mind,* p. 87). He shares Charles de Gaulle and Alexander Solzhenitsyn's view of the United States as a "mere aggregate of individuals, a dumping ground for the refuse from other places" (p. 187).

44. Bloom, *The Closing of the American Mind,* p. 31.

45. James Madison, *The Federalist Papers,* no. 10.

46. Bloom, *The Closing of the American Mind,* pp. 151-52. The similarity between America and Weimar is not the greatest source of Bloom's dismay. What alarms Bloom the most is that America might succeed where Hitler failed—that is, she might succeed in creating a universal and homogeneous state or a global tyranny that stamps out the extraordinary few and persecutes philosophers preoccupied with the hierarchy of beings. After

all, America has the charm that Hitler lacked. The success with which she is quickly Americanizing the globe is a testimony to the deadly nature of her appeal. Earlier, Hiram Caton had explored the same theme in "Explaining the Nazis: Leo Strauss Today," *Quadrant* (October 1986), pp. 61-5. See the discussion of this essay in ch. 1.

47. Hannah Arendt, *The Origins of Totalitarianism* (New York: Meridian Books, 1951).

48. Bloom, *The Closing of the American Mind*, p. 36.

49. Ibid., p. 34. The argument is further developed in Allan Bloom, *Giants and Dwarfs* (New York: Simon & Schuster, 1990). See especially his address at Harvard, "Western Civ—And Me."

50. Bloom, *The Closing of the American Mind*, p. 37.

51. For a more detailed analysis and critique of Bloom's political thinking see Shadia B. Drury, "Allan Bloom's Last Men," in *Alexandre Kojève: The Roots of Postmodern Politics*.

52. William J. Bennett, "To Reclaim a Legacy: Text of Report on Humanities in Higher Education," *The Chronicle of Higher Education* (November 28, 1984), pp. 16-21; Roger Kimball, *Tenured Radicals: How Politics Has Corrupted Our Higher Education* (New York: Harper & Row, 1990); Dinesh D'Souza, *Illiberal Education: The Politics of Race and Sex on Campus* (New York: Free Press, 1991); John Searle, "The Storm Over the University," *New York Review of Books* (December 6, 1990), pp. 34-42; Sidney Hook, "Civilization and Its Malcontents," *National Review* (October 13, 1989), pp. 30-33; Chester E. Finn, Jr., "The Campus: 'An Island of Repression In a Sea of Freedom,'" *Commentary*, vol. 86 (September 1989), pp. 17-23; Edward Shils, "The Sad State of the Humanities in America," *The Wall Street Journal* (July 3, 1989), p. 5; Gertrude Himmelfarb, "What to Do About Education," *Commentary* (October 1994), pp. 21-29; Robert Scholes, "Aiming a Canon at the Curriculum," *Salmagundi*, vol. 72 (Fall 1986), pp. 101-17, see also responses to Scholes from E. D. Hirsch, Jr., Marjorie Perloff, Elizabeth Fox-Genovese, and others in the same issue; Tzvetan Todorov, "Crimes Against Humanities," *The New Republic* (July 3, 1989), pp. 26-30; Tzvetan Todorov, "All Against Humanity," *Times Literary Supplement* (October 1985). The best essays are by Todorov and Scholes.

53. Michel Foucault, *Power/Knowledge, selected interviews and other writings, 1972-1977*, Colin Gordon, ed. (New York: Pantheon Books, 1980); Jacques Derrida, "White Mythology: Metaphor in the Text of Philosophy," in *Margins of Philosophy* (1972), Alan Bass, trans. (Chicago, Ill.: University of Chicago Press, 1982). It is important to note that Bennett also recommended the in-depth study of at least one non-Western civilization, its history, literature, and religion.

54. An exception is Peter Levine, *Nietzsche and the Modern Crisis of the Humanities* (Albany, N.Y.: State University of New York Press, 1995).

Levine recognizes the affinity between Strauss and postmodernists such as Derrida.

55. Bloom, *The Closing of the American Mind,* p. 37.

56. This is based on the Straussian reading of Nietzsche. See Leo Strauss, "Note on the Plan of Nietzsche's *Beyond Good and Evil,*" *Interpretation,* vol. 3, nos. 2-3 (Winter 1973), pp. 97-113, also reprinted in Leo Strauss, *Studies in Platonic Political Philosophy,* T. L. Pangle, ed. (Chicago, Ill.: University of Chicago Press, 1983); see also T. L. Pangle, "The Roots of Contemporary Nihilism and Its Political Consequences According to Nietzsche," *The Review of Politics,* vol. 45, no. 1 (January 1983), pp. 45-70; T. L. Pangle, "Nihilism and the Modern Democracy in the Thought of Nietzsche," in Kenneth L. Deutsch and Walter Soffer, eds., *The Crisis of Liberal Democracy: A Straussian Perspective* (Albany, N. Y.: State University of New York, 1987). Pangle's essays are by far the best and clearest account of the Straussian understanding of Nietzsche.

57. Mill, *On Liberty,* ch. II, p. 40.; A. N. Whitehead, *The Aims of Education* (London, England: Ernest Benn Ltd., 1932), p. 2.

58. Alasdair MacIntyre, *Whose Justice? Which Rationality?* (Notre Dame, Ind.: University of Notre Dame Press, 1988).

59. Alasdair MacIntyre, *After Virtue* (Notre Dame, Ind.: Notre Dame University Press, 1981), pp. 105-107.

60. Bloom, *The Closing of the American Mind,* p. 89.

61. Freud's version of the story is that the family has its origins in the union of *eros,* which is masculine and *ananke* (necessity), which is feminine. Because women need men to help them raise their offspring, they have devised means of keeping them around. Their efforts have been successful because they coincided or contributed to the transition of male sexuality from its olfactory stage (when men were attracted to women only at special intervals), to the visual stage when men were attracted to women all the time. In this way, the family was born, and became the basis of civilization. See Sigmund Freud, *Civilization and Its Discontents,* James Strachey, trans. (New York: W. W. Norton & Co., 1962), p. 86. On the similarities and differences between Strauss and Freud, see Shadia Drury, *The Political Ideas of Leo Strauss,* pp. 56-60, 64, 67, 84, 86-87.

62. Freud, *Civilization and Its Discontents,* p. 90.

63. Bloom, *Love and Friendship* (New York: Simon & Schuster, 1993), pp. 23-24.

64. Plato, *Republic,* bk. ix.

65. Bloom, *Love and Friendship,* p. 21.

66. Ibid., pp. 15 ff.

67. Bloom, *The Closing of the American Mind,* p. 133.

68. Ibid., p. 123.

69. Ibid., pp. 133, 124.

70. Ibid., p. 99.

71. Ibid., pp. 101, 114, 129.
72. Ibid., p. 129. Hobbes paved the way by repudiating the warlike spiritedness of masculine pride. Strauss has emphasized this in his book, *The Political Philosophy of Hobbes* (Chicago, Ill.: University of Chicago Press, 1952). For Strauss, the process of emasculating man is as old as Christianity. It was the latter that made pride the archetype of sinfulness. This is why Strauss believes that, for all his atheism, Hobbes has an important affinity with Christianity; see his "Quelques remarques sur la science politique de Hobbes," *Recherches philosophique,* vol. 2 (1932-33), pp. 609-22.
73. Bloom, *The Closing of the American Mind,* pp. 97, 100, 101.
74. For Bloom, equality is contrary to nature, because the latter contains an order of rank where wisdom, strength, and beauty are involved. Aristophanes's *The Assembly of Women* is Bloom's egalitarian nightmare, where "old hags (are) entitled by law to sexual satisfaction from handsome young males"(*The Closing of the American Mind,* p. 97). In Bloom's view, the feminist reign of terror is not far from Aristophanes's fiction.
75. This formulation belongs to Rawls, and is applied to justice between the sexes by Janet Radcliffe Richards in *The Sceptical Feminist* (London, England: Routledge and Kegan Paul, 1980).
76. Bloom, *The Closing of the American Mind,* p. 205; Bloom, *Love and Friendship,* pp. 209-29.
77. Gustave Flaubert, *Madame Bovary,* Geoffrey Wall, trans. (London, England: Penguin Books, 1992), p. 46.
78. Ibid., p. 38.
79. Ibid., p. 52.
80. Ibid., p. 85.
81. Ibid. p. 80.
82. Johann Wolfgang von Goethe's ballad, *Zauberlehrling,* in *The Oxford Book of German Verse* (Oxford, England: Clarendon Press, 1967), translated into English as "The Pupil in Magic" in *The Poems of Goethe,* Edgar Alfred Bowring, trans. (London: G. Bell and Sons, Ltd., 1911), pp. 131-34; Paul Dukas's symphony, "A Sorcerer's Apprentice" (1897) was inspired by Goethe's version of the story. See also Alexandre Kojève, "The Sorcerer's Apprentice," in Denis Hollier, ed., *The College of Sociology* (Minneapolis, Minn.: University of Minnesota Press, 1988), pp. 12-23. Georges Bataille and the College of Sociology believed that science had disenchanted the world, and they hoped to re-enchant it. Kojève argued that it was impossible to go from science back to magic—as impossible as being a sorcerer's apprentice who is taken in by his own tricks. Kojève assumed that a sorcerer's apprentice could not fall prey to his own tricks; he was not aware of Goethe's version of the story.
83. Willmoore Kendall, "The Open Society and Its Fallacies," originally published in *American Political Science Review,* vol. 54 (1960), pp. 972-79,

reprinted in John Stuart Mill, *On Liberty,* David Spitz, ed. (New York: W. W. Norton & Co., 1975); all references are to the latter.

84. Ibid., p. 162.

85. Although Kendall never changed his mind about the inadequacy of liberalism, he became increasingly dissatisfied with the plight of the philosopher in the closed society. In *Cicero and the Politics of the Public Orthodoxy,* written with Frederick D. Wilhelmsen (Pamplona, Spain: Universidad De Navarra, 1965), Kendall makes it clear that he no longer thinks that one is justified in upholding a public orthodoxy merely on the basis of its "brute factuality" (p. 11). He now believes that the only ground on which to uphold a public orthodoxy is that it partakes of truth. But what if there is a conflict between the truth and the public orthodoxy? Kendall surmises that Cicero faced this dilemma and that his solution was to remain true to the public orthodoxy. He understood Cicero to be saying that philosophy itself counsels the philosopher to uphold the public orthodoxy, even when it is contrary to the testimony of reason. But Kendall was no longer satisfied with this solution because he believed that it forces the philosopher to live a dual life; he must live in the face of two conflicting truths. Kendall thought that not too many can withstand such a dreadful dualism; and even the few who can, cannot withstand it for long. Philosophical truth is a "friend of the soul" and as such it must be made harmonious with the public orthodoxy if the latter is to escape the charge of being an enemy of the soul (p. 32). Man seeks a unity. This unity appears to Kendall in the form of Christianity. The latter has become *the* orthodoxy of the West, and in so doing has resolved the dilemma of the philosopher. That particular orthodoxy resolves the dualism because it is an orthodoxy that is illuminated by the transcendent truth that illuminates the human soul and makes philosophizing possible. Only an orthodoxy that is open to the "transcendent ground of Being" can be a friend of the soul. In this way, Kendall moved away from Strauss and toward the philosophy of Eric Voegelin.

86. Kendall, "The Open Society and Its Fallacies," p. 163.

87. Willmoore Kendall, "The People Versus Socrates Revisited," *Modern Age* (Winter 1958-1959), pp. 98-109.

88. Kendall, "The Open Society and Its Fallacies," p. 167.

89. See Willmoore Kendall, "Subversion in the Twentieth Century," in William F. Buckley Jr., et al., *The Committee and Its Critics: A Calm Review of the Committee on Un-American Activities* (New York: G. P. Putnam's Sons, 1962); also "McCarthyism: The Pons Asinorum of Contemporary Conservatism," in Kendall, *The Conservative Affirmation.*

90. Kendall, *The Conservative Affirmation,* p. 14.

91. Ibid., p. xxvii.

92. Ibid., pp. 14, 18.

93. Ibid., p. 13.

94. Joseph A. Schumpeter, *Capitalism, Socialism and Democracy* (New York: Harper & Row Publishers, 1942), see especially chs. 21 and 22.

95. Leo Strauss, "Epilogue," in Herbert J. Storing, *Essays on the Scientific Study of Politics* (New York: Holt, Rinehart & Winston, 1962), p. 326.

96. Kenneth L. Deutsch and Walter Soffer, eds., *The Crisis of Liberal Democracy: A Straussian Perspective* (Albany, N.Y.: State University of New York Press, 1987). Straussian ruminations about how to save America from her liberal self.

97. Joseph Cropsey, "The United States as Regime and the Sources of the American Way of Life," Robert H. Horowitz, ed., *The Moral Foundations of the American Republic* (Charlottesville, Va.: University Press of Virginia, 1986); similar views are held by very diverse writers such as Christopher Lasch, *The True and Only Heaven: Progress and Its Critics* (New York: W.W. Norton, 1991), and Amy Gutmann and Dennis Thompson, *Democracy and Disagreement* (Cambridge, Mass.: Harvard University Press, 1996). Lasch argues that the great liberal victories (desegregation, legalized abortion, and affirmative action) were not won in Congress or at the polls. He maintains that liberals themselves realized that Americans were "incorrigible" and this is why they relied on the courts and the federal bureaucracy to bring about their reforms (p. 37). Gutmann and Thompson wish to make America more democratic, and democracy more deliberative by having questions of rights discussed broadly by citizens at a political level, and not left to the Supreme Court, an institution that is "above politics."

98. Steven A. Maaranen, "Leo Strauss: Classical Political Philosophy and Modern Democracy," *Modern Age*, vol. 22, no. 1 (Winter, 1978), pp. 47-53; T. L. Pangle, *The Spirit of Modern Republicanism: The Moral Vision of the American Founders and the Philosophy of Locke* (Chicago, Ill.: University of Chicago Press, 1988). Like Maaranen, Pangle believes that modern Republicanism has a more hedonistic flavor than its ancient counterpart—it assumes a harmony between the interests of the individual and those of the whole that in reality does not exist. See accounts of these works in the annotated bibliography.

99. Saul K. Padover, ed., *The Complete Jefferson* (New York: Tudor, 1943), pp. 283-84.

## CHAPTER 5

1. William Kristol attributes the term to Michael Harrington, see Irving Kristol, *Reflections of a Neoconservative* (New York: Basic Books, 1983), pp. ix. Harrington was a socialist member of the editorial board of *Dissent*, and maintained that he was not the first to use the term, and that it was commonly used among the editorial staff of *Dissent*. See Ronald Radosh

and Michael Harrington, "An Exchange," *Partisan Review,* vol. 55, no. 1 (1989), p. 82. See also Seymour Martin Lipset, "American Intellectuals—Mostly on the Left, Some Politically Incorrect," in his *American Exceptionalism* (New York: W.W. Norton & Co., 1996). Lipset points out that the neoconservatives were not originally Republicans (even though Irving Kristol backed Nixon in 1972), but they had very tough positions on both domestic and foreign policy issues, and when they became frustrated with Jimmy Carter's administration for being too soft in foreign policy, they were wooed by Ronald Reagan and the Republicans.

2. Irving Kristol, "Confessions of a True, Self-Confessed—Perhaps the Only—Neoconservative," (1979) in his *Reflections of a Neoconservative,* p. 74. Kristol lists some of his fellow neoconservatives, acknowledging that they are not a totally homogeneous group, and that some of them might not agree with him on some specifics, but thinks that it is still fair to say that they share the general outlines of his thought. See for example, Christopher DeMuth and William Kristol, eds., *The Neoconservative Imagination: Essays in Honor of Irving Kristol* (La Vergne, Tenn.: American Enterprise Institute, 1995), includes essays by Norman Podhoretz, James Q. Wilson, and Robert H. Bork. Daniel Patrick Moynihan was once closely associated with the neoconservatives but is no longer; for an account of the rise and fall of Moynihan in neoconservative circles, see John Ehrman, *The Rise of Neoconservatism: Intellectual and Foreign Affairs 1945-1994* (New Haven, Conn.: Yale University Press, 1996).

3. *Time* (August 19, 1996) reports that "it was intellectual love at first sight when Jack Kemp met Irving Kristol" (p. 21).

4. Irving Kristol, *Neoconservatism: Autobiography of an Idea* (New York: Free Press, 1994), pp. 6-9.

5. Kristol, *Reflections of a Neoconservative,* p. 76.

6. Lionel Trilling, *Sincerity and Authenticity* (Cambridge, Mass.: Harvard University Press, 1972); Lionel Trilling, *Freud and the Crisis of Our Culture* (Boston, Mass.: Beacon Press, 1955); Lionel Trilling, *The Liberal Imagination: Essays on Literature and Society* (New York: Harcourt Brace Jovanovich, 1940); William Barrett, *The Truants: Adventures Among the Intellectuals* (New York: Doubleday, 1982); Claude Rawson, "An Embattled Tradition," *Times Literary Supplement* (September 16, 1994), pp. 3-5: a review of Diana Trilling, *The Beginning of the Journey: The Marriage of Diana and Lionel Trilling* (San Diego, Calif.: Harcourt Brace Jovanovich, 1994). See annotated bibliography for more details.

7. J. Huizinga, *The Waning of the Middle Ages* (New York: St. Martin's Press, 1924). A classic work on the thought, art, and literature of the fourteenth and fifteenth centuries in Western Europe.

8. M. Morton Auerbach, *The Conservative Illusion* (New York: Columbia University Press, 1959). An excellent critical account of the history of American conservatism.

9. Kristol, "The Adversary Culture of Intellectuals," *Reflections of a Neoconservative*, p. 29.

10. Kristol, "Capitalism, Socialism, and Nihilism," *Neoconservatism*, p. 99.

11. Kristol, "The Adversary Culture of Intellectuals," *Reflections of a Neoconservative*, p. 29.

12. Ibid.

13. Ibid.

14. Ibid.

15. Kristol, "About Equality," *Neoconservatism*, p. 171.

16. Kristol, "Capitalism, Socialism and Nihilism," *Neoconservatism*, p. 100.

17. Ibid., p. 101. Kristol thinks that as the connection between the bourgeois society and the Protestant ethic has withered, the demand for simple egalitarianism has become more powerful; the reason is that simple equality appears more just than the arbitrary inequalities of the market. See also "'When Virtue Loses all her Loveliness'—Some Reflections on Capitalism and the Free Society," in Irving Kristol, *On the Democratic Idea in America* (New York: Harper & Row Publishers, 1972).

18. Kristol, "Adam Smith and the Spirit of Capitalism," *Neoconservatism*, pp. 258-99.

19. Kristol, "About Equality," *Neoconservatism*, p. 176.

20. Kristol, "The Adversary Culture of Intellectuals," *Reflections of a Neoconservative*, p. 42.

21. See, for example, Christopher Lasch, *The True and Only Heaven: Progress and Its Critics* (New York: W. W. Norton & Co., 1991).

22. Irving Kristol, "Horatio Alger and Profits," *Two Cheers for Capitalism* (New York: Basic Books, 1978).

23. Ibid., p. 86.

24. Ibid., pp. 79 ff.

25. Kristol, "Corporate Capitalism in America," *Neoconservatism*, pp. 211-229. Kristol is not as opposed to the welfare state as he sometimes sounds, because the welfare state is as paternalistic as his ideal corporation. However, he favors only universalistic programs that do not define what poverty is and therefore avoid creating disincentives to work, and therefore undermine the work ethic. His reasoning is sound, but these universal programs are too expensive for the fiscal conditions of the 90s. See his "Social Reform: Gains and Losses," *Neoconservatism*, pp. 200-204.

26. This explains the limited appeal of Milton Friedman and Friedrich Hayek. Kristol shares their antipathy to big government but not the individualistic temper of their laissez faire economics. See Kristol, *Neoconservatism*, pp. 92-93, 102-03.

27. Irving Kristol, "Countercultures," in *Neoconservatism*, p. 143.

28. Irving Kristol, "Capitalism, Socialism, and Nihilism," and "About Equality," in *Neoconservatism*, pp. 99, 168.

29. Irving Kristol, "Countercultures," *Neoconservatism*, p. 142.

30. Irving Kristol, "Christianity, Judaism, and Socialism," *Neoconservatism,* p. 431.

31. Ibid., p. 432.

32. Ibid.

33. Kristol, "Countercultures," *Neoconservatism,* p. 140.

34. Kristol, "Christianity, Judaism, and Socialism," *Neoconservatism,* p. 431.

35. Ibid., p. 430.

36. Ibid., p. 435.

37. For further discussion of this point see "Family Values: The Undeclared War on Women," in this chapter.

38. Kristol, "Countercultures," and "About Equality," *Neoconservatism,* pp. 146, 172.

39. Irving Kristol, "Christianity, Judaism, and Socialism," *Neoconservatism,* p. 441.

40. Kristol, "Countercultures," *Neoconservatism,* p. 144.

41. Ibid., p. 145.

42. Kristol, "About Equality," *Neoconservatism,* p. 172.

43. This is the thesis of his essay "About Equality."

44. Kristol, "Capitalism, Socialism and Nihilism," *Neoconservatism,* pp. 99, 101; Kristol, "Adam Smith and the Spirit of Capitalism," *Neoconservatism,* pp. 258, 269, 298-99.

45. Ibid., p. 101, my emphasis.

46. Kristol, "Countercultures," *Neoconservatism,* p. 146.

47. Kristol, "America's 'Exceptional Conservatism,'" *Neoconservatism.*

48. Kristol, "Capitalism, Socialism, and Nihilism," *Neoconservatism,* p. 100.

49. Kristol, "The Coming 'Conservative Century,'" *Neoconservatism,* p. 365.

50. Kristol, "Capitalism, Socialism, and Nihilism," *Neoconservatism,* p. 100: Kristol rejects the "utilitarian definition of civic loyalty" because it will not "convince anyone that it makes sense for him to die for his country." See also Leo Strauss, *Natural Right and History* (Chicago, Ill.: University of Chicago Press, 1953), p. 257: Strauss praises Rousseau for rejecting enlightened self-interest as the foundation of political obligation.

51. This is the gist of Strauss's interpretation of Plato. See Leo Strauss, *City and Man* (Chicago, Ill.: University of Chicago Press, 1964), pp. 50-138. Kristol's debt to Strauss's reading of Plato is manifest in his ""Utopianism, Ancient and Modern," *Neoconservatism,* pp. 18-99.

52. Kenneth Minogue, *Nationalism* (New York: Basic Books, 1967), a lively, imaginative, and engaging exposition. See also the classic work by Elie Kedourie, *Nationalism* (New York: Frederick A. Praeger, 1962).

53. Kristol, *Reflections of a Neoconservative,* p. xiii.

54. John Ehrman, *The Rise of Neoconservatism: Intellectual and Foreign Affairs 1945-1994,* a comprehensive history of neoconservative foreign policy.

55. Kristol, "The New Populism: Not to Worry," *Neoconservatism,* pp. 360-61.

56. Ibid.

57. Leo Strauss, *Thoughts on Machiavelli* (Chicago, Ill.: University of Chicago Press, 1958). On Strauss's interpretation of Machiavelli, see Shadia B. Drury, *The Political Ideas of Leo Strauss,* ch. 6. Kristol shares Strauss's subtle admiration for Machiavelli, see his "Machiavelli and the Profanation of Politics," in *Reflections of a Neoconservative.*

58. Theodore Draper, "An Anti-Intellectual Intellectual," *New York Review of Books* (November 2, 1995), pp. 29-34.

59. Kristol "The Adversary Culture of Intellectuals," *Reflections of a Neoconservative,* p. 41.

60. Kristol, "The Cultural Revolution and the Capitalist Future," *Neoconservatism.*

61. Christopher Lasch, *The True and Only Heaven: Progress and Its Critics,* pp. 511, 512. Like Kristol, Lasch also extols the bourgeois virtues, but he realizes that these virtues rightly belong to petit bourgeois capitalism and not to corporate capitalism.

62. Kristol, "The Cultural Revolution and the Capitalist Future," *Neoconservatism,* p. 134.

63. Ibid., p. 134; also, Kristol, "About Equality," *Neoconservatism,* p. 172.

64. Kristol, "American Historians and the Democratic Idea," *Neoconservatism,* p. 314.

65. Kristol, "The New Populism: Not to Worry," *Neoconservatism,* p. 360.

66. Ed Gillespie and Bob Schellhas, eds., *Contract With America: The Bold Plan By Rep. Newt Gingrich, Rep. Dick Armey, and the House Republicans to Change the Nation* (New York: Random House, 1994), p. 185.

67. Ibid., p. 186.

68. Ibid., p. 193.

69. For an excellent analysis of the *Contract with America* and its architect, Newt Gingrich, see Garry Wills, "What Happened to the Revolution," *New York Review of Books* (June 6, 1996), pp. 11-16.

70. Michael Kinsley argued that this strategy can backfire, see his excellent essay, "The Genie's Revenge," *Time* (March 11, 1996), p. 64.

71. Michael Oakeshott, "On Being Conservative," in his *Rationalism in Politics* (London, England: Methuen & Co. Ltd., 1962), p. 169.

72. Kristol, "'The Stupid Party,'" *Neoconservatism.*

73. *Contract with America,* p. 182.

74. See for example the concluding paragraph of Kristol's "Christianity, Judaism and Socialism," *Neoconservatism,* p. 441.

75. Kristol, "America's 'Exceptional Conservatism,'" *Neoconservatism,* p. 375.

76. Kristol, "The Adversary Culture of Intellectuals," *Reflections of a Neoconservative,* p. 41.

77. Oakeshott's conception of conservatism is discussed and rejected by Kristol in "America's 'Exceptional Conservatism,'" *Neoconservatism.*

78. *Contract with America,* p. 190.

79. Kristol, "America's 'Exceptional Conservatism,'" *Neoconservatism*, p. 377.
80. Michael Oakeshott, *The Politics of Faith and the Politics of Scepticism* (New Haven, Conn.: Yale University Press, 1996).
81. Edmund Burke, *Selected Writings and Speeches,* Peter J. Stanlis, ed. (Chicago, Ill.: Regnery Gateway, 1963), p. 542-43.
82. See for example R. E. Morgan, *Disabling America: The Rights Industry in Our Time* (New York: Basic Books, 1984); Charles Murray and Richard J. Herrnstein, *The Bell Curve* (New York: Free Press, 1994).
83. Tanya Melich, *The Republican War Against Women* (New York: Bantam Books, 1996).
84. Barbara Ehrenreich, "Whose Gap Is It, Anyway?" *Time* (May 6, 1996), p. 43.
85. Kristol, *Neoconservatism*, p. 17.
86. Leo Strauss, *Socrates and Aristophanes* (Chicago, Ill.: University of Chicago Press, 1966), p. 272.
87. Ibid., p. 278.
88. Leo Strauss, *The Rebirth of Classical Political Rationalism,* edited by T. L. Pangle (Chicago, Ill.: University of Chicago Press, 1989), p. 247.
89. Ibid., p. 113.
90. Ibid., p. 114.
91. Ibid., p. 247.
92. Ibid., p. 114.
93. See Shadia Drury's review of *The Rebirth of Classical Political Rationalism* in *Political Theory,* vol. 19, no. 4 (November, 1991), pp. 671-75.
94. See Shadia B. Drury, *The Political Ideas of Leo Strauss,* pp. 82-87, 188-91.
95. Thomas Pangle, *The Spirit of Modern Republicanism: The Moral Vision of the American Founders and the Philosophy of Locke* (Chicago, Ill.: University of Chicago Press, 1988).
96. Alasdair MacIntyre, *After Virtue* (Notre Dame, Ind.: University of Notre Dame Press, 1981); Alasdair MacIntyre, *Who's Justice? Which Rationality?* (Notre Dame, Ind.: University of Notre Dame Press, 1988); Michael J. Sandel, *Liberalism and the Limits of Justice* (New York: Cambridge University Press, 1982); Amitai Etzioni, ed., *Rights and the Common Good: A Communitarian Perspective* (New York: St. Martin's Press, 1995).
97. Hannah Arendt, *The Human Condition* (Chicago, Ill.: University of Chicago Press, 1958). Arendt is the inspiration behind the American interest in the republican tradition. But the American appropriation of Arendt tends to be more democratic than Arendt herself. Representatives of the republican tradition include Sheldon Wolin, *Politics and Vision* (Boston, Mass.: Little Brown & Co., 1960), and Jean Bethke Elshtain, *Democracy on Trial* (Concord, Ontario: House of Anansi Press, 1993).
98. Ronald K. L. Collins and David M. Skover, *The Death of Discourse* (Boulder, Col.: Westview Press, 1996). A lament for the decay of the First

Amendment into a defense of pornography and hence the death of discourse.

99. Kristol, "Pornography, Obscenity, and the Case for Censorship," in *Reflections of a Neoconservative.*

100. Terence Ball, "The L-Word: A Short History of Liberalism," *The Political Science Teacher,* vol. 3, no. 1 (Winter 1990), pp. 1-7.

# ANNOTATED BIBLIOGRAPHY

Anastaplo, George. *The Artist as Thinker: From Shakespeare to Joyce.* Chicago, Ill.: Swallow Press, 1983. A book of literary criticism written by one of the few liberal-minded followers of Leo Strauss. Anastaplo is famous as a rebel against the witch-hunt of the McCarthy era. This cost him the opportunity to practice law. He teaches law at the Loyola University of Chicago.

Appleby, Joyce O. "Without Resolution: The Jeffersonian Tensions in American Nationalism." Oxford University, Inaugural Lecture, April 25, 1991. Oxford, England: Clarendon Press, 1992. A superbly balanced account of Jefferson's views, especially on Native Americans and African slaves. A good antidote to the romanticization of Jefferson by Harry Jaffa and others.

Arendt, Hannah. "Truth and Politics," in her *Between Past and Future.* New York: Viking Press, 1954. A subtle and profound essay that decries the shift in the attitude toward lying in politics. It was once believed that lying to the enemy was justified, but now all of politics has become a matter of systematic lying. This is what propaganda is about; and it is a critical component of totalitarian politics. The essay can be read as a critique of Leo Strauss's views on the need for systematic lying in politics.

Auerbach, Morton M. *The Conservative Illusion.* New York: Columbia University Press, 1959. An excellent comprehensive survey of conservative thought in America. Contains devastating critiques of Russell Kirk and others.

Ball, Terence. *Reappraising Political Theory.* Oxford, England: Clarendon Press, 1995. See especially "Constitutional Interpretation: What's Wrong With 'Original Intent'?" Ball argues that the attempt to return to the original intention of the Founders is fraught with difficulties, not least among which is the single author fallacy. The Constitution is not the product of a single author with a single intention, but a plurality of authors with a plurality of diverse and often conflicting intentions. He illustrates this brilliantly using article I, section 8, on the jurisdiction of Congress over state militias. These and many other difficulties notwithstanding, Ball argues that it is possible to reach an understanding of the original meaning of a document or text, and that a text cannot simply be arbitrarily interpreted. But this is not to say that this text can be authoritative in our own time, unless we are willing to accept all its assumptions and prejudices as if our own assumptions and prejudices don't exist. Originalism is academically viable, but legally and politically disastrous because a law cannot be efficacious if it is meaningless to those whose actions it must govern. The real attraction of originalism is not academic, but political; it is part of the desire to retrieve a lost past. And, resorting to the "last refuge of scoundrels and scholars" (that is, the argument from authority), Ball argues that Madison himself was critical of originalism in *The Federalist Papers,* number 37.

Benda, Julien. *Treason of the Intellectuals* (1928), Richard  Aldington, trans. New York: W. W. Norton & Co., 1969. Benda laments the fact that the intellectuals have all descended into the cave and have contributed to inflaming the parochial nationalist passions. He has no appetite for the rule of the philosophers; he longs for the days when philosophers were dragged kicking and screaming into the cave. He thinks that intellectual life, properly understood, is a disinterested understanding of the world that rises above political partisanship. Benda assumes that the world is irremediably evil, that human beings are flawed, and that society is not perfectible. All we can expect is that the world will continue doing evil while praising good. The treason of the intellectuals consists in their willingness to redefine evil as good whenever it suits their political causes. The book is brilliantly written with sparkling prose and moving polemics.

Berlin, Isaiah. "Jewish Slavery and Emancipation," in *Hebrew  University Garland,* Norman Bentwich, ed. London, England: Constellation Books, 1952. A moving essay in defense of political Zionism.

Bernstein, Richard. "A Very Unlikely Villain (or Hero)." *The New  York Times* (January 29, 1995). Describes Strauss as the "intellectual godfather" of the Republican party's Contract with America.

Bloom, Allan. *Love and Friendship.* New York: Simon and Schuster,  1993. Reveals the extent of Bloom's sympathies with the romantic tradition.

———. "Giants and Dwarfs," in Bloom, *Giants and Dwarfs: Essays  1960-1990.* New York: Simon and Schuster, 1990. An excellent illustration of the Straussian conception of the relation between the elite and the masses as one modeled after the relation between Gulliver and the Lilliputians. What is absolutely sacrilegious and forbidden to the Lilliputians— urinating over the great palace—is appropriate for Gulliver and beneficial to the Lilliputians because it saved all of Lilliput from being engulfed by flames!

———. *The Closing of the American Mind.* New York: Simon and  Schuster, 1987. See discussion of Bloom in chapter 4, and Shadia Drury, "Allan Bloom's Last Men" in her *Alexandre Kojève.*

Bok, Sissela. *Lying: Moral Choice in Public and Private Life.*  New York: Vintage Books, 1978. Maintains that the situations in which lying is morally excusable are much fewer than is generally believed. Politically speaking, she argues that lying is particularly destructive in a democracy because it destroys trust and makes it impossible for voters to make informed choices. The prevalence of lies in election campaigns have made voters cynical of politicians and of the political process as a whole. The damage that lying inflicts far outweighs the supposed benefits that those who engage in it believe it to have. Besides, when closely examined, their motives are not as altruistic as they would like to think. See my discussion of Strauss's views of the need for noble lies in chapter 3.

Buckley, William F., Jr. *God and Man At Yale.* Chicago, Ill.: Regnery Gateway, 1951. Speaks of the influence of Willmoore Kendall on him as an undergraduate at Yale. He also tells the story of how a janitor at the university approached Kendall and asked him: "Is it true, professor, dat dere's people in New York City who want to . . . destroy the guvamint of the United States?" To which Kendall replied, "Yes, Oliver, that's true." Then Oliver said, "Well, why don't we lock'em up?" Kendall apparently informed the faculty at Yale that the janitor had more political wisdom than all of them put together. Kendall eventually left Yale for Dallas, where he was much adored.

Burnyeat, F. M. "Sphinx Without a Secret." *New York Review of Books* (May 30, 1985), pp. 30-36. A devastating critique of Strauss's views in general and his views of Plato in particular.

Cassirer, Ernst, "Herman Cohen, 1842-1918." *Social Research,* vol. 10 (1943), pp. 219-32. Cassirer was a student of Cohen's. His essay outlines the basic concerns of Cohen's neo-Kantianism. Cassirer claims that the major problem with which Cohen had to contend is the conflict between his Jewish faith and his Kantian belief that the moral law has its source in the autonomous will of man. Cohen resolves the dilemma by claiming that religious morality is a mythical version of rational or philosophical morality.

Caton, Hiram. "Explaining the Nazis: Leo Strauss Today." *Quadrant* (October 1986), pp. 61-65. A brilliant and disturbing application of Strauss's ideas to America. Caton enlarges on Strauss's conviction that American liberalism re-creates the spineless liberalism of Weimar.

Cropsey, Joseph. "Plato on Knowledge and Society: Theaetetus." Paper Presented at the Midwestern Political Science Association, April 20, 1991, Chicago, Illinois. Eschews the usual Straussian preoccupation with the fact that Theaetetus is suffering from dysentery and therefore Socrates, the midwife, can only help him bring forth excrement. But the conclusion is the same: what comes out of Theaetetus's mouth is excremental nonsense that Plato does not seriously endorse. While sticking close to Strauss's interpretation of Plato, Cropsey seems to have a kindlier, gentler version of elitism. He suggests that even though reason cannot lend support to the good, wisdom is characterized by its devotion to goodness.

————. "The United States as Regime and the Sources of the American Way of Life," in *The Moral Foundations of the American Republic,* Robert H. Horwitz, ed. Charlottesville, Va.: University Press of Virginia, 1986. Argues that the nature of the American regime has two sources. The first is what he calls the "parchment regime"—the Declaration of Independence, the Constitution, Lincoln's Second Inaugural Address, judicial opinions, and the like. The parchment regime repudiates the regulation of religion, art, thought, science, and private life. But these are a large part of what we are. And this "ungovernable" part is the second source to which we must turn to understand the American regime. The "ungovernable" part is at odds with the parchment regime and is critical of it. And in a classic Frankfurt School motif, Cropsey argues that the parchment regime somehow manages to emasculate and vulgarize every criticism that the ungovernable part coughs up.

————. *Political Philosophy and the Issues of Politics.* Chicago, Ill.: University of Chicago Press, 1977. Colleague and lifelong collaborator with Leo Strauss. An eclectic collection of essays on everything from Plato to Welfare economics.

Dannhauser, Werner J. "Leo Strauss as Citizen and Jew." *Interpretation,* vol. 17, no. 3 (Spring 1990), pp. 433-47. A sensitive and beautifully written apology for his teacher.

Deutsch, Kenneth L., and Nicgorski, Walter, eds. *Leo Strauss: Political Philosopher and Jewish Thinker.* Lanham, Md.: Rowman & Littlefield, 1994. A collection of essays on Strauss, some of them focusing on his Jewish heritage.

Diamond, Martin. "Ethics and Politics: The American Way," in *The Moral Foundations of the American Republic,* Robert H. Horwitz, ed. Charlottesville, Va.: University Press of Virginia, 1986. Begins with the Aristotelian assumption that the proper relation between ethics and politics is that the latter is meant to inculcate the former. Believes that America has its foundation in modernity, which constitutes a significant departure from this Aristotelian conception of politics. On the modern view, politics is not intended to create a unique, special, or national character. Modernity reduces politics to securing the conditions necessary for peaceful commerce. By the same token, he argues that the devotion to commerce is not exactly the same thing as giving way to the "downward pull of ease, creature comfort, and the lower pleasures" (p. 45). There is a distinction between greed, avarice, and covetousness on one hand, and acquisitiveness on the other. It is the latter rather than the former that defines America's spirit and its founding. Acquisitiveness presupposes moderation, which Diamond regards as the bourgeois virtue par excellence. The trouble with Diamond's position is that he assumes that limiting the scope of the political to the securing of peace and order is the same as giving up on all virtues other than those that serve the needs of a commercial empire. He does not consider that the political may be a most oppressive vehicle for the inculcation of virtue, and that there may be better ways to inculcate virtue than to use the coercive arm of government.

————. "Democracy and the Federalist: A Reconsideration of the Framers' Intent." *American Political Science Review,* vol. LIII (1959), pp. 52-68. Reprinted in Horwitz, ed. *The Moral Foundations of the American Republic.* An important essay that is at the center of many of the sectarian debates among the Straussians on the American founding. Argues that the American Founders were Hobbesians who were mainly interested in "comfortable self-preservation." Their aspirations for politics were too low, and we cannot depend on them to solve our current problems. What is needed today is religion, public-spiritedness, military courage, and individual excellences.

Drury, Shadia B. "The Jewish Thought of Leo Strauss?" *Shofar: An Interdisciplinary Journal of Jewish Studies*, vol. 13, no. 2 (Winter 1995), pp. 81-85. A review essay on Kenneth Hart Green's *Jew and Philosopher*, arguing that there is nothing particularly Jewish about Leo Strauss's thought.

————. *Alexandre Kojève: The Roots of Postmodern Politics*. New York: St. Martin's Press, 1994. Argues that despite its repudiation of all grand narratives, postmodernism is in the grip of a grand narrative bequeathed to it by Kojève. Regards Strauss as a postmodern who shares the same Kojèvean narrative as Raymond Queneau, Georges Bataille, and Michel Foucault. Contains a chapter on Strauss's exchange with Kojève, arguing that it was not so much a debate between an ancient and a modern thinker, but a much more intriguing debate between a superman and a commissar.

————. Review of Leo Strauss, *The Rebirth of Classical Political Rationalism*. *Political Theory*. vol. 19, no. 4 (November 1991), pp. 671-75. A review that focuses on Strauss's endorsement of pederasty, his conviction that women are more evil than men, and his hedonistic proclivities.

————. *The Political Ideas of Leo Strauss*. New York: St. Martin's Press, 1988. A comprehensive interpretation of Strauss's writings. Reveals the extent to which Strauss's political thought is inspired by a coherent (even if vulgarized) version of Nietzsche's philosophy.

D'Souza, Dinesh. "The Legacy of Leo Strauss: Is America the Ancient Society that the Ancient Philosophers Sought?" *Policy Review* (Spring 1987), pp. 36-43. A well-written introduction to Strauss and the debate between his students regarding the American founding.

Dyzenhaus, David. "The Puzzle of Neo-Conservatism." *Policy Options* (December 1996), pp. 46-7. Argues that the intellectual father of neoconservatism is Friedrich Hayek whose work is a sanitized version of the work of Carl Schmitt. What neoconservatives want is a homogeneous populous, no competing interests, no parliamentary debates, and no liberalism.

Ehrman, John. *The Rise of Neoconservatism: Intellectual and Foreign Affairs 1945-1994*. Yale University Press, 1995. A comprehensive history of neoconservative foreign policy. Suggests that the end of the Cold War and the collapse of the Soviet Union have robbed the neoconservatives of their raison d'être. This seems to me to be true where foreign policy is concerned; but the collapse of the Soviet Union also leaves the neoconservatives free to focus on their internal enemy—liberalism.

Fackenheim, Emil, *What Is Judaism?* New York: Collier Books, 1987. An account of Judaism in light of the history of persecution that the Jewish people have endured.

————. *God's Presence in History: Jewish Affirmation and Philosophical Reflection.* New York: New York University Press, 1970.

Farias, Victor. *Heidegger and Nazism.* Philadelphia, Penn: Temple University Press, 1989. Documents the extent to which Heidegger collaborated with the Nazis, applying their "cleansing" program to the University of Freiburg. As rector of the university he was instrumental in destroying the lives and careers of professors and students alike by writing damning letters to the authorities saying that they were Jewish, consorted with Jews, or were not well disposed to the regime.

Fox, Marvin. *Interpreting Maimonides.* Chicago, Ill.: University of Chicago Press, 1990. Praises Strauss for emphasizing the esoteric quality of Maimonides's work, but thinks that Strauss's commentary is so obtuse and esoteric itself that it sheds no light on Maimonides. And what is worse, those elements of Strauss's interpretation that can be gleaned from his convoluted commentary have the effect of reducing Maimonides's whole enterprise into an absurd charade. Fox provides an alternative interpretation.

Fukuyama, Francis. *Trust: The Social Virtues and the Creation of Prosperity.* New York: Free Press, 1995. The latest incarnation of neoconservativism. Not surprisingly, it reads like a paean to corporate capitalism, which eschews the individualistic entrepreneurial spirit in favor of hierarchy, authority, and discipline.

Galston, William. *Liberal Purposes: Goods, Virtues and Diversity in the Liberal State.* Cambridge, England: Cambridge University Press, 1991. A liberal Straussian who was deputy assistant to President Clinton on domestic affairs. Clearly he does not swallow the Straussian philosophy in toto. Galston has learned from Strauss to appreciate the importance of civic virtue.

Gay, Peter. *Weimar Culture.* New York: Harper Torchbooks, 1968. An excellent account of the history and the spirit of the Weimar republic. Strauss's world was shaped by Weimar, and his conception of liberalism is typical of those Germans who loathed Weimar as the triumph of mediocrity and longed for a heroic age. What Gay says about the poet Stefan George and his "tight, humorless self-congratulatory coterie" bears a strong resemblance to Leo Strauss and his disciples.

Gildin, Hilail. "Leo Strauss and the Crisis of Liberal Democracy." in *The Crisis of Liberal Democracy: A Straussian Perspective,* Kenneth L. Deutsch and Walter Soffer, eds. Albany, N.Y.: State University of New York, 1987. Gildin believes that Aristotle's ideas are in perfect harmony with liberal democracy. He suggests that Aristotle failed to provide a justification for slavery, and accepted it only as a necessary evil. Despite its hazards, modern technology has the beneficial effect of making possible the good regime in the classical sense because it dispenses with the need for slavery. In this way, American liberal democracy can be seen as the fulfillment of the aspirations of the classics.

Green, Kenneth Hart. *Jew and Philosopher: The Return to Maimonides in the Jewish Thought of Leo Strauss.* Albany, N.Y.: State University of New York Press,

1993. Hart sets out in search of the Jewish thought of Leo Strauss only to find that the great prophets were philosophers, atheists, and dissemblers who praised God for His political utility. But instead of concluding that Strauss is no great representative of the Jewish tradition, Hart is tempted to accept the Straussian version of Judaism as the definitive account of the tradition. For a review of Hart, see Shadia Drury's "The Jewish Thought of Leo Strauss?"

Gunnell, John G. *The Descent of Political Theory.* Chicago, Ill.: University of Chicago Press, 1993. A comprehensive study of political science as a discipline in the United States, including the influence of the German émigrés.

————. "Strauss Before Straussianism: The Weimar Conversation." *Vital Nexus,* vol. 1, no. 1 (May 1990), pp. 73-104. Another version of the same paper can be found in *The Review of Politics,* vol. 53, no. 1 (Winter 1991), pp. 53-74, and in Kenneth L. Deutsch and Walter Nicgorski, eds., *Leo Strauss: Political Philosopher and Jewish Thinker,* Lanham, Md.: Rowman & Littlefield, 1994. The best available account of Strauss's early intellectual life in Germany. Gunnell argues that the fundamental problem of the academics in the Weimar period was the absence of an authoritative intellectual voice that could speak to politics and to concrete political problems and situations. That was the result of the demise of reason by the "new thinking" according to which reason was groundless or was itself based on a commitment. This new thinking led naturally to existentialism—the awareness of the irrationality and groundlessness of all decisions. This meant that reason could not provide any rational or authoritative direction for practice—the political world is left at sea. This is the central dilemma of what Gunnell calls the "Weimar conversation." Max Weber tackled the problem by saying that even though reason cannot guide action toward any particular ends, it can tell us what the consequences of our choices are likely to be. No one was satisfied with Weber's solution. Gunnell rightly argues that Strauss's solution is not the return to rationalism that it is generally believed to be. It is merely a return to the authoritativeness of philosophy in the public sphere. In other words, Strauss wished to adhere to the "new thinking" without its damaging political consequences.

Hayek, Friedrich, A. *The Road to Serfdom.* Chicago, Ill.: University of Chicago Press, 1944. Advocate of laissez-faire economics and critic of big government as the road to totalitarianism. I think he wrongly assumes that big government is necessarily strong government. Neoconservatives share his antipathy to a centrally administered economy.

Hill, Anita. *Speaking the Truth to Power.* New York: Doubleday, 1997. An autobiographical work in which Hill tells her own story about Clarence Thomas's Supreme Court nomination and her testimony before the Senate hearings.

Holmes, Stephen. *The Anatomy of Antiliberalism.* Cambridge, Mass.: Harvard University Press, 1993. A spirited and lively defense of liberalism against its critics, including Carl Schmitt, Leo Strauss, Alasdair MacIntyre, and others.

―――. "The Secret History of Self-Interest," in *Beyond Self- Interest,* Jane J. Mansbridge, ed. Chicago, Ill.: University of Chicago Press, 1990. A delightful essay on the shortcomings of selflessness. Argues that much of the evil in the world is motivated not by selfishness, but by selfless devotion to religious or ideological doctrines.

Horwitz, Robert H., ed. *The Moral Foundations of the American Republic.* Charlottesville, Va.: University Press of Virginia, 1986. An excellent collection that includes most of the leading Straussian writers on the American founding.

Jaffa, Harry V. *American Conservatism and the American Founding.* Durham, N. C.: Carolina Academic Press, 1984. Includes criticisms of Willmoore Kendall, a controversy with Walter Berns, and criticism of American liberalism.

―――. *How to Think About the American Revolution.* Durham, N.C.: Carolina Academic Press, 1978. Jaffa maintains that the United States is in crisis. It was nothing, then it became everything, and now it is on the verge of becoming nothing again. The reason for this crisis is that Americans have wondered away from the sacred principles of the Founding Fathers. The solution to the current malaise is to retrieve these original principles. Unlike other conservatives who think of the Constitution as the central document of the American founding, Jaffa understands the founding in terms of the Declaration of Independence. His emphasis on equality and freedom sets him apart from other conservatives. The conservative element in his thought is his desire to return to something good in the past, even if that is good old-fashioned American liberalism. Jaffa's ideas exerted a decisive influence on Justice Clarence Thomas.

―――, Anastaplo, G., Stone, R. L., et al. *Original Intent and the Framers of the Constitution.* Washington, D.C.: Regnery Publishing, 1994. In his essay on the original intent of the Framers of the Constitution, Jaffa puts American conservatives to shame. He shows that their position is indistinguishable from that of the leftists that they repudiate. They both share the same view of the American founding as rooted in racism, inequality, and injustice. The only difference is that the leftists repudiate it while the conservatives endorse it. Jaffa is the gadfly of American conservatism.

Kaufmann, Walter. *Nietzsche, Heidegger, and Buber.* New Brunswick, N.J.: Transaction Publishers, 1980. A lively argument to the effect that Nietzsche has contributed much to the discovery of the mind, while Heidegger was a fraud who borrowed Nietzsche's ideas and added absolutely nothing to them.

Kendall, Willmoore. *The Conservative Affirmation in America.* Chicago, Ill.: Gateway Editions, 1985. The subject of many of Harry Jaffa's polemics.

Vilifies Abraham Lincoln for ending slavery and derailing the American heritage with his egalitarian ideas.

Kesler, Charles, ed. *Saving the Revolution.* New York: The Free Press, 1987. A collection of essays on the American founding that includes Straussian authors such as William B. Allen, William Kristol, Harvey Mansfield, and Thomas West.

Kirk, Russell. *The Intelligent Woman's Guide to Conservatism.* New York: Devin-Adair Co., 1957. The message is that liberal individualism and Communist collectivism will turn women into animals, and that conservatism is the best thing for them. Tells women that they are conservatives by instinct, and that he has written this book to make them conservatives by reason as well. But unfortunately, Kirk himself is a conservative by instinct.

————. *A Program for Conservatives.* Chicago, Ill.: Regnery Books, 1954. Tells us that to be a conservative you must dislike liberals, be suspicious of change, and read Irving Babbitt (Kirk's mentor). The book is full of gloom in a world threatened by the madness of liberalism; the latter has destroyed all veneration for ancestral traditions, and in so doing, has robbed the world of order and tranquility. Kirk adores everything old and moldy and is more conservative than Edmund Burke. But he insists that he is not un-American and that the American Revolution was a conservative revolution, that the American founders were all conservatives (p. 24), and that the best men in American politics were conservatives—Lincoln as much as Calhoun (p. 34).

————. *The Conservative Mind From Burke to Eliot.* Chicago, Ill.: Regnery Books, 1953. A survey of conservative thought that exerted a certain influence on the postwar revival of conservatism in America. Kirk is a Burkian who longs for an aristocratic agrarian society and has little use for an industrial, capitalistic, individualistic society such as America. Kirk is a tolerably good collector of conservative lore, but is not a coherent or clearheaded thinker. Fancies himself to be a forlorn voice in the wasteland of modernity. On the whole, it is difficult to decide if Kirk's pomposity outweighs his illogic, or vice versa.

Kolakowski, Leszek. "Modernity on Endless Trial." *Encounter* (March 1986), pp. 8-12. Although he is caught up in the antimodern bandwagon, Kolakowski is insightful enough to recognize that the antimodern forces can be just as barbarous as the modern ones. It seems to me that he describes Strauss and Bloom perfectly (without naming them) when he speaks of faithless prophets lamenting the loss of faith in the modern world. Kolakowski realizes that the recognition of the social utility of faith cannot revive it.

Kristol, Irving. *Neoconservatism: The Autobiography of an Idea.* New York: Free Press, 1995. See my detailed discussion of Kristol in chapter 5.

————. *Reflections of a Neoconservative.* New York: Basic Books, 1983.

————. *Two Cheers for Capitalism.* New York: Basic Books, 1978.

————. *On the Democratic Idea of Capitalism.* New York: Harper & Row, 1972.

Lessing, Gotthold Ephraim. "Ernst and Falk: Conversations for the Freemasons," in Lessing, *Nathan the Wise, Minna Von Barnhelm, and Other Plays and Writings,* William L. Zwiebel, trans., Peter Demetz, ed., with a foreword by Hannah Arendt. New York: Continuum Publishing Co., 1991. Dialogue on the secret teachings of the Freemasons. See discussion in chapter 2.

————. *Nathan the Wise* (1779), Bayard Quincy Morgan, trans. New York: Frederick Ungar Publishing Co., 1955. A model of Enlightenment rationalism. See my discussion in chapter 2.

Löwith, Karl. "My Last Meeting With Heidegger in Rome, 1936," and "The Political Implications of Heidegger's Existentialism." *New German Critique,* no. 45 (Fall 1988), pp. 115-34. The first essay is a touching personal account that reveals that Heidegger was so thoughtless and so committed to the Nazi party that even while spending the day with his Jewish student in Rome, he did not remove the swastika from his lapel. The second essay shows why Heidegger's commitment to National Socialism was required by his philosophy.

————. "Heidegger: Problem and Background of Existentialism." *Social Research,* vol. 15, no. 3 (September 1948), pp. 345-69. An account of Heidegger's existentialism that explains how Heidegger gives to Nothingness a creative significance.

————. "M. Heidegger And F. Rosenzweig OR Temporality and Eternity." *Philosophy and Phenomenological Research,* vol. 3 (1942), pp. 53-77. Franz Rosenzweig and Martin Heidegger begin from the same starting point— finitude, the individual, and death. Rosenzweig called it the "new thinking" (an expression that Strauss also used). But in contrast to Heidegger, who finds the heart of Being in time and finitude, Rosenzweig contrasts time with eternity, the ever-present with the truth that redeems time and gives it meaning; the latter is God or the "star of redemption."

Maaranen, Steven A. "Leo Strauss: Classical Political Philosophy and Modern Democracy." *Modern Age,* vol. 22, no. 1 (Winter 1978), pp. 47-53. Argues that from the Straussian point of view, the best tradition in modern political thought is that of the American Founders because the latter were as aristocratic and as antidemocratic as Aristotle. The Founders were republicans and not democrats because republicanism is representative government in which the few rule, and not the majority. Jefferson believed that the representatives were the natural aristocracy, and like Aristotle, he believed that the many must elect them into office. But this will happen only if the many are enlightened. But since self-interest is the moving force of the greater number, then what they need to learn is that it is in their self-interest to choose the natural aristocracy to govern them. In this way, the author shows that America is an ancient polity.

Maimonides, Moses. *The Guide of the Perplexed,* with an introduction and notes by Shlomo Pines, trans., and an introductory essay by Leo Strauss. Chicago, Ill.: University of Chicago Press, 1963. Maimonides's own introduction to his work acknowledges its esoteric nature. See my discussion of Maimonides in chapter 2.

Mansfield, Harvey C., Jr. *Taming the Prince.* New York: The Free Press, 1989. Unusually direct and clear, which is refreshing in view of its Straussian lineage. Argues that the concept of the executive is a politically modern transfiguration of the Aristotelian conception of royalty that presupposes superiority and the right of the superior to rule over the inferior. Because modernity is unable to withstand the harsh reality of natural inequality, it has devised the concept of the executive in order to camouflage the fact of inequality as well as the dark reality of politics by pretending that the one who is endowed with supreme power is merely a "servant of the people" executing the will of the legislative and having no will of his own. Argues in favor of a strong executive as a necessary defense against the political weakness and vulnerability of republics.

Neumann, Harry. *Liberalism.* Durham, N. C.: Carolina Academic Press, 1991. The only student of Strauss who openly declares that he is a nihilist, but he denies that Strauss was also a nihilist. The book includes an exchange between Neumann and Drury on Strauss and nihilism. Despite his obscure style, Neumann has a most profound understanding of Strauss.

————. "Civic Piety and Socratic Atheism: An Interpretation of Strauss's *Socrates and Aristophanes.*" *Independent Journal of Philosophy,* vol. 2 (1978), pp. 33-37. Although he does not express it this way, the point of Neumann's essay is that the case of Athens against Socrates was quite justified. Socrates replaced the old gods of the city—martial, patriotic, and courageous—with new cosmopolitan and effeminate gods who preferred Aphrodite (goddess of love) to Ares (god of war), and compassion to anger. Christianity is the cosmopolitan and feminine religion par excellence. The success of Socrates is the reason for the crisis of modernity because the new religion contains the seeds of atheism and its attending destruction of all moral restraint. In Neumann's view, all of the monstrous things that men do can be traced to the universalistic spirit (Neumann was a refugee of Nazi Germany and had Hitler in mind). Strauss was not so explicit about this because he did not want to declare that Christianity is responsible for all the ills of modernity.

Pangle, Thomas L. *The Ennobling of Democracy: The Challenge of the Postmodern Age.* Baltimore, Md.: The Johns Hopkins University Press, 1992. A critique of postmodernism that conceals the affinity between Straussians and postmoderns. Caution: the book does not readily yield its message.

————. *The Spirit of Modern Republicanism: The Moral Vision of the American Founders and the Philosophy of Locke.* Chicago, Ill.: University of Chicago Press, 1988. Takes issue with the view of Harry Jaffa, which he regards as the "orthodox view." Unlike Jaffa, he thinks America is capitalist and Lockean. Most of the book is devoted to Locke. The latter is portrayed as a devious writer who has the uncanny ability to present his outrageously innovative ideas in traditional garb. But Pangle finds him out and reveals the shocking, antibiblical character of Locke's teaching (p. 242). Pangle insists that the biblical message is one of subjection and inequality. Locke is the enemy of the Bible and the wisdom of the ages because he undermines patriarchalism, liberates women, and destroys the family. Pangle asserts the superiority of the tradition against Locke's scandalous innovations. See my discussion of the phalocratic character of Straussianism in chapter 5.

———. "Nihilism and the Modern Democracy in the Thought of Nietzsche," in *The Crisis of Liberal Democracy: A Straussian Perspective,* Kenneth L. Deutsch and Walter Soffer, eds. Albany, N.Y.: State University of New York, 1987. Similar to Pangle's "The Roots of Contemporary Nihilism and Its Political Consequences According to Nietzsche."

———. "The Roots of Contemporary Nihilism and Its Political Consequences According to Nietzsche," *The Review of Politics,* vol. 45, no. 1 (January 1983), pp. 45-70. This is the best and clearest expression of the Straussian interpretation of Nietzsche, which in my view is the key to understanding Strauss and Bloom.

Pocock, J.G.A. *The Machiavellian Moment: Florentine Political Thought and the Atlantic Republican Tradition.* Princeton, N.J.: Princeton University Press, 1975. Traces the origins of American republicanism to the "civic humanists" of the Renaissance who emphasized civic virtue or dedication to the public good and the willingness to sacrifice personal interest to the needs of the whole. Despite the hostile exchanges between Pocock and the Straussians, they share a preference for communitarianism and civic virtue as opposed to liberalism, its rugged individualism, and its preoccupation with private interests and pursuits.

———. "Prophet and Inquisitor." *Political Theory,* vol. 3, no. 4 (November 1975), pp. 385-401, an exchange with Harvey Mansfield.

Rosenzweig, Franz. *The Star of Redemption,* William W. Hallo, trans. New York: Holt, Rinehart and Winston, 1970. Rosenzweig saw both Judaism and Christianity as different experiences of the divine. He was tempted to convert to Christianity, but he changed his mind. He decided that Christianity was forever conquering an unredeemed world in its march closer and closer to God. In contrast, Judaism was already with God. So, how can one who was born chosen, convert? See my discussion of the differences between Rosenzweig and Strauss in chapter 2. See also Strauss's discussion of Rosenzweig in his preface to *Spinoza's Critique of Religion.*

Schmitt, Carl. *The Concept of the Political* (1923), George Schwab, trans., with a commentary by Leo Strauss. New Brunswick, N.J.: Rutgers University Press, 1976. Laments the eclipse of the political. Although critical of the autonomy of politics that Schmitt upholds, Strauss shares most of his ideas and bequeaths them to his American students. See discussion of Strauss and Schmitt in chapter 3.

———. *The Crisis of Parliamentary Democracy* (1923), Ellen Kennedy, trans. Cambridge, Mass.: MIT Press, 1985. A savage critique of liberalism.

Argues that liberalism and democracy are incompatible. And while he is willing to tolerate democracy, he simply cannot abide liberalism. See my discussion of Schmitt in chapter 3.

———. *Political Theology* (1922), George Schwab, trans. Cambridge, Mass.: MIT Press, 1988. Argues that every modern conception of the state is a secularized theology. Absolute monarchy presupposes a traditional monotheistic God who punishes and pardons, constitutional regimes presuppose a deistic universe that is governed by mechanical or unalterable laws, and anarchism presupposes an atheistic theology. Schmitt joins de Maistre, de Bonald, and Donoso Cortés in lamenting the passing of royal absolutism. See my discussion of Schmitt in chapter 3.

———. *Political Romanticism* (1919), Guy Oakes, transl. Cambridge, Mass.: MIT Press, 1986. A critique of the politics of the German romantics. Insists on setting the romantics apart from reactionaries such as De Maistre and De Bonald, whom he adores. Often reads like an ad hominem attack on Adam Müller. It becomes particularly ironic when he accuses Müller of being the "zealous servant of whatever system happened to be in power" (p. 49)—this is not the sort of accusation that Schmitt can afford to make of others. He associates romanticism with decadence and claims that even though it is politically uncommitted, it is compatible only with a bourgeois liberal regime.

Sheehan, Thomas. "Reading a Life: Heidegger and Hard Times," *The Cambridge Companion to Heidegger*, Charles B. Guignon, ed. Cambridge, England: Cambridge University Press, 1993. An account of Heidegger's life, his philosophy, and his connection to the Nazis.

———. "Heidegger and Hitler." *New York Review of Books,* vol. 35, no. 10 (June 16, 1988), pp. 38-47. A review of Victor Farias's book *Heidegger and Nazism.*

Staples, Brent. *Parallel Time.* New York: Pantheon Books, 1994. An autobiographical account of the life of a tall black young man who was a graduate student at the University of Chicago. He arrived in Chicago to discover that he fit the local image of the violent criminal. People cringed as they passed by him on the streets, and secretaries looked upon him with disbelief when he introduced himself as a doctoral student. Soon he discovered that one of the most famous, most influential, and supposedly most enlightened of professors, Saul Bellows, reinforced the image again and again in his novels. Staples pretended to be the terrifying animal they took him for; he stalked Bellows, and gave him a taste of his own fiction.

———. "Undemocratic Vistas: The Sinister Vogue of Leo Strauss." *New York Times,* November 28, 1994, p. A16. Links Strauss with the conservative elite in America. The article resulted in a torrent of outrage by Strauss's disciples in the pages of the same newspaper.

Storing, Herbert J. "Slavery and the Moral Foundations of the American Republic," in *The Moral Foundations of the American Republic,* Robert H. Horwitz, ed. Charlottesville, Va.: University Press of Virginia, 1986. Denies that the

Founders were thoughtless contradictory men who declared the equality of all men while owning slaves. Argues that the Founders were painfully aware of the fact that slavery was a product of positive law and that it was contrary to the law of nature. But even though they acknowledged the injustice of slavery, they did not feel that the African slaves were their equals and therefore did not think that they were deserving of American citizenship. In other words, they were not advocates of racial equality, and did not dream of a multiracial society.

————. *What the Anti-Federalists Were For.* Chicago, Ill.: University of Chicago Press, 1981. Leading Straussian scholar of the American founding who focuses on the political thought of those who opposed the Constitution, and a strong central government. The anti-federalist opposition is fashionable again today.

Strauss, Leo. *Philosophy and Law: Essays Toward the Understanding of Maimonides and His Predecessors,* Fred Baumann, trans. New York: Jewish Publication Society, 1987. See my discussion of this work in chapter 2.

————. *Spinoza's Critique of Religion.* New York: Schocken Books, 1965. The preface is an intellectual autobiography that addresses his Jewish identity, the question of Zionism, and his theologico-political predicament, or the philosophical problem that concerned him throughout his work. He also reveals that he is no ordinary conservative when he scorns Hermann Cohen for committing the "typical mistake of a conservative, which consists in concealing the fact that the continuous and changing tradition which he cherishes so greatly would never have come into being through conservatism, or without discontinuities, revolutions, and sacrileges committed at the beginning of the cherished tradition and at least silently repeated in its course" (p. 27).

————. "An Epilogue." *Essays on the Scientific Study of Politics.* H. J. Storing, ed. New York: Holt, Rinehart & Winston, 1962. A well-deserved critique of behavioral political science as mindless nonsense that "fiddles while Rome burns." Critical of American political science for clinging to democracy while recognizing the total irrationality of the masses and the need for elites. Strauss shares their insight regarding the masses and the need for elites.

————. *What Is Political Philosophy?* Westport, Conn.: Greenwood Press, 1959. Contains the famous essay by the same name, where Strauss describes philosophy as "fearless," "shameless," and "the very opposite of sobriety or moderation" (p. 32). He distinguishes between philosophy and political philosophy, which is the public face that philosophy must assume. Political philosophy is moderate speech about shameless thoughts that are destructive of useful social conventions; it is therefore a very dangerous business.

————. "The State of Israel." *National Review,* vol. 13 no. 1 (January 5, 1957), p. 23. See my discussion of this essay in chapter 2.

————. *Persecution and the Art of Writing.* Westport, Conn.: Greenwood Press, 1952. Argues that philosophers must be secretive; their work must contain an exoteric or surface teaching that is salutary for society and a secret or esoteric teaching meant to be communicated only to the few who are the secret sharers of the dangerous but delicious truth. The reason for this secrecy is not just to protect the philosopher from persecution, but also to protect society from the corrosive effects of truth.

———. *Natural Right and History.* Chicago, Ill.: University of Chicago Press, 1950. Although the Declaration of Independence appears on the cover, the thesis of the book subverts the whole idea of equality as well as the idea of natural rights. Instead, Strauss defends the natural right of the superior few to rule over the inferior many.

———. "On the Intention of Rousseau." *Social Research,* vol. xiv (December 1947), pp. 455-87. Rousseau's numerous contradictions magically disappear when Strauss explains that Rousseau is addressing two audiences—common men and philosophers. Philosophy, science, and enlightenment are bad for society because they are too universalistic. Society thrives on the particularistic; it must therefore foster national and exclusive institutions, as well as a warlike spirit.

———. "The Spirit of Sparta or the Taste of Xenophon." *Social Research,* vol. 6 (1939), pp. 502-36. This is a clear expression of Strauss's esoteric teaching. He says clearly, that esotericism is not just an attempt to escape persecution, but a duty, because the vulgar are unfit for the truth (pp. 534-35). Strauss seems to share Xenophon's view that the singular cause of Sparta's depravity is the laxity, incontinence, ignorance, and immodesty of her women. A commonsense reading would lead to the conclusion that women must also be educated and disciplined, otherwise a society is doomed. But Strauss reaches much more subtle conclusions.

Talmon, J. L. "Uniqueness and Universality of Jewish History," in *The Unique and the Universal.* New York: George Braziller, 1965. Points to the disproportionate influence of the Jews on Western civilization in comparison with their numbers. He agrees with Toynbee that Western civilization has been Judaized, but does not share the latter's poor estimation of Jewish influence on the West. It is interesting to note that Toynbee's views are an inversion of Nietzsche's. Nietzsche also thought that Western civilization had undergone a process of Judaization. He believed that this process had led to the softening and feminization of Western culture, which he deplored. In contrast, Toynbee believed that the reverse is the case. The Judaization of Western culture accounts for its intolerance, militarism, and imperialism. Talmon argues against Toynbee's self-loathing and his inclination to prostrate himself before the supposed mildness and tolerance of Eastern religions and civilizations.

Thomas, Clarence. "The Higher Law Background of the Privileges or Immunities Clause of the Fourteenth Amendment." *Harvard Journal of Law and Public Policy,* vol. 12, no. 1 (Winter 1989), pp. 63-70. Endorses the same version of the doctrine of original intent as Harry V. Jaffa. Argues that the Constitution must be read with the Declaration as its backdrop, because the real intent of the Constitution is to phase out slavery. Shares Jaffa's critique of Justice Taney in the *Dred Scott* case because Taney ignored the Declaration and therefore wrongly assumed that the Constitution approves of slavery and protects the rights of slaveholders. Thinks that to be conservative is to conserve the revolutionary principle of equality on which America is founded. Shares Jaffa's high regard for Oliver North.

————. "Civil Rights as a Principle Versus Civil Rights as an Interest," in *Assessing the Reagan Years,* David Boaz, ed. Washington, D.C.: Cato Institute, 1988. Critical of Ronald Dworkin's critique of Judge Bork, and thinks that the fact that he is not Justice Bork is a disgrace. Lends support to the Republican party, which he regards as the party of Lincoln. Although he realizes that Barry Goldwater rejected the civil rights act of 1964, he defends the famous lines in his speech written by Harry Jaffa, saying that they are not as extremist as they appear. See my discussion in chapter 4.

————. "Affirmative Action Goals and Timetables: Too Tough? Not Tough Enough!" *Yale Law & Policy Review,* vol. 5, no. 2 (Spring/Summer 1987), pp. 402-11. Is against affirmative action, hiring goals, quotas, and timetables because they are too easy on employers and because they leave individual cases of discrimination untouched. His view is that the law should always be color blind, even if the society is not. Believes that blacks should pull themselves up by their own collective efforts—have their own businesses and schools, and not rely on government help.

————. "Toward a 'Plain Reading' of the Constitution—The Declaration of Independence in Constitutional Interpretation," *Howard Law Journal,* vol. 30 (1987), pp. 691-703. Is critical of Chief Justice Warren's decision in *Brown v. Board of Education* because it is based on sensitivity and emotion, not reason and justice.

Tolstoy, Leo. *The Death of Ivan Ilych* (1886). New York: Penguin Books, 1960. This brilliantly written story is usually considered to be a superior version of Heidegger's account of human angst in the face of death. See my discussion in chapter 3.

Trilling, Lionel. *Of This Time, Of That Place and Other Stories.* New York: Harcourt Brace Jovanovich, 1979. Trilling was not reputed to be a good writer of fiction, but "Impediments" is an interesting account of his own approach to being Jewish. It tells of a young Jewish student who erects an emotional barrier around himself that makes him impenetrable both to those of his own kind who are too Jewish for his liking as well as against those who are hostile to his kind. When a Jewish student (Hettner) with intellectual gifts that far surpass those of the narrator tries to become his friend, he erects his impenetrable barrier. And though he is not blind to Hettner's gifts, he considers him merely a "scrubby little Jew." Although he is extremely polite to him, the reader cannot but feel sympathetic to Hettner when he says to the protagonist, "what a miserable dog you are."

————. *Freud and the Crisis of Our Culture.* Boston, Mass.: Beacon Press, 1955. Argues that Americans pay lip service to individuality and nonconformity but are in reality the worst conformists. Freud's emphasis on the opposition between civilization and human biology is a liberating idea because it reminds us of the possibility of the "opposing self"—an idea that flies in the face of the cultural omnipotence of our time.

Weisberg, Jacob. "The Family Way: How Irving Kristol, Gertrude Himmelfarb, and their son, Bill Kristol, became the family that liberals love to hate." *The New Yorker* (October 21 and 28, 1996), pp. 180-89. Describes the gala event in Washington celebrating the seventy-fifth birthday of Irving Kristol, in which the "luminaries of the right"—Jack Kemp, George Will, William Bennett, Jeane J. Kirkpatrick, William F. Buckley, Jr., Robert Bork, and others—dressed in their "evening finery" went around calling each other "Comrade." Paints Irving Kristol as the Lenin of the neoconservatives, Gertrude Himmelfarb as a tenacious neoconservative scholar, and William Kristol as the Machiavellian practitioner of neoconservative politics.

Wilde, Oscar. "The Decay of Lying" (1891), in *The Artist as Critic: Critical Writings of Oscar Wilde,* Richard Ellmann, ed. New York: Vintage Books, 1968. A delightfully arrogant condemnation of modern realism in art and literature. Insists that art is doomed if it sets about imitating life and nature. Art must be creative, imaginative, and filled with flights of fancy, otherwise the world will die of boredom. A more artistic and less serious view of lying than Strauss's.

Williams, Juan. "A Question of Fairness," *Atlantic Monthly* (February 1987), pp. 71-82. An excellent biographical essay on Justice Clarence Thomas that explains his sentiments on being black in America. Reveals the roots of his pessimism about the possibility of integration or of a color-blind society.

Williams, Nigel. *Star Turn.* London, England: Faber and Faber, 1985. About a young Jewish boy growing up in the east part of London, who decides not to be Jewish. He changes his identity at a new school for "regular" English lads. He calls himself Shadbolt, behaves in a way that is confident, charming, and debonair. But the other boys just call him Jewboy and beat him to a pulp in the schoolyard. So, try as he may, he cannot become Shadbolt. When he grows up, he takes an interest in politics; he wants to change the world. His father is apprehensive for him, and wishes that he would be sensible. He dies at the hands of the British Fascist party. It may be possible to think of Lionel Trilling as Shadbolt with a happy ending because what was not possible in the old world, may sometimes be possible in the new one.

Wolin, Richard, ed. *The Heidegger Controversy: A Critical Reader.* New York: Columbia University Press, 1991. An excellent collection of essays including Heidegger's political speeches and essays by people who knew Heidegger, including Karl Jaspers, Karl Löwith, and Herbert Marcuse.

———. *The Politics of Being: The Political Thought of Martin Heidegger.* New York: Columbia University Press, 1990. A sprightly written critique of Heidegger, arguing that his philosophy is totally compatible with his politics.

Wood, Gordon S. "The Fundamentalists and the Constitution. *New York Review of Books* (February, 1988), pp. 33-40. This is an excellent piece and the most comprehensive account of the Straussian writings on the American founding. Agrees with those who think that the Founders were republicans and civic humanists rather than liberal democrats wedded to a commercial society. Repudiates the Straussian view that the shift from one paradigm to the other was part of a sinister modernist plot. He is also critical of the Straussian absolutism and anti-historicism, which he believes contribute to the radicalism of their politics. In contrast to Wood, I believe that the radical nature of Straussian politics has its source in a romanticization of the past as the enchanted rule of the superior few over the inferior many by the use of salutary fables. Strauss is certainly not a *moral* absolutist.

Yolton, John W. "Locke on the Law of Nature." *Philosophical Review,* 67 (1958), pp. 477-98. Yolton illustrates the careless nature of Strauss's scholarship, and his habit of quoting out of context.

———. "Criticism and Histrionic Understanding." *Ethics,* 65 (1955), pp. 206-12. Yolton argues that Strauss's rejection of historical understanding is exaggerated. Historical understanding does not automatically lead to a preference for nihilism over morality and cannibalism over civilization. Historical understanding makes it possible to enter the world of the other and understand it from within. Far from making criticism impotent, the historical approach allows critique to transcend the biased, superficial, and parochial level.

# INDEX